T0295705

JOBLESS GROWTH IN THE DOMINICAN REPUBLIC

Emerging Frontiers in the Global Economy

Jobless Growth in the Dominican Republic

Disorganization, Precarity, and Livelihoods

Christian Krohn-Hansen

STANFORD UNIVERSITY PRESS
Stanford, California

Stanford University Press
Stanford, California

Printed in the United States of America on acid-free, archival-quality paper

Library of Congress Cataloging-in-Publication Data
Names: Krohn-Hansen, Christian, 1957– author.
Title: Jobless growth in the Dominican Republic : disorganization, precarity, and livelihoods / Christian Krohn-Hansen.
Other titles: Emerging frontiers in the global economy.
Description: Stanford, California : Stanford University Press, 2022. | Series: Emerging frontiers in the global economy | Includes bibliographical references and index.
Identifiers: LCCN 2021039907 (print) | LCCN 2021039908 (ebook) | ISBN 9781503630529 (cloth) | ISBN 9781503631571 (ebook)
Subjects: LCSH: Precarious employment—Dominican Republic—Santo Domingo. | Labor—Dominican Republic—Santo Domingo. | Labor market—Dominican Republic—Santo Domingo. | Informal sector (Economics)—Dominican Republic—Santo Domingo. | Santo Domingo (Dominican Republic)—Economic conditions. | Santo Domingo (Dominican Republic)—Social conditions.
Classification: LCC HD5858.D65 K76 2022 (print) | LCC HD5858.D65 (ebook) | DDC 331.2097293/75—dc23
LC record available at https://lccn.loc.gov/2021039907
LC ebook record available at https://lccn.loc.gov/2021039908

Cover photo: Irene Grassi
Cover design: Susan Zucker

Contents

A Note on Currency

The Dominican peso has been slowly declining over time.

In 2012 (or the year when the field research started), the Dominican peso was on average equal to US$0.025 (that is, DOP100 = US$2.50). Average exchange rate in 2017 (the year when the field research was finished) was US$0.021 (DOP100 = US$2.10). Average exchange rate in 2013 was US$0.024 (DOP100 = US$2.40), and in 2014 US$0.023 (DOP100 = US$2.30).

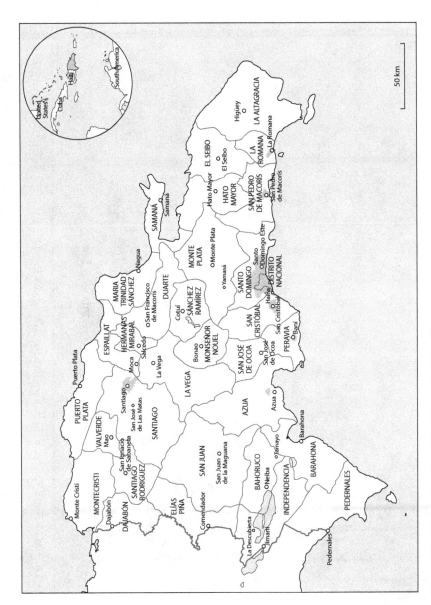

Map 1. The Dominican Republic. Drawn by Ove Olsen.

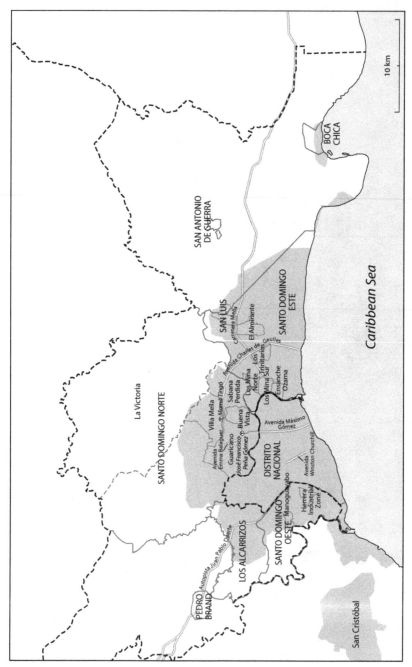

Map 2. The Distrito Nacional and Santo Domingo Province. Drawn by Ove Olsen.

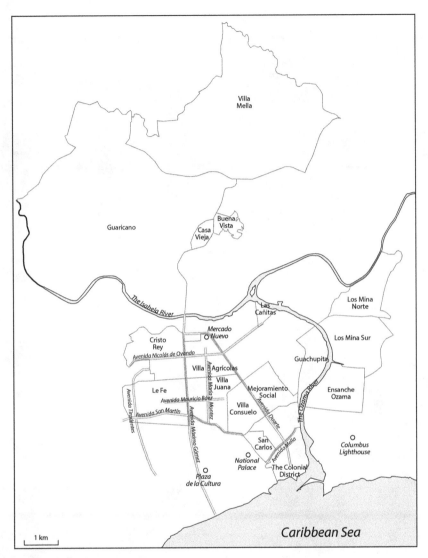

Villa
Mella

Guaricano

Buena
Vista

Casa
Vieja

Los Mina
Norte

The Isabela River

Las
Cañitas

Los Mina Sur

○ *Mercado*
Nuevo

Cristo
Rey

Avenida Nicolás de Ovando

Guachupita

The Ozama River

Villa *Agrícolas*

Villa
Juana

Mejoramiento
Social

Ensanche
Ozama

Le Fe

Avenida Mauricio Báez

Avenida Marión Montez

Villa
Consuelo

Avenida Duarte

Avenida San Martín

Avenida Trinitarios

Avenida Máximo Gómez

San
Carlos

○
Columbus
Lighthouse

○
National
Palace

Avenida Mella

The Colonial
District

○
Plaza
de la Cultura

1 km

Caribbean Sea

Map 3. Santo Domingo. Drawn by Ove Olsen.

Introduction

Many of the workshops of Santo Domingo's small producers and repairers of metal objects, furniture, mattresses, textiles, and other items are situated in some of the city's most populous neighborhoods. An example is the barrio Villa Consuelo, located near downtown Santo Domingo. This old working-class barrio houses a series of timber importers and timber merchants, and a large number of carpenter shops and furniture workshops. Most of these *talleres*, or workshops, are situated in small buildings or houses that originally were constructed for residential purposes. To run a workshop in this type of neighborhood is a challenge; the sound, or the smell, of the production may anger neighbors, the workshop premises may be too small or restricting, without possibilities for expansion—and the narrow, crowded streets render access to and from the workshop (to deliver timber, finished products, and so on) difficult. The country's small business associations and political activists have therefore—and for a long time now—been demanding that the state construct a number of parques industriales—special areas zoned and planned for industrial development. In an industrial park, firms can cooperate to secure better services and to reduce costs. However, constructing an industrial park is a large investment. In the late 1960s, the Dominican government built one in Herrera, in western Santo Domingo, but after that no more were planned until 2004, when the state decided to create at least eight new parks in different parts of the country. Three years later, in 2007, a national plan, El Plan Nacional de Competitividad Sistémica de la República Dominicana,

1

outlined the need to intensify the country's efforts to develop separate areas for industrial use. In spite of this, the history of the state's creation of industrial parks is depressing.

At the time of my fieldwork, in 2013, only three parks had been built. More correctly, two small parks had been completed and were up and running: one in the eastern part of the capital, and one in the city of San Cristóbal. In 2004, construction had begun on a third, the Parque Industrial Santo Domingo Oeste (DISDO), located in Manoguayabo in the western part of the capital, but by 2013 the park was still far from completed. It was to be a large park—clearly the state's most significant attempt to develop a separate area for small domestic enterprises—but it had evolved into a strange story.

Cristian Nolasco, a man in his forties and head of the small family enterprise, Industrias Colón, had invested in the park in 2004, as he had wanted to relocate his furniture manufacturing business.[1] His workshop, which was situated in the barrio Villa Consuelo, produced beds, chairs, and other items of wood and metal. It had always been a small venture, but from the mid-1990s to the early 2000s business went well, and Cristian was employing around fifteen workers. After these promising years, the enterprise began to stagnate and then decline. Although it continued to make the same products, over the years, demand had fallen. When I met him for the first time, in 2012, the workshop had essentially been without production for six months. Cristian and a brother or a sister still ran the workshop, but there were no employees, and it was without life. If he did receive an order, Cristian would call in some of his previous workers. Asked to explain the declining demand, he underscored a set of factors. The state had, in practice, worked against the country's domestic industry, and imports from Asia and elsewhere had grown steadily. During the last few years, the prices of timber and other raw materials had gone up, and the crisis in the country's electricity sector had aggravated the situation: the cost of power had remained high, but supply was erratic at best. Ever increasing production costs had rendered domestic family businesses less competitive, particularly given the growing import sector flooding the market with cheap commodities.

Industrias Colón is located in a small, two-story building that was, originally, a family home. Cristian's father had owned the place, and they had removed some walls and made a few other changes, converting the house into a workshop with storerooms and a couple of offices. In the early

2000s, Cristian was looking for new premises, a place where the firm could continue to develop, in which he could justify investing. However, as he explained, the places he found were either too far away or too expensive, so he remained where he was. When the government started to construct a large industrial park in the western part of the capital in August 2004, he was enthusiastic and decided to join the scheme and invest in the project. According to the plan, the park would be completed in two or three years and would house almost 200 small- and medium-sized ventures, generate thousands of jobs, and represent the nation's largest industrial zone so far. The area is located some 20 kilometers from the city center and 10 kilometers from one of the country's most important thoroughfares, Autopista Juan Pablo Duarte. Cristian emphasized the difference between a project like this and the country's many *zonas francas,* or export-processing zones: "The free zones have been created in order to attract foreign companies; the companies don't pay taxes—the only condition is that they use local labor-power. You import your machines and raw materials, and export your products, without paying taxes. The free zones have been made for large international companies. However, an industrial park is something differ- ent. In a park, we're all in the same situation, we pay taxes, but we need an industrial area, an area where we can reduce our electricity expenses and other expenses."

Nevertheless, several years later, the park in Manoguayabo was still far from finished. Further, the whole area was in a miserable state. In early 2012, the state had so far spent around 150 million pesos on the project, and the area's streets and much of the infrastructure had been constructed, but only a few of the production premises. At the time, one of the country's leading newspapers published an article on the project under the telling headline: "The industrial park DISDO has become grazing land" (*Hoy* 2012a). According to the article, construction work to finish the park had been paralyzed for more than three years, although President Leonel Fernández on several occasions had promised completion. Cables, doors, windows, and other materials had been removed and stolen, while cattle, horses and other animals had been put to graze in the area. Some five years later, in April 2017, little had changed, with the exception that the state now had spent significantly more on the project, in total more than 680 million pesos. The area continued to mostly be *"un potrero* [pasture land]" (García 2017).

What had happened? Cristian explained that one of the first problems had been a change in the original plan. Originally, the plan was that he and the others would purchase their lots, that the state, through the state institution Proindustria, would construct all the plants and premises—and that all the businesses would pay off what they owed the state within thirty years. Then the plan changed so that they just received the lots, without the state building the premises. Instead, everyone had to construct their own premises with the aid of an ordinary bank loan. Subsequently the project went through a series of other changes. "You know," Cristian said drily, one day in early 2013, "since the start in 2004 we have seen three different governments [with elections in 2004, 2008, and 2012]: During these years, ministers and functionaries have come and gone. The industrial park in Manoguayabo has been refashioned more than three times. Every time we have a new government official with responsibility for the park, he changes the plan for the construction of the streets, the pavements, the containers, or something else in the park. Although the streets already have been completed and paved, he decides to change them, relocate them. In this way, he secures a commission, makes money—since he creates a need for a new construction work. He hires an engineer to do the work, who pays him a commission. The streets were fine, finished. Yet, suddenly they had to be altered, but they don't explain why. So," Cristian rounded off, "the only reasonable explanation is corruption."

Cristian began to pay his installments to Proindustria in 2004. After three or four years, a number of firm owners stopped paying, but many others continued. Cristian stopped paying in 2010. He said, "Things have changed. If this had been ten years ago, I would have been able to obtain the money to construct premises on my lot in the park—but not now." Most of the others who had paid, perhaps 80 percent, he went on, were in a similar situation. "We're small enterprises, in difficulties, lacking capital and resources; it's impossible for us to get a bank loan to build premises or a plant." Cristian's plan, and that of many others, was therefore, when the park was finished and the lots had been legally and finally transferred, to find a buyer and sell. With the capital that he got in this way, he said, he would seek to start afresh where he was, in Villa Consuelo. He concluded with an angry smile: "Very good medicine—but it arrives too late" (*Muy buena medicina, pero ya va llegar tarde*).

***

According to World Bank data, the Dominican Republic stands out over the last thirty years as one of the fastest growing economies in Latin America and the Caribbean, as well as worldwide. The Dominican economy expanded by an average growth rate of 4.9 percent per year from 2001 to 2017.[2] Growth in the country remained high in the years leading up to the COVID-19 pandemic, and between 2015 and 2019 the Dominican Republic's annual gross domestic product (GDP) growth rate averaged 6.1 percent.[3] The rapid growth allowed the country's real per capita income to increase substantially. Real GDP per capita in 1993 stood at US$3,000 (in 2010 rates), or 7.5 percent of US per capita GDP. By 2016, the country's real income was US$7,000 or 13.5 percent of US per capita GDP. Thus, the Dominican Republic narrowed the gap with respect to US income by 6 percentage points over the last twenty-five years. By contrast, the median country in Latin America and the Caribbean, and in the world, narrowed their income gap with respect to the United States by 2 and 4 percentage points, respectively, over the same time frame. Moreover, during the period 1993–2017, the Dominican Republic saw a sharper reduction in its income gap with respect to the United States than 86 percent of countries in Latin America and the Caribbean, and 87 percent of countries in the world (World Bank Group 2018:13–14). This conspicuous economic performance, however, has not translated into equally significant improvements in working and living conditions for all. The Dominican Republic has seen growth, yet the nation remains characterized by an astonishingly high percentage of workers (citizens) in a vulnerable situation. "The Dominican paradox"—high growth, stagnant or declining wages, tenacious poverty, and a vast informal economy—has for a decade or more attracted the attention of the World Bank, the International Monetary Fund, and other institutions (Abdullaev and Estevão 2013; Parisotto and Prepelitchi 2013; Carneiro and Sirtaine 2017; Winkler and Montenegro 2021). Official Dominican employment rates have remained low compared to those of other countries in Latin America and the Caribbean (Abdullaev and Estevão 2013:5–6), and official informality levels increased from 54 percent in 2004 to 56 percent in 2013 (Carneiro and Sirtaine 2017:4).

Strong economic growth and large productivity gains, however, have been concentrated in only a few parts of the economy. Such sectors (especially manufacturing in the country's *zonas francas*, telecommunications, and financial services) have had limited impact on job generation, even though they have been growing at high rates and generating a large share of the Dominican GDP (Abdullaev and Estevão 2013:3–5). Moreover, the jobs that have been created have tended to be of the low-paid type, and real earnings have fallen (Carneiro and Sirtaine 2017:3–4).[4]

The disjuncture between the nation's high-value-added economic sectors (with limited job production) and its low-value-added economic sectors (with "informality" and enormous employment increase) is reflected in the Dominican Republic's poverty figures. In 2000, the official poverty incidence in the country was below the regional average; 33 percent of Dominicans lived on less than US$4 a day, compared with 42 percent of those living in Latin America and the Caribbean. In 2003–4, the country experienced a colossal domestic banking crisis. The financial and economic emergency that followed drove an estimated 1.7 million more Dominicans into poverty, and the poverty rate rose to 50 percent in 2004.[5] When the nation and the economy recovered after the crisis, poverty rates began to drop but only returned to the precrisis level, around 33 percent (now a level above, not below, the region's average), in 2015 (Carneiro and Sirtaine 2017:1–2).

The dictator Rafael Trujillo ruled the Dominican Republic from 1930 to 1961, and was followed by another authoritarian leader, Joaquín Balaguer, who was in power 1966–78, and then again in 1986–96. Two leaders, Leonel Fernández and Danilo Medina, dominated the years from 1996 to 2020. Both represented the Dominican Liberation Party (Partido de la Liberación Dominicana [PLD]), the country's largest and leading political party. Before Fernández won the presidential election in 1996, he had worked to make the PLD less leftist and more centrist (I return to this point later). Fernández was in power from 1996 to 2000 and from 2004 to 2012,[6] and was followed by Medina, who became president in 2012 and was reelected in 2016.

The purpose of this book is to chart and analyze how ordinary and poor Dominicans work and live in the shadow of the country's conspicuous growth rates. Jobless growth can be defined as an economic condition in which a macroeconomy experiences growth while maintaining or decreasing its level of employment.[7] I explore the popular economy in the Dominican capital and investigate how people act and survive in a part of the contemporary world that lacks "good" (decent-paying, rights-based, secure) jobs. I examine the condition of the urban masses in the PLD state and analyze the changes and conditions in Santo Domingo in the two decades from the late 1990s to Medina's second presidential term (2016—20). I interweave ethnographic analyses and forms of social history. The bulk of the ethnographic data were produced through intermittent fieldwork undertaken in the Dominican capital from May 2012 to November 2017, but the book also draws on a longer research interest in, and contact with, Dominicans. I conducted thirteen months of anthropological fieldwork in and around the village of La Descubierta in the southwestern part of the Dominican Republic in 1991–92. From 2002 to 2008, I carried out intermittent fieldwork among Dominican immigrants in New York City. I have published on aspects of the Dominican political, economic, and social history since the mid-1990s (see the works by Krohn-Hansen listed in the references section). I gathered data through field research in Santo Domingo for three and a half months, from early May to late August 2012. Thereafter I lived mostly in Oslo but returned for shorter stays: three times in 2013, once in 2014, once in 2016, and once in 2017. Each stay lasted between two and four weeks; most were about two or three. In total, I carried out almost seven months of fieldwork in the Dominican capital. The research consisted mainly of observation and informal conversations and interviews in a series of different populous and poor barrios scattered throughout the city. Most of my data were gathered in the north and east of the city (in areas such as Villa Consuelo, Villas Agrícolas, Cristo Rey, Villa Mella, Sabana Perdida, La Victoria, Ensanche Ozama, Los Mina, and Los Trinitarios), although I worked in many other areas of the capital. Some of my data were produced in neighborhoods in the south and west of the city. Many of my interlocutors were small producers, traders, or storeowners. Some were, or had been, factory workers or street vendors, while others worked in supermarkets, or as drivers, domestic workers, teachers, or office employees.

Chapter 1 analyzes the conditions and activities of the capital's many small furniture makers. Chapter 2 investigates the histories and the strategies of single mothers who either operate a small food stall or buy and sell vegetables. Until recently, most Dominicans purchased food and groceries in *colmados* and in public markets. *El colmado*, the small barrio or street-corner store, continues to be the most widespread small business in the country and is a Dominican institution. Chapter 3 discusses the major changes in the Dominican retail distribution sector over the last few decades, and analyzes the present conditions and practices of the capital's *colmados*. Chapter 4 focuses on the nation's cooperative movement. Over the last two decades, Dominican savings and credit cooperatives have become increasingly important. The chapter maps and discusses how these business ventures are organized, and how they function economically and socially. Throughout these chapters, I seek to answer a set of basic questions: How do people make a living? What characterizes their work? How do people acquire their own small economic enterprises, and how do they operate them? How do they tackle market shifts? How do they manage risks, lasting unpredictability, and sudden changes? What characterizes their relationship to (encounters with) the state?

Chapter 5, "Jobless Growth, 'No Labor' Futures, and the Investigation of Popular Economies," formulates a set of answers to a more general or broader question: How can researchers usefully examine and write about the popular economies in the many city landscapes that, since the mid-twentieth century, have appeared in Latin America, the Caribbean, Africa, and Asia? I seek to outline some general principles or tools for ethnographic inquiry into the livelihood strategies of the urban masses in today's global South.

This study explores Dominicans' income-producing strategies as labor activities and investments. I use the term "investment" in a broad sense. An investment refers, in Jane Guyer's (2004:99) words, to "a performative conversion, a devotion of present income to the hope of future gains." We always need a cultural and affective analysis of economic activities. If we wish to understand economic forms, we need to study the ideas, values, and sentiments that incite, energize, and shape specific economic actions, with their accompanying configurations of identity production (Hirschman [1977] 2013; Mazzarella 2009; Bear et al. 2015).

The Jobs Problem

In *The Problem with Work* (2011), Kathi Weeks has given us a thought-provoking and bold book.[8] Weeks challenges the presupposition that work, or waged labor, is intrinsically a social and political good. While progressive political forces, including the Marxist and feminist movements, have demanded and struggled for equal pay, better work conditions, and the recognition of unpaid work as a valued form of labor, even they have tended to accept and naturalize work as an inevitable (not to say sacred) human activity. Weeks asks why we work so long and so hard. "The mystery here," she argues, "is not that we are required to work or that we are expected to devote so much time and energy to its pursuit, but rather that there is not more active resistance to this state of affairs . . . after all, even the best job is a problem when it monopolizes so much of life" (2011:1). She argues that, in taking work as a given, we have "depoliticized" it, or removed it, to an absurd extent, from the sphere of political critique. Weeks proposes a postwork universe or society that would allow people to be productive and creative rather than unceasingly bound to the employment relation.[9]

There is a limitation inherent in the perspective developed by Weeks. Who are her "we," the "we" about whom, or on whose behalf, she writes? We (researchers and critics) need a globally oriented perspective. *The Problem with Work* focuses only on the United States—exclusively on Western late capitalist (or industrial/postindustrial) historical formations. In this book, I focus on another historical condition, another reality. I discuss the conditions of the working masses in a part of the global South.[10] But the two histories (that of today's Western core, or center, and that of today's Caribbean) have been, and remain, intertwined, mutually constitutive. They belong together, are co-present in each other, and should be understood as two sides of the same process. For some within today's world economy or late capitalist system, the problem with work is the overwork that often characterizes even the most privileged forms of employment, while for others, the problem is miserable wages or the absence of jobs.

An example of the global connections and interweavings is Dominican labor migration to the United States. Considerable emigration from the Dominican Republic to the United States began in the early 1960s, after the assassination of Trujillo. Most of these Dominicans settled in New York City, and the growth of the Dominican population there has been considerable. The Dominican Republic, *in absolute numbers*, sent more immigrants to New York City than did any other country during the 1970s and 1980s, and maintained that position through the early 1990s (by the mid-1990s the former Soviet Union was the number-one source of immigrants to New York City).[11] Since 1995, however, the Dominican Republic has continued to send great numbers of migrants to New York. The overwhelming majority of these Dominicans left the island in search of work. In much of the twentieth century, the Dominican Republic was an exporter of sugar for the world market. During the last six decades, the country has turned into an exporter of another commodity, raw human labor-power. Similar changes or transformations have occurred in the same period in other parts of the world (see, for example, Pedersen 2013). At any rate, the global capitalist system contains, or offers, limited numbers of good or decent jobs. Some people work too hard or burn out. Others are underpaid or unemployed. Many experience underemployment or are victims of jobless growth. Most mainstream economists and politicians view "full employment" as impossible, and admit that structural unemployment rates probably will grow because of technological innovation, robotization, and intensified globalization. Weeks is right when she insists that a key question should be about the societal or collective organization and distribution of (necessary) work. In addition, she is right when she maintains that it is necessary to critically rethink how we view, define, and practice *the relationship* between participation in and the performance of (waged) work *and* the allocation of (full public citizenship) rights (see also Ferguson 2015). Both questions are thoroughly political. Both demand globally oriented answers.[12]

Adopting a global perspective on the problems with wage labor today, or on capital-labor relations, means a clear rejection of a Eurocentric or North Atlantic perspective that focuses nearly exclusively on the state of affairs in former metropolitan territories. Two processes have been central in the last five or six decades, when considered from a global or postcolonial capital-labor perspective. One of these has produced an accelerated process of "proletarianization"—that is, a massive expansion of the global working class in classic Marxist forms. The other has created spectacular levels (or amounts) of "informalization". As Mike Davis put it some years ago, "the global informal working class (overlapping with but non-identical to the slum population) is about one billion strong, making it the fastest growing, and most unprecedented, social class on earth" (2006:178). Shifts in the global economy over the past forty or forty-five years have expanded and restructured the globe's proletariat. The numbers of workers worldwide doubled between 1975 and 1995, as part of what was increasingly called globalization but was mostly an expanded reproduction of capital on a global scale (Coates 2000; Harvey 2005). At the same time, the global labor force became feminized and "Southernized". As Ronaldo Munck has put it,

> perhaps the most salient feature in the qualitative composition of the great quantitative leap forward of the global labour force is its concentration on the South, or what economists still call developing regions. Whereas the number of workers in the OECD countries only increased from 372 million in 1985 to 400 million in 2000 (0.5%), the number of workers in the South increased from 1595 million to 2137 million, which represented a 20% annual growth rate. The gender composition of the global labour force also changed dramatically over the

same period, with female labour force participation surpassing 50% by the mid-1980s. The expansion, feminization and what we might call "Southernization" of the working class went hand in hand. (Munck 2013:755)

The point is that the (global) working class remains in place. The number of proletarians worldwide has grown. Many of these workers reside in the South, and many are women. They work for corporations and firms within a multiplicity of sectors. Most earn low or very low wages. It is too early to bid farewell to the classic wage proletariat.

In parallel to the Southernization and the feminization of the working class, the so-called informal economies in the South continued to expand explosively and colossally. Since the 1980s, the informal sector has grown far faster than formal sector employment. Large companies and firms have, of course, capitalized on this phenomenon through their subcontracting chains, which are now crucial to so much commodity production. It is also an integral component of China's thriving industrial economy, which is bolstered by informal sectors. There is not a sharp division between "formal" and "informal" economies, but rather a continuum based on connections, symbioses, and overlapping areas.[13]

In this book, I focus on the implications of massive urban growth through forms of informalization. The focus is not so much on the effects of the proliferation of factory workers or proletarians through accelerated globalization—or the expansion, feminization, and Southernization of the world's working class—rather, I am concerned primarily with this question: How do we best investigate and understand popular economies in the many large cityscapes that, over the course of the last few decades, have emerged in the global South? The changes in Santo Domingo provide a good case. I investigated the popular economy in Santo Domingo through studies of family businesses, trade, self-employment, and community-based cooperatives. I view this type of interest as key. Much of the real, or important, daily economy in the megacities and large cities of the South is based on these forms—myriad small enterprises, petty trade, and forms of self-employment. Since the structural adjustment crises of the 1980s, the informal sector has grown far more—and faster—than formal sector employment (Munck 2013). According to data from ILO (2018), seven out of ten workers in developing countries today make a living in informal markets. The question is, how do ordinary citizens in the South get by (especially the many who stay put and do not emigrate)? How do they work and save? To be able to begin to shape useful answers, we need what James Ferguson and Tania Murray Li have described as a reformulated, more open "approach to global political-economic inquiry in the wake of the failure of long-established transition narratives, notably the narrative centred on a universal trajectory from farm-based and 'traditional' livelihoods into the 'proper jobs' of modern industrial society" (2018: 1). I am also fully behind them when they continue: "the prevalence and persistence of 'informal,' 'precarious,' and 'non-standard' employment in so many sites around the world [today] . . . requires a profound analytical decentering of waged and salaried employment as a presumed norm or telos, and a consequent reorientation of our empirical research protocols." This is not to say—and I underscore this—that (the value or price of) wage labor does not remain key: it continues to play a huge role. The data mentioned above on *the expansion* of the global proletariat tells a clear story. Many in today's Dominican Republic are wage laborers. However, the access to well-paid or at least decent jobs is limited. Often the salary is low or miserable and the working conditions demanding or brutal. Many give it a go but subsequently gravitate into a type of street vending, trade, or other form of small-business development. This makes it imperative to seek to understand these realms of the economy, and this is what I try to do in the subsequent chapters.

For more than five centuries, Santo Domingo's economy has been a part of the global economy and, since 1844 (the year of the inception of Dominican national independence), it has been conditioned by the Dominican state-building project. *Both* transnational capitalism *and* the Dominican state-making project have given shape to contemporary Santo Domingo through particular processes that, in a certain sense, have generated more socioeconomic "disorder" than order. In the remainder of this introduction, I seek to substantiate this assertion. In the next section, I look first at some of the key features of the historical incorporation of the island's and the nation's economy into the world economy. I then outline, briefly, the last couple of decades of PLD rule.

The Emergence of "the Dominican Paradox":
Planters, Slaves, Peasants, Migrants

Sidney Mintz, with his unique insight into the Caribbean social universes, wrote in 1974 that the peoples of the Caribbean "are illiterate rather than nonliterate; countrified rather than rural; urbanized, but nearly without cities; industrialized, but without factories—and, often, agricultural, but without land. Their poverty, rural styles, and agricultural dependence make them look like most of the Third World; but the similarities are deceptive and untrustworthy" (1989 [1974]:37–38). Nearly five decades later, in large parts of the Caribbean, including the Dominican Republic, much has changed dramatically. However, a lot appears to be unaltered, too. In the mid-1930s, 82 percent of the Dominican population lived in rural areas. In 1960, 70 percent remained rural, still one of the highest percentages in Latin America and the Caribbean (Turits 2003:265). Trujillo's strategies to increase agricultural production and secure peasants' access to land helped make the dictator's Dominican Republic "a virtually self-sufficient country in agricultural terms (save wheat), in contrast to the rest of the twentieth-century Caribbean and much of Latin America" (Turits 2003:20). After the end of the dictatorship, the country witnessed colossal urbanization and international migration. However, there remained few factories in the large Dominican cities. Significant parts of today's Dominican capital, not least its many poor barrios, are *both* urban *and* rural: they are cosmopolitan, and apparently industrialized, but mainly without factories. They represent a particular form of contemporary urban landscape: not particularly industrialized, not preindustrial, and not postindustrial, and with limited public welfare and a state in debt. Many citizens run their own small family enterprises, and many live off small-scale commerce (see in addition Hoffnung-Garskof 2008).

If we wish to understand the emergence of this reality (Santo Domingo's populous and poor barrios and how they function), we need to look at global capitalism's ravages, or history, on the island. Capitalism has always been transnational, and the traversing of geographical and political borders is immanent in its historical trajectory (Trouillot 2003; Pedersen 2013). Capital is continuously looking for sites where access to labor and other resources is cheaper, where regulations are less onerous, and where sites of production are closer to growing markets and/or are more technologized. An effect is unending disruption, constant capitalist restructuring, and the dislocation of specific labor-and-life forms. The feedback loops between movement and stasis that are integral to transnational capitalism are well captured by the term "dislocation." It signifies spatial movement (such as, for example, the movements of enslaved people, labor migrants, and refugees), but also encapsulates other senses of disorder or disorientation, such as the experience of feeling out of place, or of becoming confused or lost as things move and change around you. The term allows us to encompass important social-scientific discussions of "dispossession" (Harvey 2003; Carbonella and Kasmir 2014; West 2016), but also extends these preoccupations to more phenomenological ground: the meanings and the affective forces that color any human experience of labor and life.[14]

The collective work that makes up Ann Stoler's edited collection *Imperial Debris* powerfully brought out how imperative it still is in the contemporary world to continue to ask "how empire's ruins contour and carve through the psychic and material space in which people live and what compounded layers of imperial debris do to them" (Stoler 2013:2).[15] Today's Dominican society has emerged out of, and mirrors, a long, violent history: numerous processes of dislocation within which both places and people were forcefully reconfigured by the movements of capital. The fairly simple, or "traditional," rural economy that prevailed for centuries in Spanish colonial Santo Domingo was, in Richard Turits's words, "born, ironically, of modernity" (2003:26). The colony of Santo Domingo had an early, important sugar industry, worked by enslaved Africans, which produced large quantities of sugar for European markets from around 1520. But in the late 1500s, this plantation production collapsed as rapidly as it had emerged, and, after 1580, Spanish Santo Domingo produced little sugar for export (Mintz 1985:32–35). The next three hundred years saw commercial stagnation, and in the late eighteenth century Spanish Santo Domingo contained "only" 15,000 slaves (Moya Pons 1984:246). This opened up the space for the formation of a considerable independent or "reconstituted" peasantry: essentially former slaves and their progeny as well as marginal colonists with whom they mixed, who lived for generations mostly on the fringes of colonial society and control. This scattered and somewhat unbound mulatto population, which constituted the great majority of the colony's relatively few inhabitants, exploited the island's vast, undomesticated *monte* (woodlands), which was ideal for raising free-ranging animals, hunting, and engaging in slash-and-burn farming on small agricultural plots (Turits 2003: 10, 26).

The United States occupied the Dominican Republic from 1916 to 1924, in the process helping to create an effective national military institution in a country that had previously had none. By the age of thirty-nine, General Rafael Leónidas Trujillo Molina had become the leader of the modernized military that the United States had helped to establish, the Dominican National Army. Using his position to overthrow the elected government, he ruled the country for thirty-one years. The dictatorship would not have been possible had it not been for the activities of an expanding, imperialist United States (Roorda 1998). In addition, from the 1880s onward—some three hundred years after the island's first sugar industry had collapsed—the nation again saw sudden, intense development in the production of sugar for the world market. This production meant the creation of large, advanced plantations in more parts of the country, worked primarily by foreign, contracted migrant laborers—recruited first from the Lesser Antilles and then (to cut labor costs) mainly from Haiti. The longevity and stability of Trujillo's dictatorship cannot be understood in isolation from this more recent history of sugarcane cultivation in the country, and the protracted and considerable national economic growth this production helped generate (Hoetink 1986; Moya Pons 2010:357–80).

Yet, that is only half the story. The dictator was an economic reformist ruler who sought, in part, to enrich and empower himself, and in part to expand the state and create economic development, while simultaneously securing the independent and unchained peasants protection against the threats of increasing land and agricultural commercialization. The Trujillo state promoted an alternative, peasant-based, project of modernity (Turits 2003:81–82). In the period 1880–1930, prior to the Trujillo dictatorship, a growing commercialization of agriculture and rising land values in a few areas had led to efforts to enclose, survey, and claim land in most parts of the country. By the time Trujillo seized power, thousands of peasants had already been evicted by US-owned sugar companies, which had gained control of vast areas of land. Confronting this conjuncture, the repressive Trujillo regime implemented extensive agrarian reform that favored rural dwellers and agriculturalists by offering them land and eventually property rights. The dictator thus forged an alliance with people in the countryside. This alliance was not only about rural dwellers' state-protected access to land, agricultural assistance, and strengthened public infrastructure: it also served to protect and sustain a peasant way of life. Indeed, even today, many decades later, we continue to see the reproduction of a striking amount of selective nostalgia about the Trujillo era among elderly and ordinary Dominicans in the countryside and in the cities. A surprising number of people still say that under Trujillo everybody had to work on the land, and no one was without food (Turits 2003:1–114, 206–31; Krohn-Hansen 2009).

After 1961, however, the country's leaders and elites gradually moved the Dominican Republic away from the more self-sustaining, shielded, and somewhat isolated society of the Trujillo dictatorship, and toward an increasingly open, neoliberal economy. By the 1990s, the nation "was synchronized with the rhythms of expanding global capital to an extent not seen since the late-sixteenth century colonial plantation society. And at the end of the 1990s, as at the end of the 1500s, the rural population would find themselves on the move, searching for opportunities and a better life on the margins of modernity" (Turits 2003:263). Now, however, they did not seek out the island's undomesticated woodlands, but instead migrated to the cities, the capital, New York, Madrid, and beyond. As I said, urban growth took place in a national landscape without much industry.[16] Today, more than 70 percent of the Dominican population live in cities, and greater Santo Domingo has transformed into the largest Caribbean city, with a population of almost 3 million—almost 30 percent of the country's inhabitants. In the decades after the Trujillo rule, Dominicans became, as I have stressed, New York City's largest new immigrant group. The majority worked in garment factories and grocery stores, and as taxi drivers, janitors, hairdressers, and nannies. By 1990, one in every ten Dominicans lived in New York (Krohn-Hansen 2013).[17]

This is what I am talking about when I refer to capitalism's processes of dislocation. By dislocation, I mean the unevenness of transnational capitalism's unfolding, and the ways in which both historically produced locations and historically generated persons are transformed into altered forms by the movements of capital.

As Stephan Palmié put it in *The Cooking of History*, when we speak of the Caribbean, or more generally the worlds born of Western plantations built on slave labor, "there simply is no unself-conscious aboriginal state from which adherents of an undisturbed local tradition were ever catapulted into confrontation with global modernist ideologies" (2013:147). We are speaking of layers upon layers of disturbed pasts. We should therefore see *lo criollo*, or "the creole," as in the working-class barrios in today's greater Santo Domingo, as a testimony to the stunning human will, and ability, to survive, cultivate, create, renew, transform, build. At the same time, the histories of earlier or past European and US forms of imperialism are, in Stoler's (2013:11) words, "unfinished histories": they continue to have effects and to hurt and ruin—as the history of the Trujillo state with its afterlife shows so strikingly.

The results of the processes that I have outlined above can be observed in today's Dominican capital. The basic condition of the masses is not only difficult; it reflects conspicuous socioeconomic disorganization. One of the most telling expressions of the disorder is the last decades' registered Dominican jobless growth: the nation's continuous, significant growth in GDP over a period of more than twenty-five years accompanied by stagnant or even falling employment. In the Dominican Republic today, a number of actors (transnational and national corporations and firms, representatives of some local business families,[18] and parts of the political class) make good money. However, the social inequality is glaring. In significant areas of the country, the traces of the growth are scarcely visible, and an enormous proportion of the population remains poor and vulnerable.

The PLD State

The political party that essentially ruled the Dominican Republic from 1996 to 2020 was the Dominican Liberation Party, or the PLD, founded by Juan Bosch. Bosch, who died in 2001, was not only a politician; he was also among the country's leading and finest intellectuals. His works include innovative novels and critical sociological studies. His approach to politics was based on the Boschista doctrines: his personally worked out, Marxist-inspired interpretations of Dominican history (Bosch 1988 [1970]). Under him, the PLD political program was one of radical reform to create economic and social justice for the country's masses. However, everything changed before the elections in 1996. The presidential elections of 1994 triggered allegations of widespread fraud. Two years later, the ninety-year-old Balaguer stepped down for the last time. Once again, he had been forced to resign amid the greatest possible loss of credibility (Hartlyn 1998:251–54). The transfer of power when Balaguer stepped down for the first time in 1978 (having ruled the country repressively from 1966 to 1978) was highly irregular. Balaguer only left office, thereby transferring power to the winner of the election (the opposition candidate, Antonio Guzmán) after pressure had been put on him by the Carter administration in the United States. In 1996, PLD candidate Leonel Fernández was elected to the nation's highest office. Fernández, who had been brought up in the United States, secured more than 51 percent of the votes through an alliance with Balaguer and the latter's party.[19] Before the election, he had, as previously mentioned, sought to move the PLD toward a less radical or more "moderate" position, advocating economic liberalization and the privatization of state enterprises.

The PLD subsequently won the elections from 2004 to 2016. Fernández

governed from 1996 to 2000, and then from 2004 to 2012, before Danilo
Medina replaced him. In 2020, the PLD lost the election and the presidency. Before the election (which took place July 5, 2020), Fernández
had left the party, and this contributed to a party split. Luis Abinader—the
presidential candidate for the opposition Modern Revolutionary Party (Partido Revolucionario Moderno [PRM])—won the election. (For more on
the PLD split and the election in 2020, see the afterword.)

The extensive liberalization and opening up of the Dominican economy
took mostly place under the PLD's leadership. The regime celebrated economic growth but, in practice, did little to provide work, or satisfactory jobs.
The irrationality (growth, but enduring precarity and poverty) was further
aggravated by other features of the PLD state. The PLD rule helped, in
many ways, to reproduce, albeit in altered forms, some of the most harmful
features of the country's earlier authoritarian history. The effect was a more
difficult condition for most in the country. In the remainder of this section,
I discuss three of these features of PLD rule: (1) the PLD's political use of
the state; (2) the country's corruption processes; and (3) the PLD regime's
educational and cultural politics.

The Political Use of the Public Sector

Under the PLD, the Dominican state mostly operated with the same
political logic as it did under Balaguer and other earlier leaders. Previously, a Dominican had to belong to, and work for, Balaguer's party in
order to have the possibility of securing a public job (even as a cleaner or
a nurse in a small, state-run hospital, for example, or as a civil servant or
an engineer in the central administration in the capital) (Kearney 1986;
Krohn-Hansen 2009). In the PLD state, it was also usually obligatory
to belong to, and work for, the PLD, should one want a public job.
Merit—relevant education and competence—was seldom the decisive
criterion for a job application. Instead, the state staffed its offices across
the national territory politically, through patronage. Public jobs and access to the state's resources were treated as rewards for any political work
undertaken—or for the PLD's election victory. The consequences have
frequently been described in Dominican newspapers (for some specific
examples, see Oxfam 2017:30–35). Many of the state's institutions and
enterprises have more employees than are necessary; often, the employees perform little work, have little to do. Surprisingly many continue to
have what Dominicans, for decades, have called a *botella* (bottle): they

receive their monthly paycheck from a state institution or a state enterprise, but have never shown up at the workplace.[20] These practices contribute in at least two ways to the endurance and generation of forms of precarity and poverty. First, since public institutions lack qualified personnel, they do not supply citizens with adequate services. Second, the vast state resources spent each year on unnecessary wages could instead have been used to produce (actual, not fictive) public services. In 2015, the Dominican Republic had 592,000 public employees; the number increased on average 3.7 percent per year from 2001 to 2015 (Oxfam 2017:35). The growth was particularly high in the election years 2002, 2004, 2006, 2008, 2010, 2012, and 2016. In these years, the number of employees increased on average 3.8 percent, while the corresponding figure for the years without elections (2005, 2007, 2009, 2011, 2013, 2014, and 2015) was 3.2 percent (Oxfam 2017:36–37). The figures are testimony to an immense inclination to use the state's resources for clientelistic purposes.[21]

Corruption and Impunity

The Dominican state-system has been haunted by corruption and accusations of corruption. Corruption is a pattern; it is expected. It is found at the top of the state, and deep down at the bottom of the hierarchies. That a culture of corruption reigns in today's Dominican society is not so surprising if we look at the country's history. Trujillo was, with his greed, corruption incarnate. The decades under Balaguer were replete with corruption and accusations of corruption. As historian Frank Moya Pons maintains, under Balaguer, "public officials and high ranking military officers generously doled out contracts for public works among themselves, enjoyed exemptions for the tax-free import of all the consumer goods they desired, and became rich enough to play the roles of investor and entrepreneur in unfair competition with traditional commercial and industrial groups. Government corruption during Balaguer's regime expanded so much that even the Catholic church mentioned it in its pastoral letters" (Moya Pons 2010:401–2). The Dominican Republic has hardly experienced a type of rule other than one founded on patronage and clientage (or the idioms of kinship and friendship) with accompanying networks of corruption. According to a national poll carried out by Gallup for the newspaper *Hoy* in the autumn of 2017, as many as 89 percent (of the sample of 1,200 persons) classified the country's corruption levels as *alarmantes* (alarming). Sixty percent were of the opinion that when they cast their votes, people did not care if the candidates were corrupt (*Hoy* 2017).

The disturbing levels of corruption (however normalized and predictable they may be) make the state, with its myriad institutions and agents, look chaotic and impenetrable, like a murky or lawless order.[22] The corruption makes public projects and works more expensive, and harms or even destroys them (as Cristian's story, related at the start of this introduction, illustrates). The state's money disappears and is stolen (for a book that documents, in fascinating detail, one of the most spectacular cases of vanished money and corruption scandals in the Fernández years, see the work of the brave economist and mathematician Jaime Aristy Escuder, *El lado oscuro de la SunLand* [2012]). Corruption also engenders unfair and illegal economic competition. It turns local and national markets upside down. How so? Thanks to corruption, vast amounts of commodities (everything from rice and beans to shoes and medicine) are illegally imported into the country, with the consequence that ordinary Dominican producers, firms, and stores are unable to compete, and so lose work, market shares and opportunities.[23]

Although Dominican media continuously report on concrete accusations of corruption against individuals, institutions, and firms, few economic crimes committed by politicians, military officers, police, or business leaders are brought to justice. Extremely few are convicted. It is therefore a common assertion, or conclusion, in today's Dominican Republic, that the country is ruled with "impunity" (R. Espinal 2017; Mateo 2017; Oxfam 2017). Many police officers and judges are corrupt; they look the other way if given a bribe or even cooperate with criminals (Espinal 2017). In 2017, a World Economic Forum report ranked the degree of "juridical independence" in 137 nations, and the Dominican Republic came near the bottom, in 130th place, below Congo and Haiti (Schwab 2017:95, 107, 137). Small wonder, perhaps, that many Dominicans claim that the state, in an important sense, is absent, nonexistent. As one of my interlocutors, a man in his fifties, and a fairly cynical, but successful, small-business owner, put it: "Here, we don't have security. Here reigns the principle every man for himself. There is no state! The government itself pretends that it doesn't see."

The Regime's Educational and Cultural Politics

In the years 1991–2010, the Dominican Republic spent about 2 percent of the annual GDP on public education, ranking it at the bottom of Latin American and Caribbean countries (Carneiro and Sirtaine 2017:8).[24] Despite a notable expansion in school enrollment since the early 1990s, the system has been marked by high student-to-teacher ratios, inadequate formation, and depressingly high dropout rates (Sánchez and Senderowitsch 2012). To address these challenges, and following comprehensive popular protests and demands to increase public expenditure on education, in the 2013 budget the Medina government raised spending on education to 4 percent of GDP for the first time. Despite the size of this investment (that is, the increase in the allocation of funds for pre-university education), strengthening the school curriculum remains a huge challenge. As the World Bank mercilessly put it a few years ago, "Dominican students continue to perform poorly and lag behind other Latin American and Caribbean countries, reflecting the weakness of the system in helping students develop basic cognitive skills (e.g. reading and math), particularly in early grades. In the latest regional assessment conducted in 2013, 74.1 percent and 84.8 percent of third graders performed at the lowest level [in reading and math]. These results are substantially worse than those of comparable countries, and represent the highest proportion of such results in the region" (World Bank Group 2016:49).

This has two key repercussions for many households: First, the percentage of the Dominican population between fifteen and twenty-four years old who, according to official data, were "neither in school nor in work" in 2016 was 21.4 percent, slightly higher than the Latin American average (World Bank Group 2016:51). The usual way of being put into this category, in particular for young men, is to drop out of school and join the unstable, informal job market. If they lose this informal job, poor young men rarely return to school. Second, many ordinary households, because of the educational politics, incur higher schooling costs. Over the last few decades, the Dominican Republic's private school sector has grown tremendously (Murray 2005; Sánchez and Senderowitsch 2012). This is understandable. A growing number of people, especially in the middle class, but also in the vast working class, opt out of state schools because of their poor quality, choosing instead to send their children to private schools (which are of varying quality).

In sum, such features of PLD rule helped to cement the deep feeling of discontent that appears to be so prominent in so many places in contemporary Dominican society. The PLD state was built on a patronage system, was permeated by corruption, and did little to reduce socioeconomic inequality.

Precarity, *la familia,* and Small Business

Over the last few years the concept of precarity has become a central preoccupation in anthropology (Muehlebach 2013; Das and Randeria 2015; Han 2018; Millar 2018)—although anthropologists have long studied historically and culturally specific forms of precarity and how it is experienced and lived by people in different settings. In this book, I use the concept in a broad, elastic sense to include a range of different insecure conditions with their associated material-social forms and subjectivities. I use the term as shorthand for the many forms of basic economic uncertainty that so many people in today's Santo Domingo experience, from those who are unemployed, or have just temporary, miserably paid work, to those who operate, or seek to operate, their own small enterprise, but lack capital, access to sufficient credit, or enough demand, clients, or political support. However, I also use the term to refer to other forms of insecurity. In much of the capital, access to water is limited and unreliable—both for domestic consumption and for industry. In most neighborhoods, access to electricity for households and businesses is also chronically unstable and unpredictable, or nonexistent. A great number of roads, streets, and paths become impassable if it rains. Many people live with insecurity because of the apparent lawlessness, and the widespread corruption—the endless stream of small and large bribes that must be paid to judges, police officers, and other types of public officials and politicians. Owners of small stores and workshops fear becoming victims of arbitrary inspections and fines. Many fear theft, or another kind of crime, that often goes unpunished. A good example is the story of a single mother in her forties, who ran a food stall in a working-class area in the north of the city. Three times in the last decade, she explained to me, she had been forced to take an involuntary break from work—to gather together resources so she could start up afresh—after thieves broke into her business in the night and stole her equipment. No one had ever been punished.[25]

In order to manage, people turn to family and friends. Those who start up or buy a business often use kin and friends to raise initial capital. Many develop family firms. Help with child care, a job, or a new place to live: such things are often obtained with the aid of relatives and acquaintances.

Especially important is *la familia*, the extended family. When a Dominican speaks of *la familia*, they often refer to a large but loosely organized network of persons. Above the level of the household, the basis for construction of kinship is personal kindred. This personal kindred is individual-centered and bilateral by nature: that is, it consists of persons who are related to a particular individual on both the father's and the mother's sides. These personal kindreds are only apparent when mobilized. Historically, personal kindreds have become visible in connection with life-cycle rituals, particularly funerals. They have also been among the most significant building blocks when people have made, remade, and modified everyday life. Dominicans have drawn on their personal kindred and mobilized relatives when organizing agricultural activities, trade, and migration. The use of *la familia* has also played a decisive part in the country's political life. Kindreds have been put to use to create and sustain leaderships, factions, political parties, and the state-system (Derby 2009; Krohn-Hansen 2009).

Three dimensions, in particular, of many Dominicans' family relationships shed light on why so many have been able to, and indeed continue, to use these relationships to develop livelihoods and businesses. First, kinship ties can only be used efficiently for such purposes if they function in a climate in which exchanges are backed by mutual trust, or what Alejandro Portes (1995:4) long ago described as "enforceable trust." The kinship institution must be in a strong position; people must identify profoundly with the belief that relatives should exchange favors, pool resources, and stick together. The Dominican Republic's political and social history in the twentieth and the early twenty-first centuries—in particular the many decades of dictatorship and repressive, arbitrary rule—engendered a climate within which the concept of kinship became deeply rooted. Second, Dominicans have created and developed their enterprises through alliances with a range of different types of relatives. Some have worked with a spouse or children, some with brothers and sisters, some with cousins, and some with an uncle or an aunt. Others have sought help from or worked with a half-brother, a brother-in-law, or a sister-in-law. Dominicans' kin relationships are characterized by flexibility, and this has significantly broadened people's room for maneuvering and creative action. Third, many have had access to a considerable number of relatives, in other words, have belonged to sizable families.[26] This, too, has helped broaden the space for efficient resource pooling.

Yet, why are the businesses not (at least not automatically or necessarily) eroded by excessive claims from relatives?[27] Dominicans have, for a long time now, been used to the concept of private property. As I explained, land became a commodity in all parts of the country during the late nineteenth and early twentieth centuries, and firms and businesses are privately owned. Today, Dominicans emphasize family solidarity, but they also cultivate a person's right and ability to act independently, to be an individual. Indeed, it has often been claimed that Caribbean societies in general strongly value and nurture imaginaries of the independent person (Ortiz 1995 [1940]; Mintz 1989 [1974]:37–38, 155–56; Freeman 2014). Businesses have also been shielded by people's ideas about what produces value—what produces money. Those who run family businesses generally work long hours. They know that the source of value and profit is labor. This has made it possible to create and maintain a boundary between those in the family who contribute labor (or work in the enterprise) and those who do not. This boundary is used to efficiently limit the extent of unity and solidarity between kin.

In the chapters that follow, I examine various niches in, or parts of, the Dominican economy. In so doing, I seek to throw light on how the masses in the capital worked and lived in the shadow of the Dominican Republic's noticeable growth rates, and on how they fared in the PLD state. A more basic goal is to track and analyze how some of those in today's world, who have never had access to well-paid, stable wage work, think, labor, and adapt. Chapters 1–4 are envisaged as an ordered sequence of relatively independent essays. Each focuses on a different socioeconomic field (with its actors, practices, and processes). Chapter 5 then returns to a discussion of the more general challenges that the phenomena of jobless growth and "no wage labor" futures raise for anthropology and political-economic analysis. While the chapters are meant to form an integrated whole when read in sequence, my intention is that each can also be read alone. I hope that the reader will pardon a certain amount of redundancy that must necessarily accompany this approach.

CHAPTER 1
State against Industry
Time and Labor among Dominican Furniture Makers

Marx's explorations in *Capital* show that the abstract time-reckoning of capitalism helps to produce a large number of contradictory social rhythms that must be mediated by social agents—capitalists, workers, financiers—through concrete activity. His studies of capitalist "circulation time" in volume 2 (1993 [1885]), for example, demonstrate that there is a contradiction between the rhythms of production and consumption, and those of money markets—and that decisive infrastructures of production are often left vulnerable, or are jeopardized by the patterns and rhythms of credit markets. In turn, the diversity and clashes between rhythms have an impact on both collective and individual experiences of time. At the level of the self, the navigation of capitalist time is thus replete with dilemmas and choices.

A basic anthropological task is, consequently, to examine ethnographically the various forms of labor through which inconsistent capitalist rhythms are mediated. As Laura Bear (2014a, 2014b, 2016) has instructively underscored, such an endeavor should focus on labor practices.[1] It is through specific encounters with the material world and creative use of the body, technology, and time that humans seek to reconcile disparate time-maps[2] and social rhythms. In this chapter, I examine forms of time and labor among a group of small-scale entrepreneurs—owners and operators of mainly small, precarious family businesses. These entities all produce and sell furniture and mattresses, and are situated in various parts of the Dominican capital.

The Dominican Republic's furniture industry is neither large nor powerful. On the contrary, its position today is fairly weak, not to say seriously threatened. Around 95 percent of the production units are *talleres* (workshops or small enterprises) with fewer than fifty workers, usually fewer than ten. In 2012, the national production of furniture constituted 1 percent of GDP (Rodríguez Bencosme 2013:16). A large proportion of these firms are situated in the capital, typically in its most popular and populous neighborhoods. I stress that most of my data are derived from small, precarious operations that employ few workers. In these firms, the owner has an office (or at least a desk and a couple of chairs pushed into a corner) where they attend to customers and paperwork—but the workshop is never far away; most owners spend the bulk of their time with the workers, making or repairing furniture.

Anthropological analyses of social time under contemporary capitalism are important for at least three reasons. First, such analyses provide a window through which to comprehend power differentials and forms of inequality. It is important to be concerned with capitalism's forms of time because they express the constant negotiation of the power relationships in the capitalist system.

Second, we need an ethnographically driven critique of approaches to research that seem too general or abstract. Many explorations of the social time of capitalism work only at the scale of global processes, in almost complete isolation from studies of specific places. This applies, for example, to the works of Marxist thinkers, such as David Harvey (1989, 2005) and Noel Castree (2009). The problem with their—and many others'—discussions of capitalist circulation time is that they almost exclusively seek to account for capitalism's dynamics and "fixes" in terms of large-scale processes, such as the advancing of credit through banking activities and financial operations. These analyses do not draw attention to the everyday forms of labor that make global capitalism possible. Real, contemporary capitalist circulation has to be understood as a contingent outcome of labor activity in the form of myriad localized, prosaic, and creative efforts to "fix" it according to manifold ideas about time, well-being, usefulness, advantage, and profit. Such efforts always articulate particular moral and affective forms and a particular history. By studying contemporary capitalist time through a focus on concrete (in other words, localized) labor, we can identify—and provide insights into—how global capitalism's discrepant rhythms help disrupt and dislocate forms of labor in a given place (Harvey and Krohn-Hansen 2018).

Simultaneously, we can show how the agents involved seek to adapt to, and respond to the effects of, the contradictions between rhythms.

Third, anthropological examinations of contemporary capitalist time are significant because they can help us better understand the sustained, tremendous role of the state, and how deeply the world's nation-state systems and global capitalism are entangled. This continues to apply, even though most states since the 1980s have deregulated markets and trade, and privatized assets in striking ways (Graeber 2002; Pedersen 2013). In what follows I focus, in particular, on the effects of state debt (Bear 2015a). Like so many other states, the Dominican Republic has had significant debt for a long time now. Debt relations are, by definition, about the social shaping of time. In the words of Gustav Peebles, "the crucial defining feature of credit/debt is its ability to link the present to the past and the future . . . Credit is a method of lending concrete resources to an institution or an individual in the present and demanding (or hoping for) a return in the future" (2010:226–27). A modern state's debt is bound to the calendar (Graeber 2011; Guyer 2012:491). In the Dominican case, we shall see that the construction and reconstruction of the state's debt—governed by calendar time—creates unpredictability, delays and, more generally, clashes between forms of time. The other side of this is, of course, that the country's inhabitants, including the producers of furniture, are forced to adapt. These accommodations and adjustments they must make take place in the everyday environment, and in, and through, labor.

Dominican furniture makers' labor is also political—or, put differently, their efforts to find solutions have a political dimension. How so? First, the Dominican state, with its various institutions, is a crucial actor. Producers of furniture continually need to adjust to public laws and regulations, and many apply to state institutions for loans and credit. Many also attempt to sell their products to public agencies. The outcome is that most, if not all, in the industry find themselves in almost constant negotiation—struggles over rights and obligations, resources, documents, and meaning—with representatives of the state. Second, Dominican producers of furniture and mattresses have created their own interest organization, La Asociación Nacional de Industriales de Muebles, Colchones y Afines (ASONAIMCO). Through this, they attempt to act collectively and fight for their common interests. As I show, a vast majority of those in the industry are profoundly critical of the state. According to them, the Dominican state has rendered it increasingly difficult—almost impossible—for the national industry to survive and develop. In the following section, I outline some key features of the general economic situation of the industry, before looking in more detail at social time among Santo Domingo's furniture makers.

Trujillo's Authoritarian Legacy, Structural Adjustment, and the Conditions of the Dominican Industry

The timescape of today's Dominican industry is a product of the past. Two processes have been key: first, the nation's protracted authoritarian political history; and second, the country's adoption of an increasingly neoliberal political-economic model since the beginning of the 1990s. General Rafael Trujillo ruled the Dominican Republic dictatorially from 1930 to 1961. From 1966 to 1978, and from 1986 to 1996, the country was governed by Joaquín Balaguer. The latter had been one of Trujillo's close collaborators, and his first twelve years in power were violently repressive. After 1978, the use of military repression was discontinued, and the nation has celebrated presidential and congressional elections every four years.

In 1990, the Dominican economy was in deep crisis, and the government was unable to pay its debts (Greenberg 1997:87–88). This period, 1990–93, saw the beginning of a marked opening of the Dominican economy under International Monetary Fund (IMF) stabilization programs underpinned by a large number of neoliberal reforms. The 1990 tax reforms opened national markets to foreign competition by lowering tariffs and removing most of the import quotas and licensing requirements. The Foreign Investment Law, passed in 1995, opened significant parts of the economy to foreign investment, and removed all restrictions on profit remittances (Moya Pons 2010:444–48, 458–59). Leonel Fernández, president in 1996–2000 and 2004–12, intensified this process of neoliberal restructuring.

Since the mid-1980s, tourism, export manufacturing, and migrant remittances have been the country's most important sources of foreign exchange (Gregory 2014:20–26, 136–39; Winkler and Montenegro 2021:7). Whereas tourism and export manufacturing have enjoyed state support and special incentives and privileges, traditional industries, such as the furniture industry, have been marginalized, as is illustrated by the following two examples.

The bulk of Dominican furniture production is for the domestic market. There is a tiny export market, but it is highly limited (and deals almost exclusively with Haiti, Puerto Rico, and Jamaica). With the opening of the Dominican economy, Dominican furniture production for the national market has faced increasingly tough competition from imported commodities, particularly furniture made in China, Indonesia, the United States, and Europe. Many of these imported products are cheap, or relatively so. For example, Denny Reynoso, a spokesperson for the Dominican furniture makers, declared in May 2009: "Today . . . the problem is that the demand for local furniture has gone down more than 40 percent because people buy more furniture made in China, Indonesia, and Malaysia" (Maldonado 2009). Those I met in the industry underscored that they do not oppose free trade or stronger economic competition. What frustrated them, they said, was that the changes had occurred so quickly and without any transition period that could have helped domestic producers to adapt.

The tourist companies, meanwhile, are constantly building hotels, which need furniture: beds, chairs, tables, cupboards. But local access to this market has been undermined and blocked through the state's tax policies. This is how Santo Domingo's furniture producers see the situation. According to the owners in the tourist industry, it is more economically advantageous for them to import. If hotel owners purchase furniture from local producers, they have to pay the country's normal 18 percent value-added tax (VAT). But if they instead import the furniture directly from abroad, they do not have to pay this tax. Most therefore choose to import rather than buying locally.

The Timescape of the Production of Furniture in Santo Domingo—and a History of Entrepreneurship and Labor

A number of Santo Domingo's small furniture makers underscored that a part of their basic survival strategy, given the rapidly growing sector of furniture imported from Asia and elsewhere, was to offer "Dominican," not foreign, products. What kind of mapping and navigation of time does this strategy reflect? While the first part of this section provides answers to this question, the second part examines the following question: How did these workshops and firms function in order to secure sufficient access (a) to electricity (for production) and (b) to the market? Although the main theme of temporality recurs throughout the analysis, the specific, ethnographically driven intervention explaining the connections between historically constituted structures of power, laboring practices, exploitation, and forms of time features as a shifting and contingent picture that refracts differently in each part. I seek to formulate a bottom-up, anthropological account of capitalist labor and its value(s). Specifically, I seek to develop a perspective using material from just a few firms. Social time and capitalist time may appear to be elusive categories, a bit slippery, vague, mystical, even. Ethnography, replete as it is with descriptions of mundane, prosaic, and concrete realities, has the ability to demonstrate, from the level of the individual workshop or enterprise, how society's and capitalism's framings of time and diverse rhythms are reflected in the most ordinary and trivial occurrences, and in the biographies and everyday lives and labor of flesh-and-blood citizens.

Power, Timber, Time

Before the Dominican economy started to change due to the liberalization of trade in the early 1990s, the amount of furniture imported from abroad was very limited—and came in mostly through diplomatic or "occult" (illegal) channels. The regimes of Trujillo and Balaguer protected the domestic industry through prohibitions on the import of commodities that could be made in the country: beverages, shoes, furniture, and a long list of other products. As one furniture maker put it in a conversation, in the early 1990s "suddenly the restrictions and prohibitions were abolished and the country was hit by an avalanche."

Dominican furniture products, Santo Domingo's furniture makers maintain, are different from most of the imported products in at least three critical ways: the use of materials, the production process, and forms of time. In the following paragraphs, I will explain this, and in so doing I hope to be able to demonstrate that many ordinary Dominicans, from the large working classes as well as the middle class, continue to want, and prefer, "Dominican" furniture. Most of the extant small firms survive because of these groups. My argument is this: the government's loans, tied to IMF and World Bank conditions, had a decisive significance. Pressured by financial difficulties and international lenders, the state deregulated and opened the economy, while still failing to invest in the development of the nation's workshops, small firms, and industry. The combination of contemporary global capitalism's (technical, social, and economic) ability to compress time and space, and the opening up and liberalization of the Dominican market, resulted in the growth of the import sector over the last thirty years. In many cases, the outcome for Santo Domingo's small furniture makers has been, as I have said, difficult or precarious conditions and conflicts between social rhythms and forms of time. The businesses seek to get by through their labor. As we shall see, one strategy is particularly effective: continuing to offer styles of furniture that are in tune with a certain historically constituted tradition and widespread Dominican (popular) taste. This taste expresses a way of thinking about furniture and time, and is linked to memories. Put differently, these Dominican furniture makers' labor is a labor on forms of time and history.[3]

The contemporary Dominican furniture market can be divided into three categories (Rodríguez Bencosme 2013:93). The first of these represents what may be summarized as more or less traditional forms of furniture. The preferred colors are dark, and the style is classic—or an amalgamation of classic styles. A large percentage of the population prefers this "classic" design to rustic or more contemporary (straight) lines. The furniture is made from wood, preferably mahogany (or materials that somehow resemble mahogany), and the most desirable chairs, sofas, and tables have lavish carvings. The second category comprises furniture of a more "contemporary" type—often with straight lines. Very few businesses in the Dominican Republic make these products; instead, most are imported. In 2002, this type of furniture made up about 16 percent of the value of the national market for furniture (Rodríguez Bencosme 2013:93). The third category consists of products that do not fit the other two categories owing to the use of materials or to where the furniture is used. Examples are pieces of furniture made of iron or rattan, modular kitchens, and furniture for gardens, offices, and hotels. This sector of the market has seen an increasing number of imports.

In addition to mahogany, Dominican firms use other types of wood, especially pine, oak, and, to a lesser extent, acacia. Almost all the timber used by Dominican furniture makers is imported. In 2000, in an attempt to prevent deforestation, the country passed a law (Law 64–00 on the Environment and Natural Resources) that prohibits the use of native forests for commercial purposes. Labor in the workshops is anchored in carpentry traditions: firms take the measurements of kitchens and bedrooms, receive small orders, and carry out repair work.

Small Dominican furniture makers argue that many ordinary Dominicans prefer Dominican furniture to imported furniture. They are of the opinion that the familiar national products last longer—they are more solid and hence better. Dominican furniture is made from solid wood, not from veneer, plywood, or other less robust materials. This is how Rafael Estévez, a furniture maker in the eastern part of the city, put it. He and his father had sought to diversify and develop an extra source of income by importing some furniture in addition to making and selling their own products:

> We wanted to experiment, attempt to import and sell furniture made in China. We sold a little before we imported a bit more and sold a bit more. But, as I see it, our audience [customers] prefers the furniture made here, the wood, to know that it's wood and not a type of compressed cardboard or something similar, which will get damaged rapidly. People remain traditional concerning this.

María Paulino, who runs a tiny workshop in the popular barrio of Los Mina Norte, explained:

> The creole furniture made here [*El mueble criollo de aquí*] in the Dominican Republic is the furniture that lasts. The imported furniture doesn't last, isn't equally good, I think. Here, people want their furniture to be durable—and the furniture lasts for many years, which isn't a good business for us [*laughing*] . . . But the furniture that we make is furniture that lasts—owing to the materials, the way of working, because we use wood; abroad they often use cardboard or plywood, materials that immediately are damaged if they get wet. Wood veneer is fine in a country with a lot of resources, where people change furniture each year, but not here. We don't change our furniture so quickly.

Dominicans with limited means do not treat furniture as disposable. On the contrary, when they invest in furniture, they want it to be durable. The life of a piece of furniture can be long. In popular barrios, there are usually stores selling used furniture. The desire for solid furniture made from whole wood, not plywood, has to do with typical Dominican (middle- and working-class) domestic rituals. As María said, imported products are often made from materials that are easily damaged if they get wet. When Dominicans clean their homes (typically every Saturday), they empty buckets of water and soap onto the floor. Furniture with legs or plinths made of veneer does not stand up to this treatment.

As previously mentioned, the preferred type of wood for many people is mahogany, or *caoba*, and this has been the most culturally valued material for generations: good furniture is made from mahogany. Aldo Núñez, one of two owners of a firm in the barrio of Casa Vieja in the north of the city, put it this way:

We Dominicans have always said that mahogany is the best wood. I'm from the countryside and grew up with this: mahogany is mahogany [*la caoba es la caoba*] . . . It's like a culture. The Dominican is so fond of mahogany that he even is fooled or swindled! Yes! Because you take a piece of wood and paint it and tell him that it's mahogany and he buys it.

Mahogany is more expensive; people with less money purchase furniture with less mahogany in it, or furniture that is only the color of mahogany—or they purchase furniture made from pine or rattan. Yuri Chez, who headed the furniture makers' organization ASONAIMCO until late 2012, explained:

Trujillo used a lot of mahogany and, in the past, people harvested a lot of mahogany. But in those days, a lot of mahogany was felled without any control and without any reforestation programs. In the colonial period, even exceedingly old trees were harvested—the Spaniards and the Europeans used mahogany precisely to make furniture, and for shipbuilding and housebuilding.[4] Mahogany was precious wood that was sold at low prices as if it were a cheap wood, owing to the abundance. This is the background to the tradition that we still see today, that people prefer furniture made from mahogany, that it's viewed as better than any other wood.

Dominican workshops and businesses that make furniture from mahogany work in an established tradition. Through their products, they elicit and sell emotions, notions, and memories—historically produced affective forms that are filled with a sense of history. Today, *la caoba* is the national tree of the Dominican Republic. General Trujillo (ruled 1930–61), a man from a modest background, with thoroughly traditional taste, created the twentieth-century Dominican nation-state. He was a ruthless dictator, but his protracted rule transformed Dominican society in important ways, for better or for worse (Turits 2003; Derby 2009). His regime built roads, irrigation canals, homes, schools, and hospitals throughout the country. One of the regime's central characteristics was patronage, and furniture made from high-quality mahogany featured in all the most important public buildings and offices that the regime constructed. In his home town of San Cristóbal, Trujillo built, as early as 1940, what became his favorite country house, La Casa de Caoba, or Mahogany House. Mahogany was the principal material used in the building, hence the name.

Today, the Dominican Republic is among the world's largest mahogany importers, behind only the United States, China, and the United Kingdom. The largest exporter today is Peru, which surpassed Brazil after that country banned mahogany exports in 2001. A depressingly large proportion of exported Peruvian mahogany is illegally harvested (Gordon 2016). Illegal logging and its destructive environmental and social effects led to mahogany's incorporation, in 2003, into Appendix II of the Convention on International Trade in Endangered Species (CITES). Other suppliers of genuine mahogany today are commercial plantations in India, Bangladesh, Indonesia, and Fiji.

The Dominican furniture makers I know adapt to their clientele and are flexible. Take Lorenzo Ortiz and Aldo Núñez, for example. Their customers were members of the working class and lower middle class. When they started their firm in the north of the city in 2002, they made upholstered furniture—chairs and sofas—and different styles of small tables. The chairs and sofas had mahogany legs; however, under the textiles, the makers used Chilean pine. The tables were made of mahogany.

In offering Dominican furniture, and especially products made with *caoba*, workshops and businesses help give form to experiences of time. Through the everyday use of objects made with mahogany, people inscribe themselves and their families into the national past and present narratives of the island; the national territory with its vegetation and resources; and the Trujillo dictatorship and its building of today's Dominican Republic. The construction (or the remembering) of the nation and the making and remaking of the self and the family are thus woven together, and work together. The sight of familiar furniture evokes personal memories—of one's own adolescence; of family and neighbors; of homes, kitchens, and sitting rooms. Additionally, the consumption of *caoba* operates as a language for the measurement of relative success: through purchasing and using furniture and other objects made of mahogany, it is possible to experience time as a form of personal growth and individual mobility—or as a form of spectacular political-economic triumph, as Trujillo must have experienced it when he luxuriated in mahogany at La Casa de Caoba.

As I have shown, the picture is dynamic, and the growing importation of furniture is a reality. Well-to-do Dominicans purchase furniture made in Europe or the United States. Younger, educated couples, and Dominicans who grew up or used to live in New York or Spain, may opt for a more "contemporary" style: objects with straight lines, made from chipboard or plywood. The tourist sector imports the furniture it needs. Furthermore, public institutions and the general public increasingly purchase imported products. In this landscape, small-scale Dominican furniture makers attempt to get by and survive. Their strategies grow out of particular affective and moral ideas about workmanship, materials, furniture objects, and time. Dominican solid wood furniture is considered to be long lasting. In addition, the products are part of history—or part of a variety of concepts related to both the past and the present. The manufacture and the use of this furniture helps sustain and modify memories, produce roots, and anchor and legitimize understandings of the self, including notions of growth and mobility.

Capitalism as Speed, Capitalism as Foot-dragging

In the real capitalist world, the rhythms of credit and money markets frequently imperil the health of important infrastructures of production. Infrastructure first has to be created and constructed, and then kept in good repair and renewed. These tasks require withholding significant capital from circulation for the long term and, in many states today, this is difficult to manage. It is especially hard to manage for a state that already struggles with debt problems (Mains 2012; Schwenkel 2015; Jensen 2017; Appel et al. 2018).

The best example of infrastructure challenges in the contemporary Dominican Republic is probably the nation's power sector. In most parts of Dominican society, access to electricity has, for decades, been unreliable, and short and long blackouts have been—and continue to be—part of everyday life. As a consequence of this protracted and apparently chronic crisis in the country's power sector, Dominicans experience a number of discrepant social and economic rhythms that stem from the dominant use of abstract time in global capitalism. But, and this is important to recognize, these discrepancies are also a product of something more delimited, namely, Dominican political and social history—or features of a particular historically constituted state-system and of a particular historically produced political culture. Below, I show ways in which small furniture makers seek to cope and find solutions, or "fix" these contradictions, through their forms of labor. First, I provide an overview of the history of the Dominican power sector.

Electricity rates in the Dominican Republic are among the highest in Latin America. As with so many other nations, high prices are a consequence of the country's reliance on oil for electricity generation. However, the industry also suffers from low tariff collection rates and considerable electricity theft. Massive reforms, implemented by the Fernández administration in the late 1990s, led to the privatization of the largest of the state enterprises. These enterprises, which had been confiscated from Trujillo and his associates in 1961, had been a heavy financial burden on the state for years, as mismanagement and corruption had left them more or less in shambles. As a result of the reforms, the formerly state-owned Corporación Dominicana de Electricidad (which until then owned all of the commercial electricity generation, transmission, and distribution assets in the country) was split up and sold. Nearly fifteen years later, at the time of my fieldwork, much of the nation's electricity generating system was owned by American corporations, although the Dominican state continued to control and operate most of the distribution sector. The state owned two of the country's distribution companies, EdeSur and EdeNorte, and it also retained 50 percent ownership of the third company, EdeEste.

At this time, the government also owed large sums to the IMF and other international lenders; in July 2012, the state's distribution companies' total debt to foreign generation companies broke an earlier record when it was estimated at around US$1 billion (*Hoy* 2012c). The outcome was *apagones*, or blackouts, across much of the country: the generators reduced electricity flowing to the country's distribution grid, and/or the distribution companies sought to discipline a recalcitrant population (and the government) into paying their electricity bills through shutting down services to barrios in the capital and other places where too few paid for the electricity they consumed. In May 2012, for example, owners of stores and workshops in Villa Consuelo, one of the capital's populous working-class barrios with a number of furniture workshops, protested loudly, telling reporters that the power in the area was gone each day from 7 a.m. to 8 p.m. (*Hoy* 2012b).

Some businesses were far better equipped to deal with this chronic crisis. For example, tourist resorts, free zones, and large companies have their own generators and methods of securing uninterrupted access to electricity. Most wealthy Dominicans also have backup generators to provide power when the lights go out—transforming the capital at nightfall into a patchwork of illumination, with some leafier districts brightly lit, while much of the rest of the city is in darkness.

As an outcome of the historical-political-economic-cultural production and reproduction of *apagones*, Santo Domingo's small producers of furniture are compelled to work with, and on, time—or, put another way, are driven to find time that can be put to use to produce and make money. Let us briefly look at how a couple of these businesses get by.

María Paulino's small workshop is, as I said, located in Los Mina Norte, in the eastern part of the city. She herself is in her late fifties, married, and has a grown daughter who is a student. María's husband, a retired teacher, assists her in the workshop—he buys materials, runs errands, and visits the bank. María runs the workshop, takes part in production, and deals with customers. Most of the work is manual. The workshop uses machines, but no heavy equipment. María has two permanent workers who have worked with her for years. Before she established her own workshop, nearly three decades ago, in 1992, she worked for many years in different furniture factories in the capital. In one of these, she learned how to make furniture from rattan: rattan chairs, rattan sofas, and rattan garden furniture. Ever since she started her own business in 1992, she has therefore specialized in the production of rattan furniture.

One of the biggest challenges remains *la luz*, or the electricity. Sometimes, the power is gone all day—or for two or three whole days, María said. In addition, it is unpredictable. As she put it, "When I arrive in the morning and there is power, I begin to work, filled with energy. But when the workers have arrived but wish to leave because we lack electricity and can't work, I'm at the point of despair." How have they tried to limit this loss of working hours? María has a small backup generator to provide power when it is needed; she cannot afford a large one. If the day begins without electricity, the first thing she has to do is send someone out to purchase gasoline for the generator. Sometimes she doesn't have the money, and they are unable to get to work—and sometimes the generator suddenly stops working and needs repair. Since she began, she has had to buy three different generators. Two have broken. "When you have to use the generator without intermission eight hours a day for long periods, it ends up breaking down," she explained, showing me the remains of the two earlier ones in a corner of the workshop. The one she uses now was made by a workshop in the vicinity from an old car engine.

The other firm is situated about 8 kilometers to the north of the city center, in the barrio of Casa Vieja in Villa Mella. Lorenzo Ortiz and Aldo Núñez are in their late forties and *socios*, or business partners. Lorenzo is the salesman and administrative head; Aldo is the furniture maker and spends most of his time in the workshop with the workers. As noted above, their business is concerned with making upholstered furniture and tables.

In 2012, their business had thirty-two workers, mainly young men in their early twenties; some years earlier, the number of workers had varied between eight and twenty. The workshop has seven simple machines; the production activities resemble a cottage industry more than a factory.

Lorenzo and Aldo had not even tried to work with the power supplied by the electricity companies. Ever since they started in 2002, they had exclusively relied on their own generator. As Lorenzo put it,

> I've never used the power from the street [*la energía de la calle*], because in this neighborhood where we operate they supply only four or five hours of electricity, and only in the night when I don't work—I work in the day. In brief, if I were to work with those lines, I would never be able to work.

He went on to emphasize that this was an expensive way of running the business and that their fuel costs were high, but that it nevertheless was an easy choice: "Without the generator, we would have depended on the power from the street and that wouldn't have worked, because, in this area, there is never electricity!" When they first set up the business, it had been based in Aldo's home and backyard in Cristo Rey, a bit closer to the center of the city. After only three months, they relocated the business to Casa Vieja, to a piece of land about 1,000 square meters in size that Aldo's family owned. The property was just a field that lay fallow: in those days, the area was mainly fields and vegetation, and there were few houses and no electricity. Within a month, Lorenzo and Aldo had constructed a simple workshop and installed a secondhand generator on the property. Over time, they invested more and built a storehouse, offices, and a high, solid wall bordering the street as protection against theft. Today, Casa Vieja is a poor, populous area—with many homes, a few small stores, and a labyrinth of narrow streets, both paved and unpaved.

Dominican furniture makers, as I have said, run different types of enterprises, and their technical, economic, cultural, and political strategies and solutions vary a great deal. However, what all of them—and their workers—have in common is that they are forced to live with the consequences of the country's ongoing power industry crisis. One result of this crisis is that they experience lasting contradictions between forms of social and economic time, and are forced to develop solutions through their own labor.

If the sale of Dominican furniture to families and households is undermined because of imports of foreign products, and if owners of tourist complexes, hotels, and other types of companies choose foreign furniture, there is nevertheless another possibility: supplying furniture to different parts of the Dominican state apparatus, such as ministries, the armed forces, the police, hospitals, universities, and schools. In the remainder of this section, I discuss Dominican furniture makers' work on securing contracts with government agencies. This activity highlights the same basic principle: that there is no such thing as a uniform, contemporary, capitalist time. As we have already seen, the Dominican state-system is diverse, a relatively fragmented structure of institutions and practices, and as a result it produces a wide range of different forms of political-economic time, including delays, waiting, and complete stops or blockades.

Cristian Nolasco heads the firm Industrias Colón in Villa Consuelo, a barrio situated not far from downtown Santo Domingo. His father is a trader, with a store in another part of the city, and formerly owned Industrias Colón with a partner. The latter had founded the firm in the late 1980s. In 1996, Cristian's father bought his partner's share and became sole owner. Cristian has run the firm since 1994. The enterprise makes furniture of wood and metal, in addition to mattresses. Industrias Colón has always been a small venture, but in the period from 1996 to 2000 the firm flourished and the workshop employed around fifteen workers. After these promising years, however, Industrias Colón experienced stagnation and decline before production in the workshop dried up in 2012. In late 2012 Cristian was elected ASONAIMCO's new president. When I met Cristian for the first time, the workshop had essentially been without production for six months, and Cristian had let go of his workers, but said that he could call some in if he received an order. However, Cristian is diligent, a hard worker, and he was working hard to try to breathe new life into the family firm, and to make some money in order to take care of his family. As the situation at Industrias Colón deteriorated, he decided to start a small enterprise importing and selling cosmetics. In his office in Industrias Colón there are now boxes of samples, and he sells and distributes products to hair salons and beauty parlors in different parts of the city.

Industrias Colón's customers had mainly been a few different furniture stores, but Cristian had also produced furniture for state departments and institutions. However, he recalled that some of these contracts were challenging. One day when we were chatting in his office, he took out a set of documents and three invoices and put them on his desk, explaining that the invoices were for products supplied by Industrias Colón to public institutions. Two were dated from 1997 and 2003, and were for supplying a type of simple bed to the armed forces; the amounts were significant, but had never been paid. The third unpaid invoice was from 1994 and was for a smaller amount. Cristian's father's partner, the man who had originally established the firm, had relatives who worked for the government, and contracts with public institutions had been secured through these contacts. Over the years, Cristian had tried many times to collect the debts, but without result. Given this experience, he said, he and the family had, for a number of years—at least until 2005 or 2006—sought to avoid selling to the state.

Industrias Colón's and Cristian's labor thus had a political dimension. This is representative of the larger situation: often, contracts with—and services from—public institutions could only be obtained by business owners with the aid of personal connections, kinsmen, and friends. Kinship or friendship bonds have various faces. Such ties may secure assistance or favors, but they may also result in experiences and feelings of betrayal (Yanagisako 2002:110–44).

ASONAIMCO is a member of the umbrella organization, La Confederación Dominicana de la Pequeña y Mediana Empresa (CODOPYME), a union of some of the country's small business associations. Furniture and mattress makers are organized politically through both ASONAIMCO and CODOPYME. In late 2012, Yuri Chez was elected president of CODOPYME. For many years, Chez had run a furniture firm and was, as mentioned earlier, head of ASONAIMCO before he became head of CODOPYME.

In December 2008, Dominican authorities promulgated a new law: Law 488–08: Regulatory Regime for the Development and Competitiveness of Micro, Small, and Medium Enterprises (MSMEs). This was viewed as a great victory by CODOPYME. Through the law, the Fernández government sought to provide stronger support for the development of the nation's myriad small and medium-sized businesses. The organizations had fought for such a law for many years—some said it had taken two decades. A central component of Law 488–08 says that all state institutions' purchases of goods and services must include a minimum proportion of 15 percent of the total purchase supplied by small and medium-sized domestic firms, provided that the goods and services in question are supplied in the country. Needless to say, this was met with enthusiasm. However, when I began fieldwork, almost four years after the promulgation of the law, it had not yet been implemented. In late 2011, a newspaper headline declared sarcastically that Law 488–08 had fallen asleep. According to the article, the entity in charge of elaborating and formulating the rules and directives for the implementation of the law, the Programa de Promoción y Apoyo a la Micro, Pequeña y Mediana Empresa (PROMIPYME), had not yet managed to execute the task; instead, the law had moved back and forth between PROMIPYME and the office of the president (Severino 2011). Organizations, activists, and small-business owners were disappointed and bitter, but continued fighting. Cristian pointed to a copy of Law 488–08 in his office: "Look! The 15 percent rule is great! But almost four years have passed since the law was ratified, and it has still not been implemented. The 15 percent rule isn't used."

Delays and waiting are one thing; being blocked altogether is quite another. The Dominican state's purchases are driven and governed by merciless power struggles; one outcome is that small domestic producers (like Cristian and his colleagues) not only experience delays, but are also blocked and excluded—stopped outright. To explain this, I shall round off this chapter with another example: the furniture makers' fight for the opportunity to deliver school furniture, particularly *butacas,* or tablet-arm chairs, to public educational institutions.

A number of Dominican firms produce tablet-arm chairs; Cristian's firm, Industrias Colón, used to supply them to private schools and universities. Most sales occur during a limited period of the year—in June, July, and August, before the start of the new school or academic year. Industrias Colón used to make 1,500 tablet-arm chairs of wood and metal during this period; the rest of the year, it made about 100 a month.

The state purchased *butacas* from domestic producers for schools and universities until 2006, but in 2007 it began exclusively to purchase imported products. In 2007, a *Listín Diario* headline announced, "Foreign tablet-arm chairs outcompete the national: The domestic producers say the Ministry of Education does not buy from them" (Guisarre 2007).

Representatives of the industry protested in the media and demanded that the state again start buying tablet-arm chairs made in the country. But with a minor exception in 2010 (when the state bought a small number from local firms, including Cristian's), the Ministry of Education continued to import them. All the tablet-arm chairs it bought for public schools and universities in 2011 and 2012 were made abroad, in China, Mexico, Panama, and elsewhere.

In August 2012, the country elected a new president, Danilo Medina. Although Medina represented the same political party as Fernández, and Medina's vice president was Fernández's wife, leaders and activists in the industry felt a certain qualified sense of hope. For a long time, Medina had voiced his determination to strengthen the state's support for the development of small economic ventures—what was known as the popular economy. In September 2012, the Medina administration passed a measure saying that all public purchases must include a minimum proportion of 20 percent of the total purchase supplied by small and medium-sized domestic firms, thus increasing by 5 percent the previous stipulation in Law 488–08. Implementation was scheduled to come into effect in January 2013, and in June and July 2013 it was again time for the Ministry of Education's annual purchase of tablet-arm chairs. Having received quotes from a series of local companies, the ministry decided to offer contracts to thirty-three of them; twenty-five, it announced, were small businesses, and eight were large. Representatives of the small enterprises immediately and loudly objected to this. Chez spoke on behalf of them all in the press: "The small firms had in reality not been given anything." Instead, he went on, the ministry had committed fraud; it had offered contracts to a series of fictitious—or only apparently small—ventures that in reality had been established and were controlled by a handful of large firms. This, he concluded, not only violated Law 488–08, but also was contrary to the will of President Medina (Reyes 2013). Although the accusations were harsh, they were not always repudiated, not even among the state's own representatives. In August 2013, for example, director of public procurement, Yocasta Guzmán Santos, admitted frankly in the press that "there are large companies that create small firms in order to take advantage of the programs and projects devoted to the small enterprises" (Maldonado 2013).

I confess: I was unforgivably naïve. I asked Chez about this situation in his office one day, and he explained to me that the state, as with the country's tourist sector, increasingly purchased imported, rather than domestic, products.

"But *why?*" I asked. "Is the increase in state imports due to the tax policy?"

"No," he said, "let's be frank—this occurs because of corruption." Cristian supported Chez's interpretation:

The reason is the corruption. Let me give you an example. Let's say that the price of a locally made product—for example, a tablet-arm

chair—is 1,000 pesos. The importer gets the product for 500 pesos from a free zone or a special economic zone in Asia—because, in
China, they produce thousands, millions. You sell the product to the
state for 900 apiece—which means that you, as importer and the representative of the state, have the difference of 400 to play with; both
make good money. Or they buy in Mexico or Asia for 500, and the
state is invoiced at 750 or 800. They still make a good profit. Government officials and owners of import firms make money—and the two
are not infrequently relatives or friends.

Cristian went on:

> You can't prove it—but there is far too much circumstantial evidence.
> Because, when you check, as I have done many times, when you go
> through the lists of the firms, study documents and invoices, you find
> that the owner of the import operation is the cousin—or the brother-
> in-law, or the husband of a daughter—of the civil servant. For example,
> last year we found out that one of the firms that had been offered a
> contract by the ministry in order to import tablet-arm chairs was a
> hardware store. Look! A hardware store doing business with furniture!
> But it turned out that the owner of the hardware store was married to
> a daughter of the government official.

As I see it, this neatly sums up a key dimension of capitalist time in the
field. On the one hand, the Dominican furniture makers experience contemporary capitalism's tremendous capacity to compress time and space,
and to transport and deliver goods from far away at an accelerated pace.
The constantly growing competition from the imported furniture sector
testifies to these processes, these dimensions of modern global capitalism,
as they unfold in today's Dominican society. On the other hand, or simultaneously, the processes become conspicuously slow and there are constant
delays—loss of time—especially when they (the local furniture makers)
seek to do business with, and sell their products to, representatives of the
state apparatus. Although both processes, or sets of processes, must be
viewed as products of today's neoliberal global capitalist system, both have
a Dominican shape; both mirror and embody a specific Dominican political-
economic-cultural history and reality (see in addition Gregory 2014:4–6;
Tsing 2013). Small Dominican furniture makers seek to produce and act
at the intersection of these forces, or in the gap and the tension between

the pace of the imports and the delays or blockades produced by state and nonstate political-economic agents. The opening up of the Dominican economy and the accompanying liberalization of trade made it feasible and far easier to import. The last decades' development of export processing zones and special economic zones around the world has made it easier to obtain and deliver cheap commodities.[5] The year 1978 put an end to a protracted Dominican authoritarian history, in a sense, yet the Dominican state-system continues to mirror the many decades under Trujillo and Balaguer, and to be deeply shaped by kinship and friendship ties: forms of patronage and forms of corruption (Krohn-Hansen 2009). Today, powerful groups and networks in the country make more money through imports than by doing business with domestic producers.

Organizations, activists, and others struggle indefatigably for small enterprises' rights and interests. CODOPYME is visible in the national press and on television, negotiating with politicians and organizing workshops and seminars; this is likewise the case with ASONAIMCO. In July 2013, Cristian investigated and analyzed the thirty-three firms that had been offered contracts by the ministry for supplies of tablet-arm chairs. In September and October of the same year, he and ASONAIMCO mapped and analyzed the results of a long list of processes in which the state had recently selected firms for the delivery of different types of furniture to public institutions. In a large open meeting organized by CODOPYME on 12 November 2013, Cristian presented the findings and decried unlawfulness and injustice. None of the examined processes had, in reality, he said, been correct or valid. On the contrary, the processes had enabled a small group of individuals or large enterprises to win most of the contracts with the aid of a set of companies acting as fronts (Rosario 2013).

Conclusion

Capitalism encourages time economy and the social acceleration of time; it condenses or elides temporal and spatial distances and advances through this global social integration. Capitalism and speed are, consequently, virtually synonymous terms—at least this is what we, in the social sciences and in many parts of society, typically tell one another. But, as we have seen, in contemporary Santo Domingo this picture is only half the story. The nation's small workshops and enterprises experience lots of delays and waiting—instead of speed and incorporation, they encounter slowness, blockades, and exclusion. The state's debt and financial crisis, and the accompanying negotiations with the IMF and other lenders, have resulted in (enforced) deregulation and free-trade agreements—and a concomitant massive increase in the country's imports, resulting in an entirely new import-export regime. Today, it is largely the same political-economic (often kinship- and friendship-based) networks and groups in Santo Domingo that produce and reproduce both the accelerated speed and the shameless delays, both the compression of time and space, and the foot-dragging and marginalization.

The production and distribution of *la luz* remain driven and permeated by power struggles. How the state debt is managed—and the consequences of that debt—still constitutes the core of the battle today, as does the question of who must pay what to whom, and when. In a way, the system appears to be based on calendar time *and* a pattern of belated and barely coordinated, unpredictable repayments of debt. The foreign energy companies limit or reduce power flowing to the national distribution grid, and the state-controlled distribution companies seek to discipline the citizens and the government into paying their electricity bills by means of blackouts. One result is that small and marginalized producers, like María and the rest of the owners and operators of small businesses in the barrios, experience much wasted time, as well as enduring vulnerability and doubt. The conditions for production are thus structured by contradictions between rhythms or times, or as Lorenzo put it: "I've never used the power from the street, because in this neighborhood where we operate, they supply only four or five hours of electricity, and only in the night, when I don't work—I work in the day."

Again, the timespaces of contemporary capitalism are heterogeneous. In their efforts to coordinate activities, and to produce and trade, my informants (Lorenzo and Aldo, María, and the others) draw heavily on a tradition of particular notions of workmanship, materials, and history. María summed it up by saying, "The creole furniture . . . is the furniture that lasts . . . Because we use wood . . . We don't [wish to] change our furniture so quickly." But we need to go further. Important aspects of many Dominican furniture makers' activities are part of more comprehensive (historically, politically, and culturally produced) forces, a form of collectively shaped, everyday politics of self-understanding and belonging. As we have seen, many Dominicans continue to be fond of *caoba*. The history of mahogany logging and mahogany use on the island is linked inextricably to the history of European colonialism (Pastore 2007; Anderson 2012). Prized originally by European furniture makers for its dark color, stability, and other qualities, mahogany was first targeted shortly after Columbus "discovered" Hispaniola and the New World. With the emergence of an independent Dominican Republic in the nineteenth and twentieth centuries, excessive *caoba* logging and conspicuous *caoba* use were nationalized, but remained inseparably connected to the history of the political and economic hierarchies, and the central power, in society. *Caoba* continued to function as a sign of authority and of success and esteem. The less wealthy and less powerful strata of society sought to mimic the practices and forms of consumption at the top of the social hierarchy. Today, things have changed once again. Members of the Dominican elite have shifted their tastes and habits and increasingly purchase foreign products, made not of mahogany, but of other materials. However, many in the middle and lower parts of the social hierarchy continue, as before, to seek social acknowledgment and respect, or a stake in the networks of power (however small it might be), through obtaining objects made of *caoba* or *caoba* imitations.[6] Furniture made of true mahogany is politically incorrect, nearly a bad word, in many parts of the world today, but this is not the case among many in Dominican society.

CHAPTER 2

Of Violence and Precarity

Gender, Food, Debt

It was a broiling hot afternoon in November 2013, and I was in Santo Domingo's Zona Norte (Northern Zone), in Avenida Emma Balaguer.[1] The place was situated close to the José Francisco Peña Gómez metro station, and we were just three stops south of the center of Villa Mella. The narrow street was jammed with traffic, and on both sides were two-story buildings with small businesses on the first, or ground, floor, and apartments on the second. The barrio was mostly poor. On the pavement, people sold a bit of almost everything, from fruit, cookies, and batteries to bottles of drinking water. A tiny plaza was located on one side, like an extension to the street, and in the mornings it housed a small market where people bought vegetables, fruit, and fresh meat. This was the place where Aris had lived and worked for some two decades. She, her sixteen-year-old daughter, and a partner she had had for about a year—a man of around fifty who sometimes found work as a painter—all lived together in a rented apartment in one of the buildings surrounding the plaza. Aris ran a small café in the plaza. The kitchen was tiny and without running water. Aris described it as a *caseta*, or booth. It had a flat roof made of iron, and the walls were of wood, reinforced with pieces of iron. The construction, which was painted blue and had been made for her by her grown son and his father, was about 2.5 meters long, 2 meters wide, and 2 meters high. It was like a blue box. The box had a window through which Aris served her customers. Outside there was a table and a couple of white plastic chairs, and a large piece of plastic had been hung up as protection, a kind of umbrella, against rain.

Thirsty, I bought a soft drink. The market was over and had left few traces, only a heap of trash waiting to be collected. There were two other *casetas* in the plaza, similar to Aris's. One belonged to another woman who operated the same type of business as Aris, the other housed a young man offering cell phone repairs. Aris offered sandwiches, empanadas, coffee, juice, soft drinks, *mabí* (a bottled homemade fruit drink made of lemon, water, and sugar), and cigarettes. Previously, she explained, she had had a larger menu and had offered hot food: *frito,* or fried meat; fried salami; eggs; boiled and fried plantains; and spaghetti. A sign on the wall advertised: "Café Aris. Breakfast—Coffee—Sandwiches—Empanadas—Juice—Mabí."

Aris had moved from the countryside in Moca (in the north of the country) to Santo Domingo when she was sixteen. At the time I conducted my fieldwork in 2013, she was fifty and had two daughters and a son, with three different men. Her oldest daughter was thirty-four, and had been raised by Aris's mother and lived in Moca. Aris had left her with her mother shortly after she was born, and had traveled to the capital in search of work. She had had little choice. As she put it, "I got my first daughter when I was sixteen. The father, you know, he was very irresponsible; I had to leave her with my mother so that she could take care of her while I left for the capital to work. And in this way I've managed, fighting and working and struggling, until I now have this [her *caseta*] after many efforts."

She opened the *caseta* at 6 a.m. and closed between 8:30 and 9 p.m., seven days a week. She had stopped selling fried meat and other hot food mainly because of health problems. She had trouble with her legs, with blood circulation; the killing heat that built up in the small kitchen when she fried and cooked affected her, made her feel tired and sick.

Over the years, there had been many challenges. She had had to start almost from scratch at least three times, after thieves had broken in and emptied her kitchen. Some years ago, her eldest daughter in Moca had left her husband and fled to her, along with her three small children. Aris had housed the four of them for a year (they had been seven in the apartment), before they returned to Moca. The father had refused to contribute money to provide for the children, so Aris had been forced to take out extra loans to cover expenses.

Like many people in the neighborhood, Aris regularly resorted to moneylenders. When I met her, in November 2013, she was paying off three small loans to three different lenders. She also had family—two sisters who also lived in the barrio—and the three helped one another out. One of the sisters lived on the same street. That day she had sent Aris a meal—rice, beans, and fried chicken. Sometimes Aris's son helped her, too. He had managed to get to Puerto Rico and for a while had sent Aris money. However, nowadays he did not send anything. He needed what he was able to make, he had explained, as he sought to legalize his stay in the country.

"Wageless life," as Michael Denning (2010) has called it, is the most common, or the dominant, form of life in today's Dominican society. The country is, to a striking extent, a place without (decently paid) work. From 1990 to 2019, the Dominican Republic saw one of the highest rates of growth in Latin America and the Caribbean. Simultaneously, the nation registered a decline in real wages, including a fall in the real value of the country's minimum wage. From 2000 to 2007, "average real minimum wages in over 100 countries covering 90 percent of the world population, grew by 5.7 percent, with 6.5 percent real growth in developing countries and 3.8 percent in developed countries." But in the Dominican Republic, "the average real value of the minimum wage was about 7 percent lower in 2010 than in 2000" (Parisotti and Prepelitchi 2013:13). As a result, wages have not kept up with the cost of living. According to the Dominican Central Bank, the cost of the minimum necessities for the poorest quintile of the population was, in 2010, double the average minimum wage (13–14). No wonder, perhaps, that so many Dominicans end up outside the wage economy.

   In this chapter, I investigate one form of wageless labor, or precarious livelihoods, among the city's poor. I look at the histories of women like Aris—at the activities of a group of female petty *comerciantes,* or traders, who had several things in common: they worked in the Zona Norte, they were all mothers, aged thirty-five to fifty-six, and they made their livings through preparing and selling foodstuffs. Six operated food stalls, and four ran small businesses selling vegetables and fruit. Most lived and worked in or near Villa Mella. One lived in Villa Mella, but her food stall was a bit farther south, in the Cristo Rey barrio. Another resided in Cristo Rey. It is important to stress that I chose this group not with any view of it being a generic sample representative of the Dominican urban poor, but rather as a set of individuals with distinct characteristics who could, all the same, offer insights into some of the powerful historical, societal, and affective forces and processes at work in the contemporary Dominican capital.[2]

I seek to answer four questions, or sets of questions. First, how can we best understand the historical emergence and maintenance of this precarious type of livelihood (the mother trading food, or running a kitchen on the street) in today's Santo Domingo? Second, what characterized these women's enterprises and everyday lives? What did it mean to sustain oneself and the family by operating a food stall or by selling vegetables and fruit? The third question involves recognizing that, for the women, "the business" and "the family" were two sides of the same operation. They were not separate. On the contrary, the two processes—the operation of the business and the maintenance and strengthening of the family—were tightly interwoven. The business's money was the family's money, and vice versa. This leads to the question, what can these women's histories convey about what Clara Han (2011:8) has described as "the lived tension between caring for kin and the demands of economic precariousness"? Fourth, just as these women, as I will show, continuously lived in many different networks, so too did they live and act in multiple heterogeneous forms of time, or temporalities. How can we best understand these dimensions of their lives and the challenges they faced? For example, how did their poverty and the precariousness of their economic activities and social relations influence their daily or weekly rhythms? How did temporal concerns shape how they navigated their work?

"Precarity," Kathleen Millar maintains, is a useful notion for seeking to conceptualize and understand the labor condition under capitalism "as inseparable from issues of subjectivity, affect, sociality, and desire." An interest in precarity, she continues, is especially valuable if we attempt to capture the relationship between two factors or processes: "between precarious labour and precarious life," or "between precarity as a socio-economic condition and precarity as an ontological experience" (2014:35). In what follows, I draw on Millar with the aim of tracking specific forms of precarity in the Zona Norte, and of describing a particular, historically constituted, socioeconomic condition. At the same time, I am interested in the working and living conditions of my interlocutors as inseparable from specific questions of cultural and affective forms and practices.[3]

For some three hundred years, the territory that today is the Dominican Republic was a Spanish colony. A watershed in the history of the Dominican Republic, independent since 1844, was the US occupation from 1916 to

1924. The US occupation created an effective national military institution in a country that previously had had none. Among the first class of native officers who graduated from the new military academy in 1921 was Rafael Trujillo. By the age of thirty-nine, he had become the leader of the modernized military that the United States had helped to establish. Using his position to overthrow the elected government, he ruled as a dictator from 1930 until his assassination in 1961. Four years later, in 1965, President Lyndon Johnson ordered 40,000 US Marines to the Dominican capital to stop the "communist" Juan Bosch and prevent the establishment of "a second Cuba in America."

We ought to ask, what is the longer and wider political and social history that has given shape to life stories such as Aris's? What kind of longer history is reflected in (built into) her basic condition? To be able to answer these questions, we must first recognize that it is not enough to look only at the history of late capitalism (or, for that matter, neoliberalism). So much in today's Dominican Republic testifies to how imperialism and colonialism live on and help to give shape to—and degrade—the present. Today, the legacies of imperialism—what Ann Stoler calls forms of imperial debris—are still highly evident among the poor in the Zona Norte. They have continued, long after colonialism's most obvious representatives were gone, to exercise enormous (for the most part tacit and glossed over) power, and to form and restrict possibilities and dreams. Stoler encourages us to seek to "track the uneven temporal sedimentations in which imperial formations leave their marks [and] to ask how empire's ruins contour and carve through the psychic and material space in which people live and what compounded layers of imperial debris do to them" (2013:2). Is claiming that colonial legacies remain a part of the present (are not just "dead past," but, instead, continue to leave their marks in the present) the same thing as saying that the contemporary world, the world we all live in, can be accounted for by colonial histories alone? Far from it. To claim such a thing would be ridiculous. Instead, the point is to insist that we need to explore and understand how imperial histories, despite having apparently been so overwhelmingly effaced, engender new injuries and renewed inequalities. As Stoler puts it, the point is "rather to recognize that these are unfinished histories, not of a victimized past but of consequential histories of differential futures" (2013:11).

What follows is divided into six main parts. The first three sketch some features of the history of the Zona Norte, the country's machismo, and the country's dominant, popular foodways. The last three analyze the women's businesses, everyday practices, and borrowing and debt strategies.

A Divided City

Researchers and politicians have often conveyed two kinds of narratives of the vast shantytowns that emerged on the outskirts of the Dominican capital and other Latin American and Caribbean cities in the second half of the twentieth century. One discourse explains that the exodus from the countryside and the heartbreaking urban poverty is mainly an outcome of the changing structures of the national economy. The other narrates the hopes, the values, and the political practices of migrants themselves, as they entered the city and sought to get by. Both discourses are, and I underscore this, valuable and contain important truths. But neither of these two frameworks or stories should prevent us from seeing the extent to which today's poor barrios in Santo Domingo's Zona Norte are also a product of legacies of imperialism and forms of state violence.

The Trujillo regime sought to control the movement of campesinos to the capital, and in 1953 the dictator even issued a decree prohibiting rural people from moving to cities without the permission of mayors and district governors. At the same time, an urban working class was needed not only to run but also to build and modernize the dictator's pride, the capital (which, in 1936, he renamed Ciudad Trujillo, or Trujillo City). The regime therefore stimulated migration to Santo Domingo:

> Beginning in the 1940s, the regime began construction of the north-west course of the Duarte Avenue and the rudimentary creation of the neighborhoods on either side of it: Villa Consuelo, Mejoramiento Social, and Barrio Obrero (as well as Los Minas on the far side of the Ozama River). Adjacent to the old working-class settlements on the rise of land inside the [original colonial] city's old northern wall, this would become the crucial backbone of the Zona Norte (Northern District), the popular and marginal neighborhoods of Santo Domingo in the half-century that followed. Indeed, as working-class settlements grew northward, many Dominicans continued to refer to them as the Barrios Altos (Upper Barrios), referring to those original hillside settlements inside the city walls. (Hoffnung-Garskof 2008:30–31)

These neighborhoods (the Zona Norte's settlements) have been created through a combination of state construction, private development, and informal land occupation, of which the last was the most important element. As in much of the rest of the world, rural migrants simply built their own urban neighborhoods in steep canyons, marshy riverbanks, and converted farm lands on the margins of already existing barrios and settlements, and then began the struggle to get schools, water, sanitation, and electricity.[4] In the early 1980s, two-thirds of the capital's residents lived in the congested barrios of the Zona Norte and in a few newer, outlying poor areas (Lozano 1997). After that, the more densely populated and marginal barrios continued to expand northward, westward, and eastward. Villa Mella, where many of my interlocutors lived, had been a rural community not long before, north of (that is, outside) the city. However, over the last three or four decades the area has been devoured by the Zona Norte, completely urbanized, and transformed into a series of densely populated and poor barrios. In 2010, the Dominican state inaugurated the country's first metro line, connecting the center of Villa Mella with the capital's southernmost areas. Mamá Tingó, the station in Villa Mella, is the last and northernmost stop.

In the 1950s and 1960s, seeking to prevent the Dominican Republic (and other parts of the Americas) from becoming communist was considered a top priority in Washington. After Trujillo was assassinated in 1961, free elections followed in 1962, the first of their kind since 1924. Those elections resulted in a decisive victory for Juan Bosch. Although Bosch was more a populist democrat and a reformist than a revolutionary, he was soon labeled a communist (by members of the armed forces, business leaders, and industrialists) and, after only seven months, his government was overthrown by a military coup. The Triumvirate regime that followed stayed in power with the support of Trujilloist generals and the United States. However, even this new dictatorship could not ensure stability. In April 1965, civil war broke out in the capital between pro-Bosch (Constitutionalist) and anti-Bosch (Loyalist) forces. A young political activist and Bosch supporter, José Francisco Peña Gómez, took to the radio to call the urban masses to the streets. "Over the course of four days in April, the residents of the working-class neighborhoods and shantytowns in the Zona Norte took control of the city, blocking the advance of the loyalist military" (Hoffnung-Garskof 2008:35). After US forces invaded Santo Domingo on April 29, they dealt with this threat, what Washington and its representatives viewed as an obstacle to a stable government and a good business climate in the Dominican Republic:

> They encouraged a terror campaign against leftists, unionists, and
> armed neighborhood leaders. U.S. troops held the pro-Bosch forces
> pinned down in the Colonial District but allowed Loyalist forces to
> roam the city waging a severe campaign of repression in the Zona
> Norte. "Operation Cleanup," as it was called, put the lid back on the
> urban crisis in Santo Domingo. Meanwhile Joaquín Balaguer [one of
> the Trujillo regime's most important ideologues and the dictator's last
> puppet president], returned from exile in New York, pieced together
> a new party, the Partido Reformista (Reformist Party), from the frag-
> ments of the old regime and launched a bid to regain the presidency.
> (Hoffnung-Garskof 2008:35)

Balaguer's first twelve years in power (1966–78) were violently repressive—a
sort of Trujilloism without Trujillo. The elections in 1966 were organized
in an atmosphere of extended civil war. With the American troops still
in the country, and while terrorist campaigns against Bosch's supporters
killed hundreds of the party's activists and Bosch himself feared for his life,
Balaguer won with 57 percent of the vote to Bosch's 39 percent. The urban
poor voted overwhelmingly for Bosch. The nation and the Zona Norte in
particular suffered for some eight years under Balaguer's state-sponsored
terror against their opposition to him. Paramilitary groups killed more than
4,000 Dominicans between 1966 and 1974 (Moya Pons 1990:528). The
regime received considerable US aid and registered significant economic
growth. In spite of this, a large proportion of the population saw their
meager incomes fall during the 1970s. The poor became poorer, while
the other social strata strengthened their positions (Torres-Saillant and
Hernández 1998:54–55).

The repression with which the Boschistas' and the urban masses' aspirations were met had a more lasting, destructive effect. Leaders, activists,
unionists, and students in the barrios were forced to drop their overtly political activities, or were deported (ironically enough, to the United States,
with the active assistance of the CIA and other US agencies [Hoffnung-
Garskof 2008:68–96]), or left the country voluntarily, or were killed. The
possibilities of efficiently fighting for, and building, a more inclusive and
better future for the masses in the Zona Norte, and the other working-class
areas of the capital, were sharply undermined.

With the rise in oil prices, starting in the late 1970s, and a drop in the
price of export products (such as sugar), the Dominican state soon faced

a drastic debt problem. By 1981 "it was already evident that the entire public sector was on the edge of bankruptcy" (Moya Pons 1990:537). Washington used the debt crisis as an opportunity to exercise power. The Reagan administration (assisted by the International Monetary Fund [IMF] and the World Bank) demanded a reduction of trade barriers and floating exchange and interest rates, and pushed the Dominican government to shift investments from industry producing for local consumption to export processing zones producing for consumption in the United States. In addition, Washington demanded cuts in public employment and subsidies, and the termination of a system of state supports to the country's urban poor. Eventually, after yet another debt crisis in the early 1990s had again brought the state to the verge of bankruptcy, the Dominican government, like its counterparts in most of Latin America, adopted most of Washington's policies, joining what came to be called the Washington Consensus. In the first half of the 1990s, the Dominican Republic gradually introduced a long list of neoliberal economic reforms.

Before that happened, however, the poor in the Zona Norte let their voices be heard. In 1984, the Dominican government accepted the terms of an IMF restructuring plan, cutting back on price controls for food and other necessities. The neighborhoods of the Zona Norte led the nation in five days of uproar over the changes, before the government responded by sending the army into the barrios. The army killed more than one hundred people and wounded more than four hundred (Ianni 1987). Two years later, the eighty-year-old Balaguer returned to power and remained in office until 1996. The military repression that had characterized his first twelve years in office had been curbed in 1978, and Balaguer did not resume it after his return to power. However, the regime reinstated his well-known authoritarian politics of urban renewal. In the Zona Norte and other poor parts of the city, the state constructed new expressways and housing complexes. In so doing, it evicted and forcibly removed thousands of families.

Because of the terror and, later, the general lack of economic opportunities, more and more Dominicans sought a better life abroad. Large-scale emigration from the Dominican Republic began after Trujillo's assassination, with most Dominicans settling in New York. The number of documented Dominican immigrants admitted to the United States rose from an average of about 14,000 per year in the 1970s to more than 40,000 per year in the early 1990s (Hoffnung-Garskof 2008:202).

According to a survey of the city in 1977, between 7 percent and 24 percent of families in the neighborhoods of the Zona Norte earned enough to be considered "popular" ("poor") rather than "marginal" ("very poor") by the Dominican Central Bank (Hoffnung-Garskof 2008:41). Put another way, each barrio has its own history and socioeconomic and cultural diversity, but the economic differences are usually not large. They all share a backdrop of poverty and weak public infrastructure, distinguished only by places of still worse misery in some barrios and clusters of better-off households in others.

Today's situation in the Zona Norte and the rest of the country's poor areas is the outcome of a particular, violent history. Authoritarian forms of government have been an ingrained part of the Dominican political landscape up to the present. Its hierarchical, undemocratic, and corrupt forms and practices are not dead, although their most conspicuous bearers and symbols are.[5] At least equally important—if not more so—have been the US interventions. As Greg Grandin put it, "neoliberalism in the Americas . . . did not emerge simply from the economic and technological logic of Fordism." Well before international competition justified such a move as inevitable, US corporations, according to Grandin,

> organized themselves to confront increasing labor power and demands for reform in Latin America . . . In the mid-1960s, executives from over thirty U.S. firms founded the Business Group for Latin America, which included participation by Ford, U.S. Steel, DuPont, Standard Oil, Anaconda Copper, ITT, United Fruit, Chase, and other blue-chip industrial and financial companies. David Rockefeller, whose family had extensive holdings in Latin America, served as its liaison with the White House. The idea was both to influence Washington's hemispheric policy and to apply direct pressure at the source, funding the campaigns of friendly politicians, helping allies hold down prices, and providing financial guidance to cooperative regimes. When lobbying proved insufficient, members of the group, either individually or in concert, worked with the CIA to foment coups. (Grandin 2013:123–24)

Dominican Machismo as Mimesis and Afterlife

In large parts of Dominican society, there is a double standard of accepted or tolerated sexual behavior—men are free to have relations with several women simultaneously, but women are obliged to remain loyal and faithful to one man. Both men and women in the countryside and in the working-class barrios often claim that it is a man's nature to need more than one woman, especially a Dominican man, whereas a woman can be satisfied with one man. If women enter multiple unions, it is generally not out of natural desire but because they are forced to do so out of necessity. Most people in the barrios do not marry. Instead, they live in *uniones libres,* or common-law unions, throughout their lives, officially registered as single. Put differently, any attempt to understand the material and social processes in the contemporary Zona Norte must take into account Dominican notions of gender and masculinity. An absorbing testimony to this is the Dominican American writer Junot Díaz's successful, award-winning work. Díaz's literary studies in, and critical displays of, a historically produced Dominican/Dominican American form of popular or working-class hypermasculinity demonstrate that hegemonic Dominican concepts of gender and masculinity continue to haunt and challenge even Dominicans who have left the island and grown up in the United States.[6]

None of the ten women about whom I write in this chapter was married. Each lived either without a male partner or with a partner whom they had had for a short period (ranging from a year to several years), but who was not the father of any of their children. They had mostly raised and provided for their children without regular assistance from the fathers. Men's neglect inflicts pain, economic precariousness, restricted possibilities for choice, and feelings of shame.

One case stands out among the stories I got to know during my fieldwork. In 2014, Julibel was a twenty-eight-year-old single mother with a five-year-old daughter. She worked in a store six days a week and, in order to supplement her low salary, made and sold simple household decorations and bought and sold shoes. In addition to herself and her daughter, her household comprised her mother, her mother's sister, and one of the latter's daughters with her two small children. Julibel's father had left her mother when Julibel was born, and had disappeared. When she was fifteen, he had called her, and they had established a form of on-and-off, irregular contact. She still discovered new half-siblings. Our conversation had lasted for a while and had revolved around her work and her use of small loans and credit to get by. She had mentioned some difficulties and concerns, but nothing unusual or dramatic. Toward the end of the conversation, however, things took a new direction. I had asked what seemed to me an innocent question: "Tell me, what's your hope for the future?" When she replied, she had tears in her eyes:

When I go to bed I always pray to the Lord, I begin to pray. My plans for the future are to get out of my problems, because I have, in reality, difficulties because of the man who is the father of my daughter. I don't like to talk about it, since it makes me shameful. What can I say? I met him when I was very young and without much experience. I fell in love, and I believed many things, plans he described for the future. "Look, let's do this and that, we're going to marry and have a family." I got into difficulties. He persuaded me to ask for a loan in my name for a business—he said that the loan couldn't be put in his name since he already had another loan.

Two years after the daughter was born, the relationship was over. The man had left without paying off the loan taken out in Julibel's name—and he never assisted her with child maintenance for their daughter. She said that she often woke up very early in the morning, and was unable to fall asleep again; she could not stop thinking about her problems and the debt, and about what she should do.

Julibel's case is extreme. Few men leave their partner with a significant unsettled debt. Some men are responsible and supporting partners and fathers, and some unions last. While there is considerable variation in the thinking and behavior of individual men, it seems that many women end up feeling let down by their male partner. From early on, girls are inculcated with the belief that they cannot trust men. When they nevertheless decide to take the chance or run the risk, many get disappointed.

Typically, Dominican men's relations with women are permeated by ambiguity. On the one hand, a man ought to be a seducer and *mujeriego,* or womanizer, engaged in the sexual conquest of women even when he is married or living in a stable union. At the same time, he should be responsible and a good father, providing for his *mujer,* or woman, and children. When a union or marriage breaks up, a man continues to have provider responsibility for his children. Men act in the tension between these two different cultural perspectives about what constitutes acceptable and real masculinity. Just as important—indeed, even more important than their relations with women—are the relations men have with other men. As Pierre Bourdieu (2002:52) has argued, "manliness must be validated by other men . . . and certified by recognition of membership of the group of real men." Dominican men's masculinity is produced (that is, accumulated, maintained, and/or lost) primarily in their relations with male friends and rivals, or in the public sphere. A real man ought to be publicly visible, independent, *valiente* (brave), and eloquent. In addition he should be generous and spend time and resources with his male friends, and be a *bebedor* (big drinker) and *fiestero* (fun-loving) (Krohn-Hansen 2009:138–49).

The cultural and aesthetic repertoires that help sanction and naturalize machismo among contemporary Dominicans did not arise *ex nihilo*. Rather, they have five hundred years of concrete history behind them. Spain's development of an early sugar economy in Hispaniola in the sixteenth century created the basis for the emergence of the local variant of what Raymond T. Smith has described as "the dual marriage system" in the Caribbean. The key was the establishment of a slave regime with a racial hierarchy, which enabled a discourse of male supremacy to interact with an ideology of white supremacy:

> From the beginning of the development of the slave regime, a marriage system was in place that included both legal marriage and concubinage, a system in which the elements were mutually and reciprocally defining and which articulated with the racial hierarchy. White men married white women but entered into non-legal unions with women who were black or "colored," that is, of mixed race . . . This system did not arise and continue just because it was useful or practically necessary. It is often supposed that a shortage of white women forced white men to take concubines for "natural" reasons, a supposition that does not survive close examination . . . Marriage to a white woman did not preclude non-legal unions with black or colored women, nor was it permissible for a white woman, even if single or widowed, to indulge in "natural" sexual relations with a black or colored man. The limits of possible action were contained within the structure of the meaning of the system, and at its core was the set of contrasted meanings attaching to marriage and concubinage. (Smith 1996:61–62)[7]

The Trujillo regime, in particular, engendered and gave shape to the type of striking machismo that still permeates Dominican society today. Trujillo's sense of theater and enjoyment in displaying his unmatched masculine vitality and power is legendary. Historian Lauren Derby writes that under the dictator, "public space was a hall of mirrors all of which reflected Trujillo in one of his many costumes: Trujillo the statesman in jacket and tie, the caudillo on horseback, or the army general in full military brass with his distinctive Napoleonic chapeau" (2003:5). Yet why did the regime stage and exhibit the ruler? How did a military dictator who accumulated spectacular personal wealth and relied on systematic surveillance, terror, and torture generate a degree of acceptance in significant parts of society and make many "marginal rural and urban poor feel proud to be Dominican" (Derby 2009:12)?

Under Trujillo, the Dominican Republic was still mostly a peasant nation, and many villagers and peasants viewed the dictator as a modernizer who brought public infrastructure and development, and thus helped enable the integration of the countryside into the nation-state (Turits 2003). But Trujillo's political and cultural impacts had much to do with the style of rule that he embodied, a populist style based upon native and everyday idioms of masculinity. He was born in 1891 to a family of modest means and mixed ethnic stock, and raised in San Cristóbal, a small town near the capital. Today, Trujillo has in many ways come to be seen as the incarnation of a now dominant tale or image of masculinity in the Dominican Republic, the "Dominican *tíguere,*" or tiger—an image that was generated by working-class men in the capital's barrios during Trujillo's regime (Krohn-Hansen 1996; Derby 2009:174–75).[8] One of his most frequently used slogans—"My best friends are the men of work"—was not mere propaganda. In personifying and displaying common images of maleness, the dictator made it possible for poor, nonwhite, rural and urban Dominican men to identify with him and feel dignity, be empowered, albeit only to a limited extent and only momentarily. The lengthy regime created and renewed pragmatic acceptance and forms of legitimacy through a continual mutual mirroring of masculinity that constructed links between the dictator and ordinary men. In the words of Achille Mbembe, Trujillo sought to institutionalize himself in the form of a fetish, and the regime functioned through "the logics of conviviality . . . In its own longing for grandeur the popular world borrow[ed] the whole ideological repertoires of officialdom, along with its idioms and forms. Conversely, the official world mimick[ed] popular vulgarity, inserting it at the very core of the procedures by which it [claimed to have risen to grandeur]" (1992:14).

The effect became tragic. Balaguer (as a person and politician) embodied and projected an image of masculinity that was significantly different than Trujillo's, but the former's long rule contributed, nonetheless, only to the continued reproduction and consolidation of the power of dominant Dominican concepts of masculinity. As Maja Horn has summed it up in her *Masculinity after Trujillo* (2014:20), "the Trujillato's hegemonic notions of masculinity continue to remain alive and well." These notions continue to exert an extraordinary force in today's Dominican society, among both men and women, and continue to give shape not only to hopes and expectations, but also to suffering, destroyed dreams, and economic vulnerability and precariousness.

La comida criolla

The role of Dominican women, or single mothers, operating tiny cafés or kitchens near a market or in the street has a long history. The practice is described by Dominican *costumbristas* writing in the 1920s and 1930s. *Costumbrismo* works document Dominican dialects, everyday life, material culture, and food traditions in semifictional form. Rafael Damirón's brief story "El Friquitin," published in Santo Domingo in 1938, is a good example. Damirón calls the *friquitin,* or street fried-food stand, one of the most characteristic features of life in the barrios of the capital. The *friquitin* offers small portions of fried meat, fried fish, fried plantain, and sometimes other dishes. Each street fried-food stand, according to Damirón, is a place to meet in the neighborhood—it is like a small parliament that gathers people from all social strata. In the Dominican Republic, mobile street vendors selling raw fruits, vegetables, and plantains are usually men, while vendors selling cooked products (such as fried meat, plantains, yuca [cassava], rice, and beans) are primarily women. According to Damirón, poor but ambitious women typically preferred establishing their own business (such as a *friquitin*) to being employed as a cook or domestic worker in a household.

"El Friquitin" narrates the story of a young woman from the countryside who, having arrived in the capital to work as a domestic worker, was evicted from the home where she worked and lived because the man of the house had "exaggerated his gratefulness towards her," and so his wife had decided to get rid of her. She went to Tamayo, a small community in the southwestern part of the country, to live with her partner, a young man who worked as a driver and was also a passionate cockfighter. She soon opened a fried-food stall. In the beginning, her economic resources were limited, so she took the leftovers from the cockfighting establishment for use in her *friquitin.* The business became successful, and she expanded it. She purchased cheap chicken in the public market and offered her customers fried chicken with rice and beans, spicy sausages, and little yuca balls stuffed with cheese.

Women who run food stands and small cafés in the barrios offer *comida criolla* or *comida típica*—typical Dominican food. Another *costumbrista*, Ramón Emilio Jiménez, describes in one of his texts, "Platos Nacionales" (National Dishes) from 1929, two Dominican obsessions: *el sancocho*, a soup (often considered a stew) containing pieces of meat, plantain, tubers, and vegetables; and *la bandera dominicana* (the Dominican flag), a triad of white rice, red beans, and meat (chicken or beef). Other main elements of *comida criolla* are roasted or fried pork, plantains, and tubers (such as yuca, sweet potato, and *yautía* or *malanga*). The Dominican roots, tubers, and green plantains are often referred to collectively as *los víveres*, literally, the items or foodstuffs that are necessary. Few ordinary Dominicans consider a meal complete without a side dish of *víveres*. The plantain is arguably the national foodstuff. People eat it boiled or fried, in soups, and as *mangú* (mash).

It is difficult to know exactly when or how a self-consciously "Dominican" cuisine—the Dominican *comida criolla*—developed, since knowledge of cooking and food traditions is, for the most part, produced and communicated orally.[9] We do know, however, that today's dominant Dominican foodways have grown out of a specific history of slavery. As Michel-Rolph Trouillot (1988:21) has argued about the Caribbean in general, "the 'peasant way of life' fully blossomed only upon the ruins of plantations." The colony of Santo Domingo had an early sugar industry, worked by enslaved Africans, that produced large quantities of sugar for the European markets from around 1520. In the late 1500s, plantation production collapsed as rapidly as it had emerged,[10] and the next three hundred years saw commercial stagnation. The decline of the sugar plantations, however, opened up the space for a sizable, independent peasantry, essentially former slaves and their progeny, as well as marginal colonists with whom they mixed. For generations, this peasantry lived mostly on the edge of, or outside, the control of colonial society. They exploited the island's vast, untamed *monte*, or woodlands—ideal for slash-and-burn farming, raising free-ranging animals, and hunting.[11] The Trujillato forged an alliance with people in the countryside (Turits 2003), an alliance that was only in part about rural dwellers' state-protected access to land and improved and new infrastructure. The regime-countryside compromise also served to protect and sustain the central components of a rural way of life. One important element of this was the *comida criolla*. Today in the Zona Norte and the other working-class barrios, people still have a preference for eating "the flag" (rice, beans, and meat) and plantains, yuca, sweet potato, *yautía*, and various fruits and vegetables—the tubers and other produce that are still associated with villagers' and peasants' *conucos* (small agricultural plots). A majority prefer a substantial *desayuno* (breakfast), for example a *mangú* of boiled, mashed plantains with eggs or fried salami. *Almuerzo* (lunch) is often rice and beans with meat, usually chicken, and a salad, or another traditional dish, such as bacalao (dried salted codfish), *moro* (a mixture of black beans and rice), or *asopao* (a soup of rice, pigeon peas, and meat, usually chicken). *La cena* (supper), like breakfast, usually includes *víveres*—plantain or another local root or tuber. People in the poor barrios are generally landless (although many grew up in the countryside and some still own, or have inherited, a small piece of land elsewhere in the country). Like their ancestors in the seventeenth and eighteenth centuries who headed to the woodlands in search of a livelihood, many live and work at the margins of the state. But they love their *comida criolla*.

Goodbye, Wage Labor: Structural Violence and the Potentials of Food

What characterized the women who operated a food stall or sold vegetables in the Zona Norte? Why and how had they established themselves in these niches? Most, but not all, had a history of migration. Either their parents had left the countryside, or they themselves had. Many had only very limited schooling, although there were exceptions. A few chose, as we shall see, to return to education later in life.

Four processes, or sets of processes, shed light on why many women end up with a food stall or working as small-scale traders of foodstuffs. First, the combination of poverty and specific gendered processes produces deeply precarious situations. Poor, single mothers need a form of income to be able to provide for themselves and their children. Second, the gendered division of labor in households and families means that girls learn to handle typical foodstuffs and to cook: they master the *comida típica*. Third, it is possible to start these businesses with limited resources. The amount of initial capital required to open a kitchen on the street, or to sell vegetables, is not large. Fourth, the only realistic alternative—wage labor, or working for others—is hardly tempting.

We can see these processes at work in the case of Doña Alejandra. Alejandra ran a *ventorrillo*, a small shop selling tubers and vegetables, in a barrio a couple of kilometers northwest of the center of Villa Mella. In 2013, when I met her, she was fifty-six.

Four times a week Alejandra went, early in the morning, to the Mercado Nuevo (a large market located to the south of Villa Mella, in the Villas Agrícolas barrio in the Zona Norte) in order to purchase *víveres* and vegetables. In her *ventorrillo* she sold plantains, yuca, sweet potato, *yautía*, tomatoes, garlic, salad, avocados, and other products, including cigarettes. In addition, she offered coffee and tea in the morning. The business was open from 9 a.m. to 10 or 11 p.m., seven days a week. If she was not there herself, another member of the household looked after the business. Alejandra had grown up in Villa Mella and had had just one year of schooling. In 1977, when she was twenty-one, her mother died, and she inherited her mother's small property with a modest house. She ran her business in a shack on the same property, which had been built by her partner and eldest children some twenty years before.[12] She did not pay trader fees to the municipality.

Alejandra had thirteen children. Most lived in barrios in Villa Mella and often stopped by for a meal and a chat. In early 2013, her household had four members: Alejandra, her partner (with whom she had lived for the last fifteen years, but who was not the father of any of her children), her youngest daughter, and her eldest son (who had just broken up with his wife or partner).

She had established her business shortly after her mother had died. This is how she described it. She had been a young single mother with a one-and-a-half-year-old boy, but traveled nonetheless to the market each morning with two thermoses to make a few pesos selling coffee. One of her neighbors' sons had sold *víveres* and vegetables but had decided to stop and instead try his luck abroad. The young man's mother persuaded Alejandra to attempt to start a similar business. In this manner, the neighbor had said, you can support yourself and the child without having to leave each day for the market, and you will not have to look for domestic work. The woman had even given Alejandra the large table on which her son had stocked and displayed his commodities. Alejandra had subsequently left for the market with a small sum, 50 pesos, and purchased some green plantains, some avocados, a few papayas, and a few mangos. By the next day she had sold them all for 100 pesos, and, with this, she returned to the market and bought yuca, sweet potatoes, and more plantains. The next day she had 150 pesos. She had continued to expand until she had a full table of products. She said: "I was young when I started to trade, but I decided to provide for myself. It is better because I don't like having to suffer because a man acts like an idiot" (*porque no me gusta aguantar disparate a ningún hombre*).

Ana (another interlocutor), when she became a single mother, had also begun to *negociar*, or trade, to make some money. When I met her in 2013, she was thirty-four and the mother of four children (aged sixteen, thirteen, eleven, and ten). She lived in Villa Mella, and operated a food stall in a heavily congested area in Cristo Rey, on the pavement near the junction of Avenida Nicolás de Ovando and Avenida Máximo Gómez. She had grown up and spent most of her life in the small community of Yamasá, located about 40 kilometers north of Santo Domingo. She had moved with her children from Yamasá to Villa Mella when she was twenty-seven.

Ana had almost completed high school. At eighteen, she had given birth to her first child. Her family was poor, and the young father was without work. He had left Yamasá a month after the child was born, claiming that he would seek to join the armed forces—and she never heard from him again. Ana started to trade. Each morning she made a Dominican favorite, *bollitos de yuca*, little yuca balls stuffed with cheese. Later in the day, she went out with her baby, carrying a basket of *bollitos* on her head, and sold the *bollitos*. Subsequently, she started to make *yaniqueques* instead of *bollitos*; this was another simple, traditional snack (a fried crispy flatbread made from flour, salt, and water), which she sold in the morning and evening.

She had begun to run the food stall in Cristo Rey when she was twenty-four, in 2003. At the time she had a partner with whom she lived in Yamasá, and they had three children together. The place where she cooked and served was tiny—a simple booth made from metal sheets placed on the pavement. Customers ate standing outside or took their food elsewhere. She offered breakfast and lunch. On each side of her stall, there were many more, similar stalls—well over fifty, all on the pavement. A few others sold food, but the majority sold clothes, shoes, bags, and handbags. Ana said that she used to pay a weekly fee of 100 pesos to the municipality. However, the municipality's plan had been to evict them and demolish the booths in this part of the city, so it had stopped sending an employee to charge them. Subsequently the plan had been changed, and, after that, they had not paid.

The food stall that Ana ran had originally been operated by another woman. The latter had sold it in 2003 to a friend of Ana's partner. In the beginning, Ana had traveled back and forth between Yamasá and Cristo Rey, and worked for her partner's friend. Ana and her partner had then broken up, and she had, as said, relocated to the city. She had borrowed 3,000 pesos at a high interest rate from a man in Yamasá, and, with this capital, she had taken over the running of the business. In 2013, she worked for herself and paid the man who still owned the booth a monthly rent of 2,000 pesos.

Many women had had several paid jobs before they established their own business. Josefina was a case in point. In 2012, she operated a food stall in a small market in La Fe barrio, right by the junction of Avenida San Martín and Avenida Tiradentes. Most stalls sold vegetables and fruit. Josefina, who was thirty-seven, had moved with her mother from the southwestern part of the country to Las Cañitas in the Zona Norte when she was eight. In 2012, she was a single mother and lived in Cristo Rey. She and the father of her two children had broken up eleven years earlier. She had a new partner, a sergeant in the military, but the two did not have children together and did not live together steadily. However, he contributed to the rent for her apartment.

Josefina had begun to work early. Her mother had been poor, and had cleaned and done laundry for families. From the age of twelve, Josefina had lived with and worked for her godmother, who had provided her with food and clothes. Thereafter, she had worked as a domestic worker for four years, for two different families. The first family had paid her only 500 pesos a month, the other 1,500. But, as she said laconically, "doing domestic work isn't easy. The families order and direct too much and it's a life filled with duress, and they pay little. I had enough and quit."

When she was twenty, she had begun working as an employee in the food stall that she now owned. After two years, in 1997, she had purchased the business for 10,000 pesos from the woman for whom she worked. She had not had any savings or capital, but had paid little by little, based on what she made—500 pesos, 1,000 pesos—until all was paid. Her kitchen or café was significantly larger than Ana's or Aris's and was, in addition, part of an indoor market. Josefina offered breakfast and lunch. People ate at a couple of tables, or took their meal elsewhere.

Shortly after she had bought the business, she borrowed 5,000 pesos from ADOPEM, a Dominican affiliate of the Women's World Bank, which offered loans to female small-scale entrepreneurs. With the loan, she purchased the items she needed to start her business: various foodstuffs, pots, dishes, forks and spoons.

The possible alternative forms of employment for these women—working in a firm or a small business or as a domestic helper—were not attractive. The wages were miserable and the working conditions too inflexible for a single mother. Women often decided to try and start their own businesses precisely because they already had solid experience of the alternatives. Take María, for example. In 2013, she was forty-two, a single mother with three children, and ran a *ventorrillo* selling vegetables and chicken in Buena Vista, a barrio just south of the center of Villa Mella. She had established the *ventorrillo* five years earlier. Having completed school, she had worked for many years as a saleswoman for various firms. The last firm had paid her a low, fixed monthly wage plus commission for the sales she made. However, in 2003 the firm dropped the commission without raising the salary. María quit and began, instead, to do domestic work for a family. The family paid her 6,000 pesos a month, and she worked for that family for the next five years. She finally resigned and started to develop her own business because the family asked her to begin to spend two, sometimes three, nights a week in their home as part of the job. At the time, her youngest daughter was just twelve. María could not leave her children alone at home at night.

We have seen why women chose to open or purchase a food stall or *ventorrillo*. Wage employment was not attractive because wages were low, and these women, often single mothers, needed some flexibility, something that being their own boss gave them. Another reason was that owning and operating a small business (even though it was only a precarious means of survival) rendered it easier (for better or worse) to get access to, or raise, capital through forms of credit and loans. I will return to this point. However, first I explain how these women organized their economic ventures and their everyday lives.

Precarity's Forms

The women I spoke to had two key goals: to be able to fulfill their responsibilities, and, to some extent, to be able to control their lives. The business was their means.[13] How did they cope with the constant tension between their obligations and wishes, especially their desire to be able to care for their children and other relatives, and the demands of economic precariousness? In order to begin answering this question, I first outline how three of the women—two with a food stall and one with a *ventorrillo*—ran their enterprises. What investments had they made? What did an ordinary day look like? What characterized their relationships with customers? As I show, running the business (in a narrow sense) and the management of other parts of life (such as the family) were two sides of the same process. The women hardly distinguished between the business (with its investments, income, and money) and other obligations and needs (and concomitant expenses) that they had. All money derived, and was taken, from the same source, the food stall or the *ventorrillo*.

The simple metal booth that housed Ana's food stall close to the junction of Nicolás de Ovando and Máximo Gómez in Cristo Rey did not have water or electricity. Ana fetched water from factories and businesses in the vicinity and cooked with gas, which was a major expense—she estimated that she spent between 1,000 and 1,200 pesos weekly on gas. The area was poor, and security was limited. Since 2003, people had broken into her booth five times during the night. Each time she had had to take out a loan to replace the stove and other equipment stolen.

Ana prepared two meals a day, six days a week. In the morning, she offered coffee, tea, plantain mash, boiled plantains, yuca, eggs, salt herring, and *spaghetti a la criolla*. Some days she fried meat, sometimes she offered cheese. Because her locale was so small, she prepared only one dish for lunch: "the flag," that is, white rice, red beans, meat, and salad. However, from time to time she offered *moro*, a combination of black beans and rice.

Her daily routine was grueling. She got up at about 4:30 a.m. and headed for the market in Villas Agrícolas, where each day she spent 1,300–1,800 pesos buying the foodstuffs she needed. She then left for her food stall, where she fetched water and began to cook the breakfast. Having sold the breakfast, she cleaned up and did the dishes, and then started to cook the next meal. She served lunch from around 12:30 to between 2 and 3 p.m., and then tidied up and went home. Back in Villa Mella, she cleaned the house and made supper. Her children went to school. The thirteen-year-old daughter was in charge of the cooking in the morning and at noon. Plantains and yuca were key elements both at home and in the food stall. Ana constantly brought *víveres* from the food stall to home or vice versa.

Her prices for a meal were not entirely fixed. The breakfast cost 50 pesos, and the lunch 100. "But some are poor," she explained, "and I let them have a breakfast for 40 or 30, and I sell lunches at 100, 80, even 50." Some of the customers ate on credit. In late 2013, her regulars were a group of workers from a factory in the vicinity and a number who worked in the metro station close by. The first group paid every two weeks, the other every month. Offering such limited credit appeared necessary to be able to compete, but entailed a certain risk. Sometimes people disappeared without having paid. A group of construction workers had recently disappeared, owing her 6,000 pesos, and another group of workers had owed her 10,000 when they disappeared.

Delsy's food stall was located on the same plaza as Aris's, near the José Francisco Peña Gómez metro station. The distance between the two booths was perhaps 10 meters. Delsy was born in the countryside in Monte Plata, north of Santo Domingo, and had had two years of schooling. When she was nine, she moved to Cristo Rey with her parents. In 2013, she was forty-six and lived in the Guaricano barrio, not far from where she worked, with her seven children, from relationships with two different men. Neither of the two fathers helped the family economically.

She had started the business five years earlier with a sister. The two had worked together and split daily expenses and income, fifty-fifty. Subsequently, the sister quit, and Delsy continued alone. A nearby supermarket owned her booth, and the rent was 4,000 pesos per month. The booth was without water, and she stole electricity via an illegal connection.

In the morning, she sold hot chocolate, coffee, *sancocho*, and *víveres* with fried meat. Later in the day, she offered "the flag," and *moro* with meat. The breakfast cost 60–100 pesos, and the lunch 90–120. She had two plastic tables beside the booth where her customers ate. Some were regulars, but she refused to sell on credit, "because people don't pay."

She had two employees, one of whom was one of her daughters. She paid both of the workers 6,000 pesos a month. This was uncommon. Ana, for example, worked alone. Josefina paid a young girl from the vicinity 150 pesos per day for doing the dishes. Two women, two friends, in the vicinity often helped Aris a bit, but she did not pay them. Instead, she gave them a cup of coffee or a meal.

Delsy's business was open from 5 a.m. to 4 p.m., seven days a week. Sunday, she said, was her best day; many wanted *sancocho* this day. They started to make coffee and hot chocolate and to prepare the *víveres* in the kitchen between 4 and 5 a.m. She bought most of what she needed, the *víveres* and the meat, at the daily market on the plaza. She spent 4,000–5,000 pesos a day on foodstuffs. At around 10 a.m., she began cooking the day's lunch. Each day she sent lunch from the food stall home to her children.

When María opened a *ventorrillo* in Buena Vista in 2008, she started first in her own home. However, when she later relocated to another part of the same barrio, she realized that she had to find a place to rent: in the new area, she sold less. She found a shack for rent in a busy area, close to other small businesses, residential areas, and the metro. The rent, which she paid annually, was 60,000 pesos, and she borrowed from moneylenders to afford it. She did not pay fees to the municipality, and she stole electricity by means of an illegal connection.

She sold chicken and pork, rice, soft drinks, and a long list of vegetables. The business was open 8 a.m.–2 p.m. and 4–7 p.m. Monday to Friday, and 8 a.m.–2 p.m. Saturdays and Sundays. Besides her work, María was a part-time student of theology at one of the city's universities. Every Friday she had classes 6–10 p.m. When she did not attend the business herself, her daughter worked in her place.

In 2013, her eldest son was twenty-three and ran a barbershop and a small cafeteria. He had his own vehicle. The two met at the market in Villas Agrícolas early each morning to buy supplies. She spent about 3,500 pesos on vegetables daily. The son transported the goods to her shack in Buena Vista. Every day, for around 2,000 pesos, she also bought chicken, which she had delivered. María said that the local demand for chicken was striking and constant: "It's as if people can't get enough of this meat." In spite of this, the bulk of her income was from the sale of vegetables. Her profits were higher when she sold vegetables than when she sold chicken: "The 2,000 pesos I spend each day on chicken give me a total profit of only 150–180 pesos. In comparison, if I purchase vegetables for 40 or 50 pesos, I sell them for 60, 80, or 120." Many of the customers were regulars, but she allowed only a handful to purchase on credit. These paid her every two weeks or every month.

Operating a food stall or a *ventorrillo* was a raw deal. The women worked almost constantly, and they virtually always owed money. Nevertheless, they were convinced that they had done the right thing. Thanks to their business, they were able to provide for themselves and their families. As Ana put it, when I asked whether her food stall was worth the work:

"Yes, I earn something."

"How much do you make?"

"Well, how can I tell you? If we look at the money I take home and the food I sell on credit I'm sure I make more than anyone around here working as an employee."

"Do you see the money, the progress?"

"No, I don't see it. How can I explain? I don't see the [accumulated] money—but I see it nevertheless because it's from this [the food stall] I get everything, from this I get what I give my [old] mother."

The income varied considerably from one day to another and was un-predictable—although at least if sales were bad, the family could eat the leftover food. This meant that the possibility of having to go hungry had been virtually eliminated. What we must understand is that, compared to employees working for the minimum wage or less (6,000–10,000 pesos a month), these women handled significant amounts daily. They bought and sold for two or three thousand pesos, or several thousand, a day. With the sums of money and the foodstuffs that circulated through their hands, they fulfilled their crucial obligations. The business paid the rent, put food on the table, paid for school equipment, and enabled care.

Much has been said about the significance of the mother–son bond in Caribbean societies. However, the daughters are typically more reliable for providing support for their parents in their final years. There comes a time when a poor single woman or man gets to an age where they find it difficult to work and produce in the same way as they did before. In contemporary Santo Domingo, there are enormous numbers of poor women and men who mostly or entirely depend on their family's—primarily their children's—support and care. For the women with whom I worked, it was an affective and ethical imperative to visit, and assist, their old mother. Aris traveled to Moca to be able to spend time with her mother and her oldest daughter. María's mother was in her late sixties, could no longer work, and lived in Villa Mella. María gave her meat and money—perhaps 400 or 500 pesos—two or three times weekly. Likewise with Josefina. Her mother, who lived close by, was old, and Josefina spent a significant amount each month on her medicines. Ana spent each Sunday visiting and caring for her mother, and keeping in touch with her kin and old neighbors in Yamasá. Her mother lived with two of Ana's brothers—one who, as she put it, did not work, and another who was born with a handicap. Ana and a third brother helped the mother with money. From Monday to Saturday, Ana ran her food stall in Cristo Rey. With money from the food stall, she purchased secondhand clothes and textiles at a market on Sunday mornings and then took the bus to Yamasá, where she resold the goods to villagers, or to kin and acquaintances. In the evening, she traveled back to the capital. Each week she helped her mother with 500 pesos.

Another important expense was the children's education—school uniforms, books, daily transport, and fees. Two of the women had even taken up studying again themselves. María studied theology; Josefina, who originally had had only a few years of schooling, completed high school in 2006, and then began to study pedagogy at a private university. In 2012, she was taking classes each Saturday and had completed three-quarters of the course.

Another goal was to live in one's own house. While Ana was still living with her ex-partner (the father of three of her children), they had managed to obtain a land lot in a poor part of Villa Mella. They began building a house and moved into it immediately. By 2014, Ana's house was still only a bit more than half-completed. Her wish was to be able to finish it. Josefina said that she had saved up to purchase a land lot. She had managed to put aside 50,000 pesos, but then had had to give up. The business had done badly, and she had needed the 50,000 to buy supplies, pay for her daughter's schooling, and pay off debt.

Navigating the tensions between the challenges of economic poverty and social and moral imperatives and desires was a daily negotiation and struggle with time (Han 2011, 2012; Bear 2016). It was a routine, an embodied habitus, consisting of labor, practices, rhythms, disruptions, nervousness, hope—a way of life. Women constantly took out small and large, short-term, high-interest loans in order to make ends meet. Over the last couple of decades, the use of such loans among owners and operators of small, precarious ventures in the Zona Norte has increased. In 2013, in areas like Villa Mella and Cristo Rey, this form of finance was rife. In the next section, I discuss why the women continually borrowed money and the consequences this had.

Juggling Debts, Navigating Time

The loans that are mostly used in the poor barrios of today's Santo Domingo are not bank loans—although some of the women with whom I worked had tried the loans offered by banks and financial institutions catering especially to low-income and poor women or entrepreneurs running a small business.[14] Instead, most borrowed from moneylenders and loan sharks, or so-called *empresas financieras,* or finance firms.[15] The *empresas financieras* were especially important and had a striking presence in most of the city. Their loans were usually small and short-term, with enormously high interest rates. The firms offered their services in particular to persons who owned and operated some form of small enterprise. People paid off the loans in fixed daily or weekly amounts, picked up by debt collectors on motorcycles. According to Alejandra, whose *ventorrillo* was located in an outlying and poor corner of the original Villa Mella, the use of these loans started to take off in her part of the city in the late 1990s and early 2000s, and spread almost like a *moda,* or fashion. She herself used them all the time.

As Clara Han has shown brilliantly, the nature of such a process—continual borrowing and use of credit—within the lifeworlds of the urban poor is "double-edged." Although the loans and credit forms of my interlocutors in the Zona Norte resulted in perpetual indebtedness (and striking exploitation because of the payment of exorbitant interest), they also offered "*material and temporal resources* for livelihoods affected by labor instability" (2011:8–9, emphasis added).[16]

The loans provided access to cash. Among the urban poor, as James Ferguson (2015:136) has argued, even very small injections of cash "can both catalyze and stimulate a range of social and economic activities and enable people to better meet their needs as they themselves define them." Put differently, fresh capital in the form of cash in the pocket enabled the maintenance and reproduction of chronically precarious business ventures, social relations, and networks, as well as forms of mutual assistance and care. A central difficulty that my interlocutors faced was constant economic unpredictability. One day they sold a lot; another day they invested money, time, and labor but sold little and ended up with little or no money. Regardless, the family had needs, and the next day they had to invest again. Forms of credit and loans represented, as Han maintains, material and temporal resources that people drew on as a way to surmount difficulties. As I said, all my interlocutors borrowed, and the normal was to have (and be forced to pay off) several different debts simultaneously. Below, I look more closely at the situation of two of them.

When Aris established her own food stall, she borrowed money from two different Dominican banks catering especially to (female) micro-entrepreneurs—the Banco de la Mujer, or Women's Bank, and the Banco ADEMI or the Savings and Credit Bank ADEMI. Before this, she had sold clothes as a traveling vendor. From the first bank she borrowed 20,000 pesos, and from the second, 30,000. In addition to coffee and soft drinks, she sold hot meals—fried meat, eggs, *víveres*, and s*paghetti a la criolla*. Her son in Puerto Rico sent her money, and the business went well and she paid her monthly installments. But, after a while, she got into difficulties. Thieves broke into her booth and destroyed or stole her equipment, and subsequently she fell ill. She was unable to work and could not pay the installments. She went to the banks' offices and cried, but to no avail. The banks' debt collectors sought her out and put pressure on her, and she ended up having to sell assets in order to be able to pay—she sold a cupboard, a display cabinet, and a series of other objects. Finally, she came to an agreement with both institutions. She never again approached a bank for a loan. She explained: "You know that the banks [work well] as long as you comply with the requirements 100 percent—but when you get ill or something happens so that you fall behind with the payments, there are many problems, lots of difficulties."

Instead she used the services of *empresas financieras*. In July 2013, she owed money to three different firms. From one firm she had borrowed 10,000 pesos; the repayment period was sixty days and the daily amount 220 pesos. The other loans amounted to 5,000 and 3,000 pesos, with repayment periods of forty-six and twenty-four days, respectively, and daily payments of 135 and 150 pesos. In other words, two of the loans had annual interest rates of over 90 percent, and the third a rate of 200 percent. These conditions were typical.[17] Aris used one of the loans to invest in a new freezer for her food stall. The price was 35,000 pesos; she paid the store 5,000 and paid the rest in the form of monthly installments of 2,500. The other loans she used to pay off debt, buy supplies, and cover the family's needs. She obtained the loans without needing guarantors—that she owned and ran a small business was enough. The firms practiced a certain flexibility. If Aris one day lacked the money to pay what she owed, she told the collector, the payment was postponed, and she was not charged extra. As she put it: "They know me and that I pay. The day I say I can't pay, it's because I've made almost nothing." This flexibility was the decisive reason why she preferred the finance firms to the banks. Borrowing from the firms meant tougher conditions, she acknowledged, but the firms and their loans were nonetheless easier to live with, or adapt to (*es más forzado para uno, pero uno se va desenvolviendo más fácil*).

Aris sometimes purchased supplies on credit. However, she did not like to ask her neighbors for credit or loans. "All around here owe money," she said. "I prefer borrowing [from one of the firms] to buying on credit" (*Para coger fiado yo mejor cojo prestado*). "Here, I know all. I see the other owners [of small businesses and stores] the whole day. If I buy on credit and cannot pay in the evening or the next day, I feel ashamed. But if the collector arrives, I pay him if I have the money, and if not, he leaves, you know, and then I don't see him until the next day."

She knew well that her ability to keep afloat was dependent on both the firms' loans and the trust and solidarity of her relatives, neighbors, and friends. Much of her life was a continual struggle to balance the two considerations: She needed money, but she would not be able to manage over time if she did not preserve her mutually obligating social relationships (Guérin 2014). It was almost impossible for her to explain how much she earned. Each day she used the income from the food stall to buy new supplies, run the family and reproduce her networks, and pay off loans. As she put it, "What I make, I use to repay the loans" (*Entonces ya lo que uno produce es para pagar los prestamitos esos a diario*).

María also borrowed from firms rather than commercial banks, and used to have several different loans simultaneously. She used the loans to pay off other loans, invest in the business, pay the rent, pay for supplies, and buy school equipment and clothes. The typical interest rates were intimidating. She used, for example, to borrow 20,000 pesos from a local firm, Inversiones Taveras, about every two months. The repayment period was forty-six days and the daily amount 520 pesos (in early 2013, the firm had just raised this from 500 to 520 pesos).

She paid annual rent for the shack where she ran her *ventorrillo*. For the year 2013, she paid 60,000—a significant sum. In order to raise the capital and pay in January she took up several new loans in November and December 2012. In addition, she paid 3,500 pesos monthly as rent for her apartment. To be able to pay this, she usually organized a *san,* or rotating credit association, in the vicinity where she lived. The *san* or *sociedad* is a popular Dominican institution (Sassen-Koob 1987:265–66; Krohn-Hansen 2013:50–51) that typically includes a fixed number of individual members, men and women, who are all kin and/or friends. The purpose is to increase the members' ability to save. Each contributes a fixed amount of money, daily, weekly, or monthly, and each in turn receives the pooled contributions. María's *san* included twenty-five members who each paid 200 pesos daily.

One of the women, Delsy, had incurred large debts. She appeared to have lost control of her debt situation and as a consequence was in a downward spiral. Her problems had started in earnest when she borrowed a huge sum—250,000 pesos—in order to make it possible for one of her daughters to leave for Italy in search of work. The daughter found a job in Italy and sent her mother 10,000 pesos monthly. Nevertheless, Delsy was unable to repay the loan, and the original debt of 250,000 only continued to grow. In the meantime, she took out a stream of small and medium-sized, high-interest loans. She spent everything she made, as well as the money her daughter sent, on paying off what she owed. In late 2013, she estimated that she owed money to almost forty individuals and firms: "Everything I have is borrowed. I never have anything, not even 10 pesos. My life is to borrow . . . I owe my soul and my life" (*Todo lo mío es emprestado. Nunca tengo ni 10. La vida mía es coger emprestado . . . Y ya debo mi alma y mi vida*).

These women needed to juggle a series of economic and moral demands. Their situation was chronically precarious and required immense self-control and discipline. At the same time, the representatives of the firms regularly sought them out in order to offer them new loans.[18] In this situation, one can easily lose control, as Delsy had done.

The persistent need to take out loans was reinforced by the difficult times. As I mentioned, wages had not kept up with the cost of living. From the early 1990s to the time of the fieldwork, the country saw a decline in real wages. My interlocutors said that they sold less than they had done previously, that the customers lacked money, and that it consequently had become harder to live off the business and get by. In María's words, "the times have changed. When I started this business [in 2008], I sold for 10,000 pesos, 8,000 pesos daily—but not any longer. Now I sell for 6,000, 7,000, 6,500, sales have dropped." Josefina claimed: "Look, previously I invested less and earned more, now I invest more and earn less. The situation is not as before, the prices have increased. Previously, I borrowed less, but now I have again to take up loans."

Declining real wages and the lack of jobs also led to sharper competition for customers and tougher conditions for everyone. For example, on a stretch of street where some years earlier there had been just two or three who offered meals or vegetables, there were now five, six, or perhaps many more. When Josefina in 1997 began to run her food stall, the small indoor market where she operated had three cafeterias or small food stalls in total. Fifteen years later, the number had grown to seven.

Josefina described, like the others, how she always lacked cash. She had a credit card with a credit limit of 20,000 pesos. If she was without cash, she explained, she could still purchase supplies in the supermarket, pay her phone bill, and pay her electricity bill with the credit card. Her system was as follows. She never let her credit card debt grow to more than 3,500 pesos, or at most 4,000. On Saturdays, she studied, and therefore her stall was closed. But for the rest of the week, and on Sundays, she ran her food stall. She used everything she earned on Sundays to pay off the credit card debt.

However, this did not prevent her from experiencing the effects of the demanding times. Her cafeteria did not make as much as before, and in mid-2013 she had serious economic problems. Her solution was a new and costly loan. She borrowed 90,000. The repayment period was two years and the monthly amount was 5,540 pesos; in other words, the 90,000 cost her 133,000. She used the loan to pay off old debt and purchase new supplies—but also to attempt to develop a new source of income and in this way diversify her economic strategies. She purchased a small pickup truck and rented it out to a driver for 400 pesos per day. As part of the agreement, the latter transported her supplies from the market to her food stall without charging. The man rented the car six days a week. The first year Josefina paid 9,000 in monthly installments for the truck, and by September 2014 she had paid it off. The rent from the car became extremely important for Josefina. In her words: "It's with the vehicle that I manage. The food stall doesn't make money [anymore]. Do you know why I haven't closed it? It's because of the 400 I get six days a week from the car. If I only had had the cafeteria, I would have had to shut down." It was hard to survive, but people adapted and improvised and constantly put into play new, although recognizable, strategies.

Conclusion

The reality in today's Zona Norte mirrors the many repressive decades under Trujillo and Balaguer. Neither of those leaders, however, would have been able to take power if it had not been for the important assistance they received from the United States. At the same time, I have underscored that we must go further back in history if we aim to properly understand the social and material life in the Dominican Republic today. The discourses and practices that help to authorize and maintain conspicuous machismo in most of today's Dominican society reflect five hundred years of violent history. These discourses and practices help to engender, and give form to, much uncertainty and misery. An outcome is that women are driven to attempt to provide for, and raise, their children as single mothers with limited or no economic or other assistance from the fathers.

Many women seek to secure a livelihood by exploiting a part of the potential inherent in the popular Dominican foodways. Viewed in this way, my interlocutors form part of a long, proud, gendered subaltern tradition. As we have seen, from the late sixteenth century, Spanish Santo Domingo saw the emergence of a sizable population of independent creole peasants who lived for centuries mostly at the margins of the state. This semisettled population's slash-and-burn farming, hunting practices, and forms of animal husbandry laid the foundations for the creation of what today is the popular Dominican cuisine. The central rural foodways were further fortified under Trujillo and have since been of central importance in large parts of the cities.

Although it is possible to see striking historical continuities embedded in today's forms of precarity, it is also a fact that the situation has changed in the past two decades. Many who depended on a small food stall or a *ventorrillo* for their livelihoods maintained, at the time of my fieldwork, that conditions had worsened. The proportion of the population that had shared in the growth of the national economy remained small, and far too many people lacked sufficient income (although remittances that constantly arrived from family members in the United States, Spain, and elsewhere alleviated the situation). An outcome was that an increasing number of people competed for a sharply limited buying power. As María summed it up, "I'm telling you—sales are not as before; they've dropped a lot—a lot. Why? People have the same income as two years ago, while the products have become more expensive, and rents have increased." Alejandra said, "People purchase very little, and there are so many *ventorrillos*! In addition, there are the . . . vehicles, the mobile vendors offering *víveres* and vegetables from their pickup trucks, who sell at lower prices [than I do] because they buy the products in larger quantities. If I sell a product at 50 pesos, they sell it for 40."

At the same time, a new credit economy had overtaken the poor barrios. As one of the women explained, the use of short-term loans from the finance firms spread in earnest to her part of the Zona Norte from the early 2000s onward. This was not a credit economy with a long history in these areas. But when I started my research, signs of these firms were everywhere. Their representatives and debt collectors on their motorcycles were a regular sight in the street, and the women had the various finance firms' business cards taped on walls and refrigerators. The loans were extremely expensive, but the firms allowed a certain amount of flexibility: if you were without the necessary money one day, you could postpone paying them what you owed until the next day, or the next week, without extra charge.

On the one hand, this flourishing credit economy helped to deepen poverty. The loans were associated with dramatic exploitation, and enormous profits for a small number—the owners and operators of the firms providing the loans. On the other hand, the loans represented, in the eyes of Alejandra, María, and the others, material and temporal assets. Given the chronically unpredictable and uncertain economic and social situation in which they found themselves, the cash infusions to which the firms allowed constant and easy access offered possibilities to resolve problems and allow them to continue working and making money. With the cash from the loans, they could keep both the family and the business afloat. The women were thus part of multiple heterogeneous material-social networks. Another way of formulating this is to say that they were part of, and were forced to navigate, a series of heterogeneous temporalities (Das and Randeria 2015:11). The loans, no matter how intimidatingly expensive they were, represented tools in the daily efforts to navigate time, and get by. Did these ways of handling life reflect *new* forms of precarity and precariousness? Of course—but new forms that simultaneously mirrored layers upon layers of violent history.

CHAPTER 3

The End of the *Colmado*?

What will become of the Dominican *colmado*? Will it survive? *El colmado*, the small village or street-corner store, is a national institution. Typically, a *colmado* stocks basic foodstuffs, cleaning products, toiletries, soft drinks, beer, and rum. Some offer more items. Until recently, a majority of Dominicans purchased food and groceries in *colmados* and in public markets. The *colmados* continue to be extremely important in today's Dominican Republic and are still the most common small business in the country. However, since the late twentieth century, especially in the largest cities—including in the capital's working-class barrios—independent and chain supermarkets have become far more important and have increasingly taken over the groceries' market. Many *colmados* in Santo Domingo now sell relatively little food and have grown correspondingly more dependent on sales of drinking water, soft drinks, beer, and rum, in addition to sandwiches, cookies, and snacks.

A *colmado* is never a self-service shop. Customers enter the store and are attended to by those behind the counter. Most often one or two people work behind the counter, and most, if not all, of the goods are stored behind the counter. Usually the store is small and packed, with boxes of fruit, vegetables, or some other kind of commodity taking up part of the space in front of the counter. More goods are often stored on the pavement in front of the store. Bottles of rum and whiskey are typically displayed in a very visible place, for example, just behind the counter.

In 2014, Fomerio Díaz owned and operated two *colmados*, one in the east of Santo Domingo, in Los Mina Sur, and another in a barrio in Haina, a seaport town located just southwest of the capital, on the way to San Cristóbal.

I had met him through the Asociación de Detallistas de Provisiones del Distrito Nacional, the capital's association of *colmado* owners and operators—the oldest one in the country, founded under Trujillo in 1942. Fomerio had been a member for many years, and sat on the association's board. Born in 1960, in the countryside near Baní, he moved in 1978 to Santo Domingo, where he started working in a *colmado* belonging to his eldest sister's husband. He worked there for four years, and slept in the store. To begin with, he was paid 15 pesos a month; subsequently it was raised to 30, then 90. The store was located in Guachupita, a poor neighborhood in the Zona Norte. By 1982, he had managed to save some money, and he borrowed a bit more, managing to get together 750 pesos. With this capital, he purchased, together with his brother-in-law, a *colmado* in another part of Guachupita. The two men became *socios*, or business partners; they paid 1,500 pesos for the store and each owned half the business. As the brother-in-law already had an established reputation in the business and was trusted by the suppliers, they were able to stock the store on credit. Fomerio ran the *colmado* and worked almost continuously. The store opened at 7 a.m. and closed late in the evening, usually around midnight, seven days a week. Four years later, they sold the business and divided the money, and Fomerio bought a new *colmado* alone, this time on a street in the Mejoramiento Social barrio, not far from Guachupita. He paid 5,000 pesos for the business. His regular supplier, a wholesaler who operated in the area, lent him most of the 5,000 and stocked the *colmado* on credit.

However, the new *colmado* was in rented premises, and the landlord's son was, according to Fomerio, a drug addict who used drugs on the patio outside the apartment where Fomerio lived with his wife and two small children. He felt that it was not safe for them, so a few months later he sold the business and purchased another *colmado* a few streets away. The new *colmado* was large. He named the store the Bodega Original and kept it until 2003, when he sold it. The business went well, and in 1996 he purchased a second *colmado* in the eastern part of Santo Domingo, in Los Mina Sur, which he called Bodega Henri. When I met him for the first time sixteen years later, in 2012, he still owned the *colmado* in Los Mina Sur and lived with his family in the vicinity. Shortly after selling his Mejoramiento Social store (the Bodega Original), in 2003, he purchased another one in

Haina. For the first two years he ran it himself but, once it was established, he found an *encargado* (manager) to take over.

Fomerio's biggest fear was that he would wake up one day to find a gigantic supermarket chain next to one of his stores. As he put it: "Tragically enough, in this country there is no law or regulation that determines a minimum distance between stores. It's a threat, because everywhere they open one of these commercial centers, or these enormous stores, the small *colmados* get into difficulties and disappear. Personally, I haven't yet experienced it—but others have."

A handful of larger independent (not chain) supermarkets had opened in some of Santo Domingo's more upmarket areas from the late 1960s to the late 1990s, but more significant changes began in the early 2000s, when Santo Domingo saw the creation and development of a rapidly growing number of large supermarkets owned and operated by chains. These large stores first opened in the central parts of the city, but have increasingly spread into the working-class barrios and the more outlying and poorer areas as well. This means that the economic climate for most of the *colmados* in the country's largest cities, and especially in the capital, has become significantly harsher. The supermarkets, which outcompete the *colmados* through lower prices and high-profile marketing, are increasingly taking over the sale of groceries and food, not only to the middle class but also to significant parts of the urban masses. Many *colmados* in Santo Domingo's barrios now sell relatively little food. As a veteran *colmadero* in one of the city's old working-class barrios put it, in a conversation in 2012: "The *colmado* today isn't like it was previously. Today the neighborhood only uses the *colmado* to buy water, soft drinks, juice, bread, cookies, many small things." However, in spite of this (exaggerated) claim, the same man was convinced that the *colmado* had a future in Dominican society—that it would survive, albeit in altered forms. Another interlocutor, a man in his thirties who was the son of a *colmadero* and who owned a small supermarket in a barrio in the east of the capital, said: "The *colmado* will live on! This country has a kind of *colmado* culture."

Colmados have changed since the late 1990s, and the way in which most are run in the barrios is different now. Still, in my view, they will remain a significant part of Dominican society and of the Dominican capital in the years to come. Statistical data seem to support this assumption. In the mid-1990s, surveys indicated that there were around 320,000 small businesses in the country and that some 70,000, or more than one-fifth, of these were *colmados* or even smaller enterprises, known as *pulperías* and *ventorrillos*. Of the 70,000 total, 40,000 were *colmados*, while 30,000 were *pulperías* and *ventorrillos* (Murray 1996:4–7). A decade later, in 2005, the number of small businesses had grown to about 615,000, and the number of *colmados* had increased significantly, to almost 67,000 (Ortiz and Mena 2007:15–16). In 2013, the total number of small businesses was more than 770,000, and the proportion categorized as *colmados, pulperías*, and *ventorrillos* remained high at 15 percent (although it was 5 percent lower than in the mid-1990s); in 2013, the country had more than 115,000 *colmados*, bodegas, and *pulperías* (Ortiz et al. 2014:19, 35).

There are at least four reasons, or sets of reasons, why the *colmado* will live on. First, it has a proud national history. It has been a cornerstone of the Dominican search for, and construction of, *progreso*, or modernity. My use of "modernity" here follows that of James Ferguson:

> I treat "modernity" not as an analytic term . . . but as what anthropologists call a "native category"—in this case, a native category shared by an enormously heterogeneous population of natives. As vague and confused as the term undoubtedly is when considered as an analytical tool, it remains the center of a powerful "discourse of identity" . . . and a key word that anchors a host of discussions . . . about an emerging global social order. (2006:177)

The lengthy Trujillo dictatorship (1930–61) changed the nation. A backbone of Trujillo's (mostly rural) Dominican Republic remained the small, local (village or neighborhood) *colmado*. In the second half of the twentieth century, and particularly in the decades after the dictator's death in 1961, the country saw extensive urbanization. In the new populous and poor barrios in the cities, the *colmados* continued to be of central significance: Most city residents bought their groceries and food in them or in public markets. In sum, while the explosive emergence of chain supermarkets in Dominican cities since the late 1990s has helped to radically redefine the Dominican food retail industry, the *colmado*, with its powerful history, continues to possess remarkable force and vitality in significant parts of the thoroughly transnationalized, contemporary Dominican social formation.

The second important reason why the *colmado* will survive is that it has shown itself to be resilient and flexible, resembling a "total" phenomenon (in the Maussian, or classic anthropological, sense of this expression [Mauss 1923–24]). Such institutions do not disappear easily; instead, they survive through continual small and large adaptations and changes. The objective of every *colmado* owner is quite simply to sell, to make money. They have always adapted to their surroundings. *Colmados* were, and still are, neighborhood institutions within which ordinary Dominicans make and remake neighborhood relationships, maintain already established friendships, and develop new ones. The owner of the store and the customers greet one another and find time for a chat. Through these conversations, news and gossip about the area's families and businesses circulate. The stream of encounters in the *colmado* helps convert the small rural village, or the store's immediate vicinity in a city barrio, into a community—a loosely organized order of shared information and understandings. The processes and relationships that give the *colmado* its characteristic shape should not, therefore, be reduced to mere economics. The cultural, affective, aesthetic, recreational, and political components are equally important. It is a site for the production and maintenance of forms of kinship and gender—and of relationships between friends.

A third significant reason why the *colmado* will not vanish anytime soon is that it is also a site for the popular production and experience of *lo criollo*—what it means to be Dominican—in contexts shot through with marked and growing globalization and transnationalism. Writers on the Hispanic Caribbean have argued that there is a cyclical theme in many Cuban and Dominican national discourses that culturally and morally constructs the nation (or what happened/happens on the island) in terms of complex encounters or struggles between two sets of historical forces: On the one hand, there is imperialism, slavery, and foreignness; on the other, independence, freedom, "nativeness," and *lo criollo* (Ortiz 1995 [1940]; Benítez-Rojo 1992; Derby 1998).

In the Dominican case, Lauren Derby (1998) has traced a powerful vernacular discourse on forms of food and the nation. This discourse shaped and used an opposition between big sugar plantations and the *conuco*, the peasant's small plot of land, a source of independence and of the Dominican masses' preferred foods. Small farming produced, and continues to produce, the Dominican *víveres*: staple foods, such as roots, tubers, and green plantains. The plantain continues to be perhaps the most important, the most creole or Dominican, foodstuff. Historically, the *colmados* sold these products, and a set of strong connections exists in many ordinary Dominicans' cultural and affective world among nativeness, the *conuco*, the *víveres*, the plantain, the *colmado*, *lo criollo*, and Dominican identity.

One sees the traces, and the lasting power, of these visions and stories in today's Dominican society. Steven Gregory, in the early 2000s, studied an area of the country that, since the early 1980s, has changed radically and strikingly through the development of international tourism. The *colmados* in Boca Chica, he writes, "were viewed by residents as particularly Dominican cultural spaces and contrasted to the tourism-oriented bars and entertainment venues" (Gregory 2014:71). Few foreign tourists and expatriates frequented the *colmados,* even those located in the heart of the tourist area. The *colmados* are important because they make it possible for the Dominican masses constantly to cultivate and experience familiarity and belonging, a sense of rootedness, in a shifting, interconnected, and profoundly globalized world.

The last and probably most important reason why the *colmado* will continue to exist is that it still fills an economic niche. Since the first half of the 1990s, the Dominican Republic has mostly experienced high and sustained economic growth. This national economic performance, however, has not translated into equal improvements in material conditions for all. Poverty remains widespread, and vast parts of the population in the countryside and in the cities continue to be economically vulnerable. As I show, in this socioeconomic landscape, the *colmado* offers commercial services that significant parts of the population need and use—despite the emergence of the supermarkets. In addition, the country lacks jobs, and most workers earn miserable wages: many continue to seek to secure a livelihood through running a small *colmado,* even though it requires long working days and (most often) means economic risk.

As is evident, a central argument here is that the *colmado*'s past continues to possess force and to exercise power, and that it is an intrinsic part of the present (albeit in permuted forms). In what follows, I explore the situation for the *colmado* in today's Dominican capital in light of the institution's history. The next three sections trace (1) its rural roots, (2) history in the capital, and (3) history in an important part of the contemporary transnational Dominican social formation—namely, the Dominican community of New York City. I then return to Santo Domingo and analyze the last decades' changes in the retail industry and the implications of these for *colmados.*[1] My aim is twofold. First, I try to provide some answers to questions such as: how have these businesses been created and run? what have been their most striking characteristics? and how have they changed over the last three decades? Second, and more ambitiously, I seek to demonstrate that the *colmado* offers a window for tracking and understanding the ways Dominican society and the Dominican economy have changed since the mid-twentieth century, that is, since the last years of the Trujillo regime. The patterns of the *colmados* have mirrored, and continue to mirror, broader historical transformations. But these businesses also help give the latter processes their form. Businesses and social configurations have been, and remain, two sides of the same historical process.

Peasants, the Trujillo Regime, and the *Colmado*

The Dominican *colmado* first emerged in the countryside and in the country's *pueblos,* or villages, and small towns. As late as the early 1960s, approximately 70 percent of the Dominican people still lived in rural areas (Turits 2003:265). The word *colmado* is probably derived from the verb *colmar,* "to fill to the brim" (Murray 1996:19). Sometimes, people use the word *bodega,* or even *pulpería,* instead of *colmado,* but the category *pulpería* is usually associated with a smaller and simpler, more rural, store. In any case, the country has, for a long time, been dotted with these types of small commercial enterprises—*pulperías,* bodegas, and *colmados.*

A solid will and propensity for commerce has characterized the Dominican and Haitian rural masses—and, more generally, Caribbean peasantries. In their *pulperías* and *colmados,* Dominican peasants and villagers buy not only salt, matches, cooking oil, bacalao, and similar products, but also (at least for significant periods during the year) a substantial part of their daily food. Dominican peasants used to sell (not store) a significant part of their harvest, although this meant that they subsequently had to resort to the *colmado* and the public market in order to put food on the table. As Gerald Murray (1996:24) has argued, this orientation toward commerce helped in two ways to increase the number of *pulperías* and *colmados* in the Dominican countryside. First, it meant that there was a material basis for entities that sold basic foodstuffs. Second, it meant that many people dreamed of, and sought to open, their own small business, such as a *colmado.*

Often, an important *colmado* belonged to a local political head or a member of a powerful extended family in the community, and its ownership and operation constituted the most decisive source of authority and leadership in the area. The local (informal or formal) leader ran his store either from his home or in adjacent premises. Many people bought on credit or owed him money. The *colmado* owner/leader exchanged goods, services, credit, and debt for profit, political loyalty, and votes.

In 1991–92, I carried out fieldwork in La Descubierta, a rural village in the Dominican southwest, located on the border with Haiti. The history of La Descubierta in the twentieth century illustrates these overlaps and connections between trade, forms of leadership and authority, and kinship history. When I was there in the early 1990s, the community had a population of around 8,000, but in the early twentieth century the region was sparsely populated.

The most powerful extended family in La Descubierta during the greater part of the twentieth century was the Ramírez family. Three members of that family were key political leaders: first Emilio Ramírez from the early 1920s to the first half of the 1930s, then his nephew Jesús María, under Trujillo, and then the latter's niece, Miriam, from 1976 to 1996, under Balaguer.[2]

In La Descubierta in the early 1920s, the only trader of significance was Emilio Ramírez who, with his wife, owned and ran a *colmado* that he supplied with goods bought in the town of Azua (Ramírez 2000:18). In this thinly populated area, it is unlikely that anyone else had the money and contacts required to provide goods from as far away as Azua—which had to be brought in by packs of mules. Emilio also raised livestock, and traveled regularly, with a brother and the brother's son, Jesús María (who became a political leader under Trujillo), to Haitian market towns to sell cattle.

Emilio's local authority and political leadership was born and matured in this landscape of trade networks and relative economic power. Although he never possessed much, and slept in a hammock, in this frontier world of scattered stockbreeders and peasants his store and home became a center to which all sorts of activities gravitated. Supplying local people with goods, credit, and work, Emilio was consulted for advice on personal matters, trade, and politics, and he offered hospitality to those who visited the hamlet from outside. In 1924, the first presidential elections in the Dominican Republic were held after the eight-year US military occupation of the country from 1916 to 1924. Emilio backed and campaigned for Horacio Vásquez, who won and remained president until Trujillo's coup in 1930.

Emilio died in 1943. However, even by the mid-1930s his nephew Jesús María had become La Descubierta's most influential man. As a villager and ex-military man said to me in the early 1990s, talking about the Trujillo regime: "The principal of all was Jesús María Ramírez. He was the friend of Trujillo." After having served as a soldier in Santo Domingo and the Cibao region in the late 1920s, Jesús María returned to La Descubierta in 1930 and set up a small butcher's shop. In 1933, he bought his first plot of land. He thereafter continued to accumulate land and develop agricultural activities in La Descubierta. In 1938, Trujillo appointed him as president of the local division of the Partido Dominicano, the state (and only permitted) political party, and he continued, subsequently, to work for, and build, the state in this part of the country up to the dictator's assassination in 1961.

The most important *colmado* in the village in the 1940s and 1950s was that of another Ramírez, Alejandro, who was brought up with Jesús María. The explanation for Alejandro's accumulation of wealth, people told me during my fieldwork, was that his father had been a well-to-do cattle rancher and trader in another community in the southern borderlands, but had sent Alejandro to live with Emilio Ramírez and his wife, who had raised him, in their store, to be a trader. In 1930, the father established a new *colmado* in La Descubierta with Alejandro in charge. Later Alejandro ran it alone, and gradually bought property until he was one of the community's two largest landowners; the other was his cousin, Jesús María. If someone in the community died, Alejandro's store would offer the relatives provisions for the nine-day wake on credit, with a piece of their land as surety, and later Alejandro would often acquire the land. The general consensus was that people felt he bought his land rightfully but bought it cheap. Later, in the mid-1960s, Jesús María sold his land to Alejandro's successors, who thereby doubled their property holding.

In La Descubierta, the *colmado* functioned as a local community center. Villagers and peasants sought it out to purchase food and other items, socialize and chat with neighbors and relatives, and exchange the latest gossip. As I have shown, the *colmado* owner (and his store) was often a key part of local stories of belonging and identity—of the everyday production of narratives of the past and present, of trade, transactions, justice and exploitation, of successes and losses.

After 1961 Dominican society changed in pronounced ways—although the country also saw significant historical continuities (Torres-Saillant 1999; Krohn-Hansen 2009; Horn 2014). Today, more than 70 percent of the Dominican population lives in cities. At the same time, there are still many small towns and villages where the *colmados* and *pulperías* continue to play a decisive role as grocery stores and meeting places.

In the early 1990s, these small stores were numerous in La Descubierta, but almost all were precarious enterprises, tiny *pulperías* or *ventorrillos*, with extremely small turnovers. In the center of the village were five *colmados*. The two largest belonged to Ramirito Ramírez and his brother-in-law,

Manuel Piñeyro. The former was Alejandro Ramírez's youngest son. Manuel Piñeyro was married to Miriam, niece of Jesús María (the Trujillista leader) and elder sister of Ramirito's wife. Miriam was a lawyer and, since the 1970s, the top local representative in La Descubierta of the Balaguer state and its Reformist Party—the elected provincial deputy for Congress.[3]

Urbanization and the *Colmado*

In Dominican vernacular, *progreso* (progress) is a term used to talk about social class and social mobility: "Building a concrete house to replace a shanty, moving from the countryside to the city, moving to New York, sending children to school," and even participating in particular, desired types of consumption, are all kinds of *progreso* (Hoffnung-Garskof 2008:11–12). In the 1960s and 1970s, Dominican urbanization and emigration took off (Lozano 1997; Hoffnung-Garskof 2008). Dominican migrants sought *progreso* by moving to the cities, to New York, to Spain, and elsewhere. Urbanization shaped the contemporary *colmado* found in Santo Domingo's barrios in two decisive ways. First, urban growth created a gigantic market for food. In 1920, the Dominican capital had barely 30,000 residents. Ninety-two years later, in 2012, greater Santo Domingo housed nearly 3 million people—some 28 percent of the nation's population. Second, urban expansion and the creation of new barrios resulted in a situation where more and more people lived and worked far away from what had previously been the principal urban supplier of food to families and households: the public market. The Dominican state's policy was to provide the many new working-class barrios with streets and parks, but not markets (Murray 1996:2). The niche was filled by *colmados*; their owners purchased vegetables, fruit, and the staples generically called *víveres* in the public markets, and sold the products in the barrios.

Colmados were often based on a family's labor: a boy or a young man would leave the countryside and start working in a relative's *colmado* in one of Santo Domingo's new barrios. It was a pattern—a form of chain migration. As one man, an owner of several *colmados* in Santo Domingo, put it, in the 1950s, 1960s, and 1970s, a poor young man in the countryside generally had two options if he wanted to leave the village and try his luck: joining the armed forces or going to work in a *colmado*. In the city, he slept and ate in the *colmado*. After a trial period of half a year, his relative started paying him a tiny salary. They worked almost continuously, opening the store at 7 a.m. and closing late in the evening, seven days a week.

In 2012, Manolo Troncoso was the head of La Federación Nacional de Comerciantes Detallistas, the national association of *colmado* owners. He also ran two *colmados* in one of Santo Domingo's old working-class barrios, San Carlos. He had left his village and begun working in a *colmado* in San Carlos in 1963, when he was twelve. Eleven years later he had managed to put aside a little money and, borrowing additional funds from a brother and a friend, he purchased his first business, a *colmado* in San Carlos. Edwin Gómez was approximately twenty years younger than Manolo, and owned and ran two small supermarkets in Santo Domingo. He was thirteen when he relocated, in the mid-1980s, from the hamlet where he had grown up to Los Trinitarios, a poor neighborhood in the eastern part of Santo Domingo. His father, who already lived in Los Trinitarios, had sent for him. Together they established a small *colmado*—first in the house where they lived, and then in new, rented premises.

When Manolo Troncoso bought his first *colmado* in San Carlos in 1974, he paid only 6,000 pesos. A good (large) *colmado* in those days, he said, cost only 10,000, perhaps 12,000. Forty years later, one needed at least half a million pesos—perhaps as much as one or two million. Many have raised capital with the help of relatives and friends. Some have resorted to *prestamistas*, or moneylenders, although the interest rates are high. A few, especially since the 1990s, have been able to borrow from a bank. Those with established reputations in the business, whom the suppliers trust, can stock their store on credit.

The *colmados* in Santo Domingo have been run mainly in two different ways. Some are operated as family businesses, or mom-and-pop stores. Others are run by *un administrador*, a manager. Some men own several *colmados* in various barrios—perhaps five, six, or seven. They use managers to operate their stores.

Owners who run their *colmados* through managers experience a constant challenge, a dilemma even. A man is recruited as a manager because he is regarded as *serio* (honest) and enjoys the owner's *confianza* (trust). He may be a friend or a close relative. But the *colmado* works almost entirely with cash. Not infrequently, the absentee owner can become a bit uncertain or start nurturing suspicions that the *colmado* manager is stealing from him. Is he being cheated? Edwin Gómez explained that he and his father had owned five *colmados* in the east of the capital, but decided to sell four of them and just keep one and instead gradually develop that into an independent supermarket. The reason, he said, was that it had been difficult to find "good people" to run their *colmados* and that they had been dissatisfied with the results. As he put it (exaggerating), "The *colmados* lack control. There is no registration. What you do, quite simply, is leave the money in the cash register, put two or three people to work there, and everybody does as he pleases." Put another way, sentiments or affective forms operate as forces of production (Yanagisako 2002, 2013). *Colmados* are established and developed based on feelings of trust and loyalty. But distrust and feelings of betrayal are also sentiments—and such feelings may result in *colmados* being transformed or sold.

Until the late 1990s and early 2000s, the *colmados* in the capital sourced their merchandise from the city's wholesalers—the owners and operators of the *almacenes*. Many wholesalers themselves once ran a *colmado,* but this has changed, and many *almacenes* in Santo Domingo have disappeared. Instead, the *colmados* are now regularly visited by distributors and purchase directly from them. However, *colmaderos* still go at least weekly to one of the public markets to buy *víveres*, vegetables, and fruit.[4]

The majority of the *colmado* owners are men, and most of the employees are men. But this does not mean that a *colmado* owned or operated by a woman is surprising; far from it. As I have shown in the preceding chapters, many Dominican women run small businesses, and many own and run their own *colmados*. In the mid-1990s, research indicated that 42 percent of the country's small businesses (outside of the *colmados*) belonged to women, while only 18 percent of the *colmados* were owned by women (Murray 1996:123). There are at least two reasons why the business has been, and continues to be, dominated by men. To be able to open a *colmado*, one needs a certain amount of capital—more than what is required to start up a number of other businesses—and women have generally had less access to capital than men. Second, employees and assistants in the *colmados* not only sell the merchandise but also carry, transport, and store it—tasks considered more appropriate to men than to women.

Many customers are women and children from the vicinity, buying food for the day's meals. The majority purchase only few things, often just one or two items, and in small amounts. The Dominican *colmadero* opens bags, boxes, and cans, and sells, for example, a single cigarette, a few spoons of coffee, or a bit of tomato paste in a paper. Often a small boy or girl is sent to the *colmado* for a single missing ingredient. Those working in the *colmado* know their customers, or at least many of them. Often there is a sign on the wall that states that the store does not provide credit, but many *colmaderos* nevertheless allow some of their customers credit, such as those who live in the area and are known to have an income—a weekly or monthly wage, for example.

Some go to the *colmado* to eat a cracker and some cheese or salami or a sandwich, and in the evening, particularly on the weekends, some barrio *colmados* function as a meeting place for the neighborhood's men. They chat, joke, play dominos, drink beer and rum, and listen to music. Many *colmados* have a couple of chairs and perhaps a table in the shade, and also play music.

The *colmado* has always been a key site of popular culture, where people discuss local and national politics and elections, for example, or religion, or sports. The *colmados* played a significant role in the historical transformation of popular Dominican *bachata* music into the influential transnational style that it is today. This guitar-based music, with its melancholy ballads, so popular among the rural and urban poor, was not viewed by the Dominican elites or the music industry as a musical genre worthy of respect and attention until the late twentieth century. In addition, for many years *bachata* was excluded from FM radio and from television. Therefore, one of the few opportunities to listen to and enjoy this music in public was at the neighborhood *colmados*. According to Deborah Pacini Hernandez (1995:54), "in the 1950s almost every *colmado* (neighborhood store) and *barra* (bar) throughout the country was equipped with a jukebox . . . Trujillo's brother-in-law Francisco Martínez de Alba imported thousands of these jukeboxes and placed them in *colmados*, free of charge, in exchange for 50 percent of the earnings. It was a highly desirable arrangement, because the jukeboxes did not require any capital investment by the owner of the colmado except for the cost of buying records." The *colmados*, with their record players, sound systems, and jukeboxes, served, in other words, as key locations for the cultivation and dissemination of *bachata* and other forms of popular music.

The *Colmado* from Santo Domingo to New York

Today, more Dominicans live in New York than in any other city in the world, barring the Dominican capital, and for a long time (at least since the 1960s), there has been an intense traffic of people, commodities, values, and ideas between the society on the island and Dominican New York (Hendricks 1974; Krohn-Hansen 2013). According to the US Census Bureau, in 2007, more than two-thirds of the city's Dominicans lived in

the Bronx (38.9 percent) and Manhattan (28.8 percent). Most Dominicans residing in Manhattan today live in the neighborhoods north of Har-
lem, in Washington Heights and Inwood, and most Dominicans residing
in the Bronx are found in the borough's southern and western parts.

In the 1960s and 1970s, a significant number of Dominicans in New
York were factory workers, employed in light manufacturing, particularly
in the garment industry (Grasmuck and Pessar 1991). From the late 1980s
onward, however, the number of Dominican immigrants in manufacturing
declined considerably (Hernández et al. 1995:42–45), and more and more
Dominican New Yorkers moved into other parts of the economy, such as
the service sector. Many became self-employed. In 1991, the sociologists
Alejandro Portes and Luis Guarnizo estimated that 20,000 businesses in
New York City were owned and operated by Dominican immigrants, particularly bodegas or small groceries,[5] small and medium-sized supermarkets,
car services, beauty parlors, restaurants, travel agencies, and sweatshops
(Portes and Guarnizo 1991:61).

A central part of how New York ended up with a considerable number
of Dominican-owned small businesses is the history of the Dominican corner grocery, or bodega. A Dominican *bodeguero* and small-business activist
and leader in Upper Manhattan claimed, in one of our conversations in the
early 2000s,[6] "I've always said that the basis of the emergence of today's
strong Dominican community in New York was the bodega. The bodegas
produced the large homes that Dominicans now own in New Jersey. The
bodegas created the large [Dominican-owned] supermarkets." But this
helped only to consolidate and reinforce the already well-rooted Dominican
experience and vision of the *colmado* as indispensable, adaptable, and replete
with potential. Let me explain.

In a 1976 *New York Daily News* article about the new Dominican core
areas in Washington Heights in Upper Manhattan, journalist John Lewis
claimed, "Evidence of the changes can be seen everywhere. Irish grocery
stores are now Spanish [*sic*] bodegas. Along the central shopping district
on W. 181st St. several older, well-known stores have closed because the
merchants said that they could not compete with Hispanic merchants who
cater to the needs of the growing Hispanic population" (Lewis 1976).
Dominican immigrants entered New York's small-business economy at a
time when it was undergoing significant change. During the 1960s and
1970s, many neighborhoods were losing their traditional retail businesses,
as white owners retired or moved away to the suburbs. At the same time,

the population of potential customers in these same neighborhoods was growing as a result of new (post-1965) waves of immigration (Sanjek 1998:65). In other words, the city was a profitable frontier for immigrant entrepreneurship and Dominican immigrants were among those who were willing to pioneer.

The Dominican immigrants in a way transplanted the Dominican *colmado* to Manhattan and the Bronx, although there are four key differences: First, the *colmado* on the island and the "Dominican" bodega in New York do not look the same; they have dissimilar storefronts, with the bodega in New York usually located in a five- or six-story building. Second, the bodega in New York is largely self-service; the *colmado* is not. Third, in the *colmado*, a person may come in and ask, for example, for "ten pesos' worth of sugar." In the bodega the customer must buy the whole bag. Finally, the typical bodega in New York does a better job of preserving the food it sells, since regulations are stricter.

Some of the more basic social and cultural features, however, are almost identical. Like his colleague on the island, the Dominican *bodeguero* in New York greets customers when they enter, often by name. Sometimes he asks a customer, "And how's the family doing?" José Delio Marte, a Dominican immigrant who, in 2002, had been operating bodegas in Washington Heights for more than three decades, said of the *colmado* and the bodega: "Look, it is the same thing. Physically, they are different. But the practice, to greet the customer, to chat with him, to sell some of the same products that we have there [in the Dominican Republic], and the wish to sell—this shows that it is the same thing."

The Dominican bodegas in New York's core Dominican areas display and sell commodities that remind people of the homeland—products such as the typical Dominican *víveres, casabe* (bread made from bitter tapioca flour), *galletas* or cookies, and Dominican sweets.[7] At the same time, the Dominican bodega in New York has become a hybrid—or an entirely practical, historical, and transcultural entity. The dominant language in the store is Spanish, but customers can also shop in English. In arranging their signs and storefronts, many Dominican *bodegueros* in the core Dominican areas in Washington Heights and Inwood draw on national identity. Quite a few storefronts employ the word *dominicano,* or "Dominican." Others use the name or logo of a Dominican product, the name of a Dominican place, or the Dominican flag. Even where a storefront exploits the word "Dominican" or a Dominican symbol, however, it usually advertises in English as well as

Spanish. The result is that the typical "Dominican" bodega storefront in Upper Manhattan is replete with mixtures of Spanish and English, with a Dominican name, image, or flag in between. Other Dominican *bodegueros* employ another strategy; they have storefronts using the US panethnic terms *hispano* or *latino*.[8]

Like the *colmado* on the island, the Dominican bodega in New York has been a site of popular culture and a site for the making and remaking of belonging. People visit the bodega and linger over a snack or a drink, sharing gossip and news from the area and the homeland. In the early 2000s, Mario Solano ran a small bodega on a street corner in Washington Heights. The area was mainly residential but also had a few small shops and commercial establishments. Most of the customers were Dominican immigrants; they lived in apartments close by or worked in the vicinity. Mario allowed neighbors to post small notices inside the store, most advertising a room for rent. He also distributed fliers for events and fiestas organized by Dominican New Yorkers with ties to the Dominican community of Cotuí. Although Mario had lived mostly in Santo Domingo before he came to New York, he had ties to Cotuí, and some of his close friends were from that town.

Mario sold empanadas and *chicharones* in his bodega, made by Dominican women who lived nearby. He also made ham and cheese sandwiches in the store. His most important commodity, however, was beer, and he allowed customers to consume their beer inside the store, although he knew that this was illegal and therefore constantly feared a sudden inspection by the police. On Saturdays and Sundays, men from the neighborhood dropped in and stayed for hours at the back of the bodega to drink and listen to *bachata*.

However, this does not mean that the Dominican bodega economy constitutes an "enclave," an isolated or parallel sociocultural universe. Dominican bodegas and other small businesses have not been purchased, sold, and run in isolation from New York's ethnic and racial diversity, but as part of it. Bodega owners and employees have had to interact with representatives of the city's police and other authorities, with representatives of large and small companies, and with landlords and moneylenders, and these, most often, are not Dominicans.

Many of the relationships that characterize the Dominican bodegas have been transnational: they have been bought, sold, and operated through practices and processes that connect communities and households on the island with stores, individuals, and networks in Manhattan and the Bronx.

A veteran in the Dominican bodega economy drew a colorful picture to describe this:

> If we analyze it, we can see that our businesses, the sort of businesses we all do, go from hand to hand. If you are my brother and I have a business and the business is good, and if you would like to obtain your own business, then—what I do—I say: "Well, let me give them a call, let me go to the bank and ask them to give my brother a loan." Or I say to my brother: "I sell you 50 percent of the business and keep the other half. You give me a sum weekly—you send it to me in Santo Domingo." In the Dominican Republic, there are hundreds of people like that, people who have retired and own 50 percent of a business here, or they own one-third, and they are sent their money monthly. So, the last one who has arrived is the one who remains, he's the one who is here. And when he leaves, a new person begins. When he is finished, a new person comes, and that's how it is. The family—all the members of the family are dreaming. I have seen families in Santo Domingo—for example, in San José de las Matas I met a boy, he's fifteen years of age. When he is twenty-two, he will take over a bodega in New York. He said, "That's how we do it. Carlos has finished. He gave the bodega to Juan. Juan will give it to Francisco, who is now nineteen." Then Francisco must give it to the fifteen-year-old I met. Juan gave me my 50 percent. Francisco will give Juan his half. In Santo Domingo, there are businesses which operate that way.

Most of New York's Dominican *bodegueros*, like so many others in post-1960s United States, have made only modest sums. Many have only managed to survive, and a large number have failed and lost their money. A tiny minority have experienced great economic success. In the early 2000s, more than half of New York City's small and medium-sized independent supermarkets were owned and operated by first-generation Dominican immigrants. Dominicans started taking over independent supermarkets around 1980. A great majority of Dominicans who controlled supermarkets two or three decades later had begun in a bodega, as an employee or as an owner and operator (Krohn-Hansen 2013:57–66, 201–29).

In sum, after Trujillo's assassination in 1961, Dominican society saw rapid urbanization and substantial emigration to New York and elsewhere. The *colmado* and the Dominican bodega were central parts of these historical and social transformations, allowing ordinary Dominicans easy access to food and other products. At the same time, they made it possible for the Dominican (urban and diasporic) masses to cultivate and experience community and belonging in a shifting, interconnected, and profoundly globalized world.

The Situation after 2000: A Changed Landscape

The years 1991–93 signaled the beginning of a restructuring and significant opening up of the Dominican economy under International Monetary Fund (IMF) stabilization programs supported by a series of neoliberal reforms, and in 2004 the Dominican Republic, along with Costa Rica, El Salvador, Honduras, Guatemala, and Nicaragua, signed DR-CAFTA, a free trade agreement with the United States.[9] In the wake of these shifts, the country saw a changing retail landscape.

In the decades from the late 1960s or the early 1970s to the late 1990s, the Dominican capital saw the appearance of a substantial number of *supermercados*. These were not chain stores, but small, or relatively small, independent supermarkets, often owned and operated by one or two persons or, more commonly, a family. In many cases, they were enlarged *colmados*, remodeled on the new principle of self-service, with one or two checkouts. Some were operated by ethnic Dominicans, some by Spanish immigrants, and yet others by first- or second-generation immigrants of Chinese descent. Most of these Chinese-owned businesses were simple stores situated in the working-class barrios.[10]

A handful of larger independent supermarkets opened in some of the capital's better-off areas from the late 1960s to the late 1990s, but more decisive change did not occur until the early 2000s.[11] During the few years from the early 2000s to the time when I started my fieldwork, Santo Domingo saw a rapid increase in the number of large supermarkets run by chains. As one man, Eusebio, whose family owned and operated an independent supermarket in El Almirante, in the east of the city, put it in 2013:

> Here in the Dominican Republic the expansion of the most important chains took off in earnest in the early 2000s, and we saw that they came ever closer to our areas, although we operate in the poor barrios. Therefore, we began to worry: "What do we do?" We saw how the chains published large advertisements and special offers.

Chain names like La Sirena, Super Pola, Nacional, Jumbo, La Cadena, and Olé are now well known in almost all parts of the capital (and in large parts of the country, for that matter). That said, the food retailing system in Santo Domingo and in the country as a whole remains highly diverse and fragmented. Large and small independent supermarkets, tens of thousands of *colmados*, a large number of *pulperías* and *ventorrillos*, and a multitude of public markets continue to play a part, and the chain supermarkets are not all owned and run by only one company. The two market leaders are the Grupo Ramos (which runs La Sirena hypermarkets, the Super Pola supermarkets, and the discount chain, Aprezio) and the Centro Cuesta Nacional (with the labels Nacional, Jumbo, and Jumbo Express). Both are Dominican-controlled companies, although both were started by a Spanish immigrant, one in 1965 and the other in 1935. In 2020, the Ramos Group operated seventy food retail establishments in various parts of the country, and the Centro Cuesta Nacional thirty-four, most of which were in greater Santo Domingo.

Owners of independent supermarkets told me that there had previously been more independent supermarkets in the city: some of the larger ones had been sold to chains; others had gone out of businesses, unable to compete when an enormous chain supermarket opened in their neighborhood. However, as I said, many small and medium-sized independent stores continued to operate, and a few independent supermarkets have continued to grow despite the competition.[12]

The supermarket's cultural history has not attracted a great deal of scholarly attention. A shining exception is Kim Humphery's (1998) *Shelf Life*, which examines the supermarket as a retail space and as an arena of everyday shopping in Australia, and at the same time engages with broader issues of the globalization of retail forms.[13] The supermarket emerged as a particular retail form in the United States in the 1930s. According to Humphery, the first supermarkets were created by independent retailers in an attempt to challenge the power of the chains:

> The first of such stores were the King Kullen stores established in New York in 1930 by Michael J. Cullen . . . The King Kullen stores were warehouse-size shops, situated in the working-class, suburban outskirts of New York . . . Cullen made all sales in cash, provided no delivery service and filled the shop with nationally branded, and nationally advertised, merchandise. By 1936 Cullen was running 15 such supermarkets based on the new "retail culture" of volume, cheapness and national uniformity . . . By 1935 there were about 300 supermarkets

in operation in the United States, a figure that rocketed to 6,175 by 1940. (Humphery 1998:68–69)

The rapid nationwide spread of these new stores was mainly due to the entry of the big retail firms (such as A&P, Kroger, and Safeway) into supermarket retailing.

Some fifteen years later, from the mid-1950s onward, the supermarket emerged in England and other parts of Western Europe. As Humphery demonstrates, however, the supermarket's history in England was different than in the United States, and likewise Germany, France, Australia, and so on. There was a continual transculturation or hybridization process embedded in the apparent production of uniformity.[14] While supermarket retailing has become an increasingly global phenomenon, the process of globalization has never been a simple transference of the supermarket form or concept from one place to the next. On the contrary, myriad cultural and economic differences have helped to drive, and give form to, the process (Tsing 2009; Bear et al. 2015).

The Dominican history resonates with this picture, as the example of Grupo Ramos, the larger of the two market-leading companies, shows. The Ramos Group has demonstrated a conspicuous ability to expand. In mid-2011, the company had a total of twenty-one retail establishments, of which seventeen were *multicentros* (hypermarkets) operating under the chain name La Sirena, and four were Super Pola supermarkets. Only four years later, the number had grown to forty-seven, and by mid-2020 it had risen to seventy: twenty-five La Sirena hypermarkets, eight Super Pola supermarkets, thirty-five smaller and simpler Aprezio discount stores, and two shopping centers. In addition, the company controlled two major distribution centers and operated its own bread factory.

La Sirena *multicentros* offer groceries along with general merchandise (homeware, electrical appliances, clothes), an affordable cafeteria, and a range of other businesses (cell phone stores, a bank, a pharmacy, a florist). Most of the customers belong to the lower middle or working classes. The company purchases goods—from both national and foreign suppliers—in large quantities, and is therefore rewarded with lower prices per unit, so it can retail them at highly competitive prices.

Like most other Dominican firms, the Ramos Group is a family firm. The firm was founded in 1965[15] by Román Ramos Uría, who had moved from Asturias in northern Spain to Santo Domingo six years before. He was twenty-four when he established the business. He had been working as an employee in La Sirena, a small store located in downtown Santo Domingo that sold fabric. The year was a politically turbulent one,[16] and La Sirena's owners decided to sell the business. Román bought it and paid what he owed over a five-year period. After a while he stopped selling fabrics and diversified into other products, including cosmetics, cleaning products, and glassware.

The business went well, and a brother, Jesús Ramos Uría, arrived from Spain and started working with him. The two developed a system of self-service and transformed La Sirena into one of the country's first department stores. In 1979, they launched into the grocery business, purchasing a medium-sized supermarket in the city center, which they called Supermercado Pola, after Pola de Allande, their hometown in Asturias. Six years later, they opened their second La Sirena, in the country's second-largest city, Santiago, together with a *socio*, or partner, Luis Fernández Galán. In the late 1990s, they restructured the company's activities, merging all their businesses into one centralized company with a clear division of labor.

In 1999, the firm opened its first hypermarket in La Avenida Churchill close to areas that were (and remain) more middle class. It was an instant success, and the rest is history. The Ramos Group decided that the *multicentro* was the future and started opening more and more La Sirena hypermarkets. Until late 2011, Román and his partner, Luis, were the company's directors. Thereafter, their children took over.[17]

Today, La Sirena and the other chains have developed into national forces—into makers and remakers of particular ideas about, and visions of, what it means to be Dominican. The chains' selections of merchandise mirror, and help to define, Dominican forms of consumption, a Dominican lifestyle and taste. Their daily special offers are advertised in the press and on TV, and their cafeterias offer Dominican favorites: rice and beans, green and sweet plantain, *pollo al carbon* (roast chicken), *carne guisada* (beef stew), *sancocho* (traditional meat and vegetable soup), and *ensalada de aguacate* (avocado salad).

The success of these chains has meant tough competition for *colmados* in the largest cities, and especially in the capital, where business has become much more difficult and precarious. The chain stores outcompete the *colmados* through lower prices and high-profile marketing, and are increasingly taking over the sale of groceries and food. As René Japa, the head of the Asociación de Detallistas de Provisiones del Distrito Nacional, the capital's most important association of *colmado* owners, put it in a conversation in 2012:

> We have only to look around us here [a barrio close to the city center]. The *colmados* around here are strangled by two large chain stores in the neighborhood—right by, down there on Avenida Mella: one La Sirena and one Plaza Lama. "You strangle us!" The *colmados* already sell less food; therefore, they direct their efforts toward beverages. But selling beverages isn't enough if you want to make some money.

According to another veteran in the industry, Alexis Reynoso, who ran two *colmados* north in the city:

> The *colmado* today isn't like it used to be. Previously we purchased large quantities of goods, *guandules* [pigeon peas], milk, and so on. But not any more. Now we buy only very small quantities so that we have the products in the store, because the prices of the large chains are lower, outcompete us—and the chains operate with special offers on fruit, vegetables. Today you enter the *colmado* and find it replete with toilet paper rolls, napkins, diapers, [and] disposable dishes, because, in the supermarket, you must buy the whole package, while, in the *colmado*, you can buy only one or two diapers: "Give me one diaper!" Previously, it was different; previously we bought large quantities of all these goods. We purchased lots of *guandules*, cooking oil, sugar, bacalao, herring, all these products—and vegetables, and the *víveres*, because people preferred to buy in the *colmado*.

In his stores, Alexis sold items such as soft drinks, beer, rum, tinned food, eggs, rice, and beans, in addition to diapers, toilet paper, napkins, and small amounts of sugar, cooking oil, salt, bacalao, herring, *víveres*, and vegetables.

Jobless Growth and the *Colmado*

It is difficult to run a *colmado* profitably today. The conditions are brutal. Nevertheless, the capital's marginalized areas are still teeming with them, and, as I have said, the number of *colmados* in the country has continued to increase steadily. What kinds of businesses are contemporary *colmados* in the capital, and what socioeconomic strategies do they harness in order to manage?

Villa Juana is one of the Zona Norte's older neighborhoods, a profoundly working-class barrio. To the west is La Fe, to the east Villa Consuelo, and to the north Villas Agrícolas. The area, which is densely populated and has constant heavy traffic, contains a multitude of workshops and businesses. There are *colmados* everywhere, most located on street corners. From the entrance of one *colmado*, you can often see one or two others—sometimes just across the road, or on each corner of a crossroads. In 2014, in the heart of the barrio, where Avenida María Montez and Avenida Mauricio Báez intersect, the Ramos Group had an Aprezio—one of its smaller, discount supermarkets. Nearby there was a large public school, the neighborhood's police station, and a series of *colmados*, mainly located in the side streets. Throughout Villa Juana, exterior walls of *colmados* were typically painted in one or two conspicuous colors: green, red, yellow, blue, or red and white— and often the Coca-Cola logo, or a Presidente logo (one of the country's chief brands of beer) decorated one of the walls. The store was open to the street, unless it had closed for the evening. The long counter inside was usually wooden, and behind it were the goods and those who worked in the store. On the counter there were usually a couple of boxes of *galletas,* or cookies, perhaps some plantains or avocados. Often the store played merengue and/or *bachata*. Outside, in the shade, there was usually a plastic chair or two, and perhaps a bench made of wood or stone—sometimes groups of people congregated outside to chat and drink beer or soft drinks.

The shopfront displayed the *colmado*'s name, which often signaled a certain hope, or belief in the future, or else might be a common first name or surname, seeking to convey that the store belonged to a local family and to the barrio, and was thus an important part of its customers' everyday lives. In the area around the intersection of María Montez and Mauricio Báez in Villa Juana, the *colmados* had names such as La Solución (The Solution), Los Hermanos (The Brothers), Los Muchachos (The Boys), Albert, and Aurora. Other typical store names in the Zona Norte were Juana, Ana María, Nuevo Renacer (New Revival), Las Flores (The Flowers), and La Esquina Caliente (The Hot Corner).

The prices were indeed a bit lower in the supermarkets than in the *colmados*, and a large proportion of the Dominican population remains poor. In this context, *colmados* nevertheless have three advantages over supermarkets. First, they continue to open boxes and bottles, and sell merchandise in small quantities. Second, in order to take advantage of the supermarkets' offers, one needs cash; the *colmado* provides credit (at least to some). If you are paid your wage once a month, you may lack money in the last week before your next payment; the owner of the *colmado* near where you live knows your situation and your family, and lets you purchase foodstuffs on credit.[18] Third, the *colmado* is situated close by, often on the same street, if not in the same building. If one lacks one's own vehicle, this is a considerable advantage. In sum, it is expensive to be poor. The *colmados* survive because of the widespread, chronic shortage of money and other resources in households.

Colmados, or some of them, survive in the teeth of tougher competition because they are able to adapt and change, as they did in earlier periods. Two such adaptations have been striking. First, a large number in the capital now offer a delivery service: the *colmado*'s phone number and the phrase *Servicio a domicilio* (Home Delivery) are painted on the shopfront, and those behind the counter hand out the store's business card to new customers. In the vicinity, people have the *colmado*'s card on their kitchen wall or the refrigerator. The store has one or two light motorcycles and one or two young men, often in their teens, who deliver merchandise to houses or apartments. The customer calls the *colmado* from their home, and the man arrives with the order shortly afterward. Supermarkets do not deliver. Manolo Troncoso, the head of the national association of *colmado* owners, explained in 2013: "The home deliveries started after 2000, around 2005. This didn't exist earlier. It's to attempt to increase the sale, because people don't just pick up a 5 gallon [20 liter jug] of water and take it home, on the shoulder, therefore the *colmadero* delivers it, on a motorcycle with an employee." Indeed, today, most people living in barrios buy drinking water, usually in 20 liter containers, and *colmados* typically deliver them to nearby households. Some customers live in apartment buildings, perhaps on the fourth or fifth floor of a building without an elevator; in such cases, the man carries the water into the kitchen and replaces the empty container with the new one. In the words of an experienced *colmadero*, "the home deliveries are tied to the vertical expansion of the city, the growth of tenement buildings. In the tenements, people have to get up their water. Instead of going down, they call the store. It's an urban phenomenon." Not all *colmados* sell 20 liter containers of water but, in almost all neighborhoods, a number do. Those who deliver stock piles of 20 liter containers of water on the pavement outside the store.

The other adaptation has existed much longer, at least since the 1970s or 1980s. Dominican law does not prohibit consumption of alcohol in the store. Some *colmados*, a minority, have been converted into what Dominicans call *súper colmados*. These are *colmados cerveceros*, cheap, popular places to drink beer and rum, almost like bars. In Villa Juana, they had names like Súper Colmado Ana María, Súper Colmado Juana, and Súper Colmado El Baratón (Super Colmado The Bargain). Music from the *súper colmado* can be heard in the vicinity till late at night, and the store often has a tiny dance floor. Yet, even this type of *colmado* offers more than beverages, at least in the daytime. Ramón ran a *colmado cervecero* or *súper colmado* on a street corner in Villa Juana. I often stopped by in the morning, and one Wednesday in November 2016 I arrived at around 10 a.m., bought a bottle of water and a couple of *galletas*, and sat down on one of the barstools at the counter. Ramón was playing loud merengue music. Several customers were eating in the store. Ramón's *colmado* was almost completely open to one of the streets, and on the pavement immediately outside, three women in their late twenties operated a busy food stall. Four men had bought themselves a *desayuno*, or breakfast of fried meat and mashed plantain. They had taken the food into Ramón's *colmado* and were sitting at the counter while they ate. Two had purchased drinks from Ramón. A young police officer in uniform had also bought his breakfast from the three women and walked around on the pavement and in the store, eating and chatting with people. A neighbor came in and asked for three cigarettes. Ramón gave him the cigarettes, and he paid and left. Another man entered with a plastic box of *galletas*. He put the new supply into one of the containers that Ramón had on the counter, got his payment from Ramón, and left again. The shelves behind Ramón were filled with bottles of rum, whiskey, and wine. In two refrigerators, there were bottles of beer, soft drinks, and bottles of water. Other items were in stock, too, such as toiletries, napkins, cooking oil, and a selection of tinned food, and Ramón prepared and sold ham and cheese sandwiches to order. In the evenings, the business sold almost only beer and rum.

A basic characteristic of the income-generating practices that support Santo Domingo's poor is that they are highly precarious and insecure. Under such conditions everyday life becomes, as James Ferguson (2015:93–94) has aptly put it, largely a matter of "survivalist improvisation": people seek (or struggle) continuously to avoid the worst through mundane forms of "flexible improvisation." A common reply to questions about how someone is doing in Santo Domingo's barrios is quite simply: *En la lucha* ("Fighting," or "We're fighting").

In order to be able to improvise and manage, people depend on having contacts. They need to be part of, and they continuously renew, relations and networks that are rooted in mutual trust. Relatives and friends exchange information and services, and help one another in case of an emergency or crisis. To stop by the *colmado* to buy something, or to have a chat, or to play dominos or drink and hear the latest news and gossip, resembles "work"—it is a part of "the job," of the daily, merciless toil of managing through survivalist improvisation. The *colmado* is the best place in the vicinity for the production and nurturing of important contacts and networks. One evening in December 2016, after attending a political meeting in Villa Mella, three friends gave me a ride back to the center of Santo Domingo. I told them about my interest in the future and fate of the *colmado*, and the three insisted, "The *colmado* isn't dying!" They then gave examples of what the *colmado* offers, before one of them summed up: "The *colmado* solves a lot of things" (*El colmado resuelve muchas cosas*).

The *colmado* helps to solve problems in two ways: first, through allowing limited forms of credit, it makes it easier (or more feasible), for many people to purchase food and other necessities, even when they lack money; and second, it offers a space where the poor can use their relationships to obtain assistance, a small loan, a favor, a temporary job—in brief, to tap into local, national, and transnational resource circuits.

Conclusion

Today's *colmados* and the rural and urban masses' lack of stable, sufficient sources of income are two faces of the same historical process (Gregory 2014:71–72). It would be a mistake, however, to reduce the *colmados* to a product of the economy, to a function of the barrios' forms of marginalization and poverty. They mirror and embody a specific political, demographic, social, economic, moral, aesthetic, and affective history. Seeking out the *colmado*, hanging around in the *colmado*, chatting with the *colmadero*, listening to the *colmado's* merengue or *bachata* music—all of this reflects a taste, a preferred style, particular habits and sentiments. Socializing and conversing with others at the *colmado* is a choice; doing so is, most often, fun, and it continues to operate as a powerful image, as a vision and a representation, of what it means to be *criollo/a*, or Dominican.

The *colmados* would not have existed had it not been for the self-exploitation and the drudgery of those who labored to keep them open. Most *colmados* are still open seven days a week, from 7 or 7:30 a.m. until midnight or later. In spite of this, the income is most often insecure and modest. Many who purchase or open a *colmado* fail and lose their money.

Many are run by a family, but a large number depend almost exclusively on paid labor. This is the case, for example, if a person owns and runs two or more *colmados* simultaneously. A typical scenario is, as I have said, that an owner operates his store through *un encargado*, or a manager. The latter is not paid a wage; rather, there is usually an agreement that allows him a percentage of the *colmado*'s profits. The consequence is that the manager's income is varying and vulnerable. Fomerio Díaz (whose story I sketched at the beginning of this chapter) ran his two *colmados* (in Los Mina Sur and Haina) with the aid of paid labor. His system was typical. His share of each store's *beneficios limpios*, or surplus, was 55 percent. Two men worked in each of the *colmados*. The manager got 25 percent of the profits, and the other, classified as under the manager in the command chain, got 20 percent. The two opened, operated, and closed the store, seven days a week. In addition, each of the stores had two employees in their late teens with motorcycles for deliveries who were paid a low wage—in 2014, it was 6,000–7,000 pesos per month. They were also sometimes given small tips by customers.

In sum, those who work for *colmaderos* have long working days, limited or meager earnings, and few rights. Personnel turnover is often significant. In today's Dominican Republic, employers can fire employees with relative ease, but they do have to give workers severance payments that increase in relation to length of employment (Itzigsohn 2000:19).[19] But a manager, or any person who works in a *colmado* for a percentage of the profits, is not considered an "employee" and therefore is not entitled to a severance payment if the owner decides to fire him. The exception is the young deliveryman, who is paid a fixed wage and is consequently considered an "employee" and given a severance payment. Fomerio defended himself and his colleagues: "Since we [the owners of the *colmados*] don't work with[in] the parameters of an employer–worker relationship, we cannot give severance payments." To find and keep sufficiently reliable, loyal, and stable labor is difficult, according to the typical (class-conscious) *colmadero*. However, in today's Dominican reality, with the pervasive and permanent lack of good jobs (or jobs with decent pay and rights), there are always more than enough people who wish to *buscar mejor vida*, or try their luck, and dream of working in, or opening, a *colmado*.

After 2000, chain stores increasingly emerged as key sites for the production of concepts and images of *progreso* in the Dominican capital. Does this mean that the *colmado*, which earlier functioned as an inextricable part of nearly all Dominicans' constructions of *progreso*, or a modern identity, has become culturally associated with a sidetrack, or a deadlock, or worse, something "backward"—the antithesis to *progreso*? The answer is no. It is true that the country has seen a significant change. Particularly in the cities, and not least in the capital, supermarkets have increasingly taken over the selling of groceries, even in the working-class barrios. Many *colmados* in the capital now sell only small amounts of food, but the masses continue to use them, and a large majority desire, and seek, a form of socioeconomic improvement or *progreso* (no matter how restricted this may appear, from one class's perspective). In the quest for improvements (through food on the table, schooling, a better home, ones's own vehicle, migration abroad), the *colmado* is necessary, a tool like no other. It enables dreams, hope, *progreso*. It is historical—it seems as though it has always been there—although it has consistently adapted to new times and hence has changed over time. It has been, and still is, a place for resolving the important problems that arise in daily life: "The *colmado* solves a lot of things."

CHAPTER 4

For Cooperatives
Mutual Aid, Social Enterprises, and Empowerment

During the last two decades, the significance of the Dominican cooperatives has increased. The national cooperative movement has strengthened
its position: it publishes its own newspaper, *El Cooperador*, and the economic turnover of the country's cooperatives has grown spectacularly
(CONACOOP 2018:3–15). This is in accordance with the picture in
many other nations. As Alice Rose Bryer (2012:23) put it some years
ago, "it is widely recognized that the macro-economic significance of
these business entities [cooperatives and other 'participatory' economic
forms] has increased rapidly in the last decade, with Europe and Latin
America as key centres of growth." In the early 1990s, the national entity
that organized most of the Dominican cooperatives (La Confederación
Dominicana de Cooperativas) was discredited and in crisis, but a group
of cooperative activists and leaders decided to start afresh and rebuild a
national movement. In 1995 they founded the Consejo Nacional de Cooperativas ([CONACOOP] the National Council of Cooperatives) and,
since then, the organization's head has been Julito Fulcar.

Fulcar, who grew up in the western part of the country in San Juan de
la Maguana as a son of a peasant, became a teacher in the mid-1980s and
then joined the teachers' national savings and credit cooperative—at a time
when he needed a loan and had applied for one from the cooperative. In
the mid-1990s, he already had ample experience as a political activist and
as a spokesperson for popular organizations. By the late 1980s to early

1990s, he had been working for three years in an export processing zone in Baní and had organized a clandestine labor union among the workers. He belongs to the Modern Revolutionary Party (which emerged in 2014 in the wake of a bitter conflict in one of the traditional, large Dominican parties, the Dominican Revolutionary Party, or PRD), was elected a deputy to Congress for his province, Peravia, in 2016, and reelected in 2020. Fulcar and the other CONACOOP leaders fight against poverty and other forms of social injustice, and strive for an economy with a human face. However, they are far from revolutionary, and they are not rebels (Fulcar 2011; CONACOOP 2011).

CONACOOP advances and defends the cooperatives' legal rights and economic and other interests in Dominican society; it offers training and seminars, and gives its members information and advice. The country's cooperatives are independent entities, but the great majority belong to CO-NACOOP. A large number are savings and credit cooperatives. A study from 2018 showed that about 80 percent of the nation's cooperatives essentially functioned as savings and credit cooperatives (CONACOOP 2018:24–25). The others were farmers' or peasants' cooperatives, consumer cooperatives, housing cooperatives, and cooperatives for those working in transport.

In this chapter, I examine Dominican cooperativism by posing several questions: How do the cooperatives operate economically and politically? How do they run their businesses? What possibilities for improvements for the masses do they represent? I wish particularly to show three things. First, the Dominican *cooperativa*, or cooperative, is a shifting entity—an open, elastic category. Second, the question is not whether these collectively owned and operated enterprises are entirely integrated into, and dependent on, the market, or on contemporary global capitalism's processes and mechanisms. Instead, the question is: how, specifically, is each cooperative incorporated into the market, and how does each one make use of it? Third, the cooperative movement represents a democratizing potential. How so? Through acting collectively, ordinary Dominicans strengthen their ability to obtain services and rights. In addition, the cooperatives offer their members training in the exercise and practice of a stronger—more genuine—form of democracy (compared to the one to which they are accustomed, for example, from the large political parties and most of the state-system).

For Marcel Mauss, the militant socialist and author of *The Gift*, according to his biographer, Marcel Fournier, the socialist cooperative remained both a necessity and a dream. It was a way to realize the socialist ideals here and now:

> Aware that "action always precedes theory," he [Mauss] emphasized two fields of action where it was possible to begin "the total emancipation of the proletariat within capitalist society": the trade union and the socialist cooperative. These movements seemed to be purely economic, but "as formulations of the future society," they were the expression of a "new form of social consciousness" with "the advent of a new legal organ, new principles of action, new incentives for sacrifice and solidarity." The trade union had an "awe-inspiring role." . . . The socialist cooperative also represented "more than a powerful, colossal interest group." It was "something infinitely rich, phenomenally fertile," where a great "economic vigor" and an "incomparable force of idealism, justice, impartiality, and intellectual and moral energy manifested itself all at once." Mauss presented syndicalism and cooperation as ways "to live the socialist life immediately," that is, "to have the proletariat in the capitalist regime live right now, as much as possible, its future life, in the form of the most complete communism, the most rational solidarity, the most conscious and the most autonomous action." (Fournier 2006:101–2)[1]

In other words, a cooperative had to have "social goals," rather than only business ones. For Mauss, for a cooperative to be defined as socialist, it had to struggle against wage labor. "A socialist cooperative," he argued, "is 'a society whose members are driven not only by the legitimate desire to improve their well-being but also by a wish to abolish wage labor by every path and every means, political and economic, legal and revolutionary'" (Fournier 2006:108).[2]

Mauss was deeply engaged in the French and European cooperative movement from the end of the nineteenth century to the late 1930s or early 1940s. In 1896–97, he joined L'Avenir de Plaisance (The Future of Leisure), a small consumer cooperative in Paris—and he continued thereafter to take part in organizing consumer cooperatives, and remained inspired by the impressive consumer cooperative movement in Britain (Fournier 2006:107, 124–27; Carr-Saunders et al. 1938; Robertson 2016).

Since the late 1970s, researchers have increasingly explored how (worker, consumer, and other kinds of) cooperatives fare under, and how they challenge, the neoliberal economy (Narotzky 1988; Kasmir 1999,

2012; Checker and Hogeland 2004; Stephen 2005; Vargas Cetina 2005, 2011; Bruyer 2012; Ranis 2016; Rakopoulos 2017; Harvey 2018). The questions have revolved around Mauss's interests: To what extent do par- ticular cooperative movements embody a critique of, or an alternative to, capitalism and capitalist practice and subjectivity? What values—or what intellectual, moral, and affective worlds—do specific cooperative activities represent? To what degree do cooperatives help to solve ordinary citizens' economic and other problems? Is collective cooperative action the result of experiences of crisis? of necessity? Or is the creation of the cooperative rather a product of dreams and burning desires? This literature shows, in Sharryn Kasmir's (2005:90–91) words, that altered or new relations in production or consumption can, in some cases, "unleash other forms of consciousness," that is, ways of thinking that critique hegemonic notions of economic rationality and profit.

The Dominican labor movement has mostly been weak and fragmented. Under Trujillo (1930–61), the working class was, overall, unable to ad- vance demands or achieve significant economic and political results. Be- sides the tight control imposed by the regime across the national territory, working-class unification was difficult to bring about, given the spatial and geographical dispersal of the sugar workers who had made up the decisive parts of the working class and their ethnic and linguistic diversity (some were Dominicans, but a large number were from Haiti and the English-speaking Lesser Antilles) (Cassá 1990:41–205).[3] In the decades after Trujillo's death, the subordination and fragmentation of the Dominican laboring masses has changed conspicuously little, despite a certain increase in industrialization (through the import-substitution industrialization in the period up to the 1980s, and thereafter through the creation of export processing zones) and the development of a less repressive rule (from 1978 onward, after the end of Balaguer's first twelve years in power) (Espinal 1987; Cassá and Murphy 1995). This raises the same questions: Why, and how, have working and poor Dominicans put cooperatives to use over the last couple of decades? What activities and possibilities do the cooperatives represent? In the fol- lowing pages, I discuss these questions.

The Cooperative Movement in the Dominican Republic

The first Dominican regime to legally recognize and regulate the na- tion's cooperativism was the Trujillo rule. As late as the early 1950s, the state formally classified and registered cooperatives only as (versions of) "not-for-profit corporations" (CONACOOP 2010:34). However, in 1955, the regime passed a new law (Law 4332), which, for the first time, provided the country with a separate legal framework for "cooperatives." With the aid of two other laws passed two years later, in 1957, the dictatorship thereafter authorized that public functionaries and employees (including members of the armed forces) could deposit money, and save, in a cooperative, and that trade unions could establish cooperatives. A third law, passed in 1957, made it obligatory to teach cooperativism as a subject in the nation's primary schools and high schools. Two years after Trujillo's assassination, in 1963, the government established a new state institution, the Instituto de Desarrollo y Crédito Cooperativo (Institute for Development and Cooperative Credit [IDECOOP]), charged with the administration, regulation, and control of the entire cooperative sector—a role it still plays today. All new cooperatives in the country must be formally approved by IDECOOP, and the institution oversees and controls all cooperatives' accounts, election procedures, member-meeting practices, and other practices.

The Dominican cooperatives are collectively owned businesses, regulated by the state through IDECOOP. Beyond these basic features, however, there are important differences. This diversity has to do with the cooperatives' activities (types of commercial enterprises and/or member services), size (number of members and turnover volume), and culture (values, goals, practices). While, as I said, an overwhelming proportion of the country's cooperatives are savings and credit cooperatives, many offer other services, too—for example, supplying their members with special offers from various firms and corporations, such as favorable insurance schemes, discounts on medicines or furniture, cheaper food and groceries, and so on. These cooperatives sometimes call themselves "multiservice" or "multiactivity" cooperatives. The size of the entities varies enormously, from the smallest (rural or urban) community-based cooperatives with only a couple of hundred members, or fewer, to a small group of colossal, nationwide entities with more than 30,000 members. Examples of the latter are the national savings and credit cooperatives of teachers, nurses, and doctors (Cooperativa Nacional de Servicios Múltiples de los Maestros [COOPNAMA], Cooperativa de Servicios Múltiples de Profesionales de Enfermería [COOPROENF], and Cooperativa Nacional de Servicios Múltiples de los Médicos [MEDICOOP], respectively). However, according to figures from 2010, a great majority (more than 80 percent) of the cooperatives are small, or fairly small, with fewer than 5,000 members (CONACOOP 2010:61).

Cooperatives also differ because they have been shaped in different ways by the wider history of Dominican collective forms. The Dominican labor movement, based on the organization of *gremios* and *sindicatos* (labor and trade unions), grew in significance in the 1920s. In the years before that, from the 1880s onward (in the wake of the growth of the large-scale production of sugar for the world market and the accompanying, albeit limited, urban growth), the urban poor sought increased social security and progress primarily through other types of collective organizing (and not so much through *gremios* or *sindicatos*). In his study of the country's labor movement, historian Roberto Cassá has described three of these types: the *sociedades de ayuda mútua*, or mutual aid associations; the *logias* (lodges); and the *clubes* (clubs) (Cassá 1990:69–77). The *sociedades* were the most important. These sought to achieve a certain, collective protection for their *socios* (members) against illness and accidents at work. The members paid a regular proportion of their wage to the common fund, and the money was used to secure food, cover medical costs, and pay for members' or their close relatives' funerals. Many mutual aid associations extended these activities, investing in members' and, more generally, the poor's education, and organizing cultural events and fiestas. In the capital, and in the sugar-producing eastern region of San Pedro de Macorís and La Romana, people also founded and developed lodges. While representatives of the elites and the educated classes were mainly freemasons, Dominican workers, and sugar workers from the English-speaking Caribbean, were usually Odd Fellows. As in the mutual aid associations, members of the Odd Fellows' lodges paid a regular monthly contribution to the collective. In return, the lodge assisted when members fell ill, and covered funeral expenses. In addition, there were the clubs, which organized recreational activities, such as fiestas, but did not practice mutual aid. Workers and artisans, or members of the popular strata, owned and operated their own clubs, associations that, in a way, mimicked the clubs of the higher classes. According to Cassá, mutual aid associations, lodges, clubs, and other types of organizations were constantly borrowing inspiration and organizational elements from one another. This activity and cross-pollination also helped to shape the emergent labor unions (Cassá 1990:69).

Voluntary associations, including mutual aid *sociedades* and social and cultural clubs, remain an enormously widespread and important phenomenon in the Dominican capital's populous and poor barrios today. The same applies to Christian congregations and denominations. These collective forms, with their recognizable patterns, are widespread, and there is continual traffic back and forth—of persons, activists, leaders, families, ideas, practices, strategies, organizational solutions—between many of the new, smaller savings and credit cooperatives, and these other communities. In other words, cooperatives import and adapt elements from other organizations. Some started as a form of loosely organized mutual aid among a set of friends and subsequently transformed into a formally approved cooperative. The structure and composition of many cooperatives' boards resembles those of clubs, and most monthly member meetings open with a shared Christian prayer.

Most cooperatives have been created as an outcome of particular events—most often particular challenges or changes of an economic or commercial nature. At the same time, many cooperatives are essentially results of network-driven processes among groups of friends, neighbors, and/or colleagues. Both these features (the cooperatives' conjunctural and pragmatic aspects, and their informal networks and processes) make the cooperatives a thoroughly dynamic and diverse field. The following history of the creation of a cooperative among a group of storeowners in the capital offers an illustration.

As I have shown in previous chapters, the Dominican capital grew significantly in the second half of the twentieth century. When the chain supermarket took off in earnest in the city from the early 2000s onward, a group—in the beginning no more than seven men—of owners and operators of small and medium-sized independent supermarkets in some of the eastern and central parts of the city began meeting informally for conversations and discussions. They had several questions, or concerns: What could and should they do in order to survive in the new business environment? How could they compete with the commodity prices and the spectacular marketing activity of the emergent chains? or were they already doomed to failure? At first, the men were just a loose network, but in 2002 they founded their own business organization, La Unión Nacional de Supermercados Económicos (UNASE). The founders were all first- and second-generation owners and operators of small and medium-sized independent stores—and most of these were situated far from the center of the city, in populous and poor areas, such as Los Mina, Los Trinitarios, and El Almirante. One of the founders, Eusebio, described how it had started:

Here in the Dominican Republic, the expansion of the most important chains took off vigorously in the early 2000s, and we saw that they came ever closer to our areas, although we operate in the poor barrios. Therefore, we began to worry: "What do we do?" We saw how the chains published large advertisements and special offers . . . The next thing that happened was that a few of us began to meet to talk about how we could tackle the chains, because they were taking our customers, and if this continued we would have to close. Then came the idea to buy our supplies together.

Already in 2003, the number of *socios* had grown to thirty (Lara Batista et al. 2003), and a decade later there were forty-two, of whom thirty-four were ethnic Dominicans, and eight were Dominicans of Chinese descent. Most owned and ran one store, while a few ran two. The objective was to achieve lower prices in members' stores. In the early 2000s, most suppliers rewarded their best customers (the chains) with more favorable prices. The larger volume one purchased, the lower the price per unit. By joining forces, the UNASE members strengthened their bargaining position. The group bought as a collective and distributed the supplies to the *socios'* stores; in this way they were able to secure the same price for all their members, and so UNASE stores could remain competitive. For the first four years, one of the members housed the organization's headquarters and its distribution center, but in 2006, UNASE obtained its own premises, purchasing, with the aid of a bank loan, an industrial building in the east of the city, in El Almirante barrio. After they had secured their own premises, the group continued to be inventive. They transformed UNASE into a state-approved (that is, IDECOOP-approved) cooperative, and today it is La Cooperativa de Consumo y Servicios Múltiples de los Supermercados Económicos, or the UNASE cooperative, which acts legally and economically, owns premises, and purchases and distributes goods to the *socios'* stores.

The decision to establish a cooperative was exclusively practical, purely for commercial reasons. The members realized they needed to constitute themselves as a cooperative if they wished to save the common initiative or the collective. Before they became a cooperative, the group paid far more in taxes than it now did when it purchased supplies. How so? The members or store owners had also been taxed for the internal distribution of supplies. As they put it, they had, in reality, been taxed twice each time they bought and received merchandise—first when they had bought as a collective and then again when they had distributed internally to the individual stores—so most of what they had won, or saved, through better prices from the suppliers had nevertheless disappeared in tax; it had not been worth the effort.

In El Almirante, the group had around fifteen employees in the office and in the distribution center, all of whom were paid salaries. Every two years the *socios* elected a new board: a president, a general secretary, a treasurer, and four others. Every two months there was a meeting for all the members. Members referred to the group or UNASE as different things, as a *cooperativa*, a *familia*, an *unión* (an association), a *red* (network), or a *sombrilla* (an umbrella).

The UNASE members were capitalists and employers. The majority owned and ran their store(s) together with (extended) family (their parents, brothers and sisters, a couple of uncles, for example). The family typically had a modest background; the present owners, or their parents, would have started with little, often just a *colmado* (a small neighborhood or street-corner grocery store).[4]

However, the dominant pattern was not a cooperative of and for capitalists. Most of the Dominican cooperatives brought together, as we have seen, employees, workers, and groups of poor. In the rest of this chapter, I look only at this latter type (the working-class variant). I begin by analyzing ethnography from two small cooperatives. One is a savings and credit cooperative based in the Villa Consuelo barrio. The other is situated in Puñal[5]—a poor, rural community a 15-minute drive north of Villa Mella, on the outskirts of Santo Domingo. Many peasants and households in Puñal grew *cereza* (acerola cherries), which they sold at the market in Santo Domingo. Many in the community also went to the city daily, or almost daily, to work or to study. The Puñal cooperative organized the area's *cereza* producers and struggled to improve their earnings and living conditions.[6] I look at these two cooperatives in order to answer my central questions—why people resorted to cooperative solutions, and the possibilities and limitations that the cooperatives represented. I focus on four key dimensions: business operations, ideological-moral processes, political practices, and forms of search for respect.

The Cooperative Divina Pérez and Friends

It was a Friday morning in late June 2012, and I was in the rented premises of La Cooperativa de Ahorros, Créditos, y Servicios Múltiples Divina Pérez y Amigos (COOPSERMUDI), a small savings, credit, and multiservice co-operative. The premises, which comprised a small hallway and three offices, were located on the second floor in a tired, commercial building on Avenida Máximo Gómez in Villa Juana. The cooperative had moved its headquarters from the working-class Villa Consuelo barrio to this place two years earlier, but had now decided that it needed more space, especially for the member meetings, and had therefore just obtained new, larger premises in the heart of Villa Consuelo, the cooperative's old barrio. The cooperative relocated a month later. The cooperative's name was displayed on a sign on the front of the building, and in the hallway there were leaflets with information about the cooperative and its goals and services. The office had three employees: a security guard, a young receptionist, and the cooperative's administrative head and accountant. It had just under one thousand *socios*. Most resided in the northern, eastern or western parts of the city, or in the city's working-class barrios—in areas like Villa Mella, Los Guaricanos, Cristo Rey, Los Mina, and Los Alcarrizos. Some lived in other parts of the country, such as Haina, Monte Plata, and Higüey, and a handful had emigrated and now lived abroad. The members were men and women; young, middle-aged, and old; and worked in a broad range of sectors. Some were teachers and engineers, or operated small businesses, such as *colmados*, and were slightly better off. Many worked as drivers, security guards, or domestic servants. Others ran food stalls or worked as street vendors. Many had kinship or friendship ties in the cooperative. This was natural. To become a member, one needed to be *recomendado/a* (recommended) by someone who already was a (trusted) member of the cooperative.

The two women sitting with me in the hallway were the reason I had come. I had asked them to tell me about the history of the cooperative. Giovanna was the cooperative's elected head, and Sonia was the adminis-trative head and accountant, a position she had filled for many years. Both were around fifty. Giovanna's father and Sonia's husband had been among the most important founders of the cooperative. Giovanna told about how the cooperative had emerged from an informal collaboration of mutual aid between groups of relatives in the late 1990s.

Giovanna's father's mother (Divina Pérez) died in 1996, having lived the last fifteen years of her life with one of her daughters and the latter's fam-ily. The grandmother had been the glue that had held the family together, and the house where she had lived in the barrio 27 de Febrero had been a gathering place for the relatives—her six adult children with their families, and nephews and nieces. When she died, a number of the remaining children and relatives decided to continue to keep in touch. The aim was twofold. They wanted to hold the family together, although they lived in different parts of the capital, and some even outside the city, and they wanted to save together in order to create a shared fund to cover expenses that resulted when someone in the family died. Giovanna explained:

> The family then started to meet, my cousins. They had monthly gatherings, and rotated between the homes. In those days, we paid 50 pesos to the fund per person, in case of a death, or for mutual aid, and some—those who did not have insurance—paid 250 pesos monthly to see if they could obtain a type of insurance some time later.

They started in 1996 and lasted at least four or five years. At each reunion, they paid their contributions, exchanged news on the families, and shared a meal. A few lived in San Cristóbal, a couple in Yamasá, and the rest in the capital. The group elected a head or president, and two others were treasurer and secretary.

The conversion of this loose kinship and mutual aid network into a formally approved cooperative was a gradual process. It started in the early 2000s, when a few of the participants attended some meetings about cooperatives. Thereafter, an IDECOOP employee began to regularly attend the group's monthly meetings, and the meetings were increasingly used to exchange information on, and speak about, the history and the organizational forms of the cooperative movement. Soon after, together with IDECOOP's representative and a lawyer, the group drew up a legal charter. The inauguration of their formal cooperative took place at a reunion in the home of one of the participants in 2003. Around thirty attended, and the cooperative's startup capital was only 70,000 pesos.

The group made two decisions. First, it wanted the cooperative to be open to nonrelatives so that the number of members would grow sufficiently. Second, the group recognized that "saving" could not be the cooperative's only activity or goal. If the cooperative was to develop, it would have to be able to enlarge—or diversify—its economic field of operation. Both these decisions were reflected in the cooperative's long, official name: "The Savings, Credit, and Multiservice Cooperative Divina Pérez and Friends." A year after its establishment, in 2004, the cooperative received formal approval and a license from IDECOOP.

In the years that followed, the number of members increased steadily.

Giovanna said, "We began putting to use chains [of contacts] to recruit new *socios*. My husband recruited his family. All the wives of the various cousins, with their relatives, became members." In addition, the members recruited friends and colleagues: "We spoke to them about the cooperative and encouraged them to join, and brought them along and got them inscribed [signed up]." Although a number of the founders ceased to be members after some years, some because they emigrated, the number of members continued to grow. By 2012, each new member had to be recommended by an existing member, show their national identity document (*cédula*), and pay the subscription amount of 250 pesos. Two accounts were automatically opened in the new member's name: one functioned as a running savings account which the member could use to deposit or withdraw cash when, and as, they wished, and the other could not be touched unless the member wanted to terminate their membership and leave the cooperative. The amount saved in this second account served as security when the member applied to the cooperative for a loan, and allowed the cooperative access to capital.

The regular member meetings were held in the afternoon of the last Sunday in the month, at the cooperative's headquarters. Attendance varied, from thirty or forty to more than a hundred. The meetings were used to inform members about activities and plans, and to discuss these matters, mingle, and socialize. In addition, the members paid their dues and installments, and there was often a prepared talk, by a member or a guest, on a subject such as health, education, economic planning, or insurance. Once a year, the cooperative celebrated its general assembly. The general assembly, which had a much larger attendance, elected the cooperative's leadership—specifically, the members of the cooperative's three governing bodies, the Administrative Council, the Credit Committee, and the Surveillance Council.

The most important was the Administrative Council, which consisted of seven members. It headed and represented the cooperative, shaped its strategies, supervised the management of its economic resources, informed the members, and worked closely with the office manager (Sonia). The president of the Administrative Council was the head of the cooperative as a whole. In 2012, Giovanna had been in this position for the last five years. She had been reelected once; each election period lasted three years. Many of the board members belonged to one of two large, extended families that, in practice, shaped, not to say controlled, how the cooperative was governed. For example, Giovanna's daughter headed the cooperative's youth group.

The Credit Committee gathered two or three times per month in order to consider, and decide on, the members' applications for loans. The Surveillance Council, which met once a month, reviewed and controlled the cooperative's decisions and activities, including the activities of the two other bodies. Elwin was the Surveillance Council's president at the time of my research. He said, "We [in the Surveillance Council] have to inspect the whole enterprise—review the economy, evaluate and control assets, and assess whether decisions are in accordance with the rules." If a *socio* had solicited a loan with security in a particular property, a member of the Surveillance Council would most often visit and inspect the property. Elwin offered an example: a few days before we spoke, he had gone to view and photograph the home and the store of a *colmado* owner who had applied for a loan. The loan application had looked all right, he said. The amount that had been saved in the cooperative (as security) was sufficiently large. But they had nevertheless felt that they did not know the man well enough. The *colmadero*'s father had been a member for years and was trusted. He had recommended his son as a member. The son, however, had attended few member meetings, and Elwin had not wanted to run any risk.

A large part of the cooperative's economic activity was connected with loans to members. To be able to obtain a loan, one needed to be a member, to have saved in the cooperative, and to have sufficient income to be able to service the ensuing debt. The cooperative's rules stated that a member could borrow about three times the amount that they had saved in their account. For example, if a member had saved 25,000 pesos, they could borrow 75,000. Some who previously had repaid several loans, and who enjoyed significant trust, could borrow a bit more—perhaps four or five times the sum that they had saved. Giovanna's first loan had been for 4,000 pesos in the late 1990s (before the kinship network had been transformed to a formal cooperative). She had borrowed the money to be able to complete her university education. In those days, she said, 4,000 pesos was a substantial amount, and she had repaid the money in installments.

When asked why they used a cooperative rather than a bank, members underscored three reasons. First, they emphasized that, for people who lacked sufficient resources or necessary documents, it was easier to obtain a loan in a cooperative. As one woman put it, "if the bank sees that you don't own much, it doesn't lend [to] you. In a bank, there is much more paperwork and more requirements or obstacles. Therefore the poor join a cooperative and attempt to conduct their affairs and resolve their problems there." Or, in the words of Elwin, "here in the cooperative, there is less bureaucracy. We, too, do all the paperwork, but it's done in a manner that is far easier [for the person who needs to borrow], with fewer obstacles." Second, the interest rates on loans were generally higher in the banks than in the cooperatives. Usually, the difference was significant. Third, if the cooperative earned a profit or surplus, it paid a dividend to all its members. Giovanna explained: "If the cooperative at the end of the year has made, for example, 1 million pesos, this money belongs to everyone. This million is distributed to each and every one of the *socios* who have their money here in the cooperative."

Many of the loans to members were small, only a few thousand pesos. A medium-sized loan for the Divina Pérez and Friends cooperative in 2014 was about 150,000 pesos, while 500,000 was a large loan. The money was used for all kinds of purposes—to invest in the home, to purchase a small business or a property, to pay for schooling, to buy a car or a television set, and so on. Some borrowed to develop a source of income, such as a sewing workshop, a food stall, or a small bakery.

The most important source of income for the cooperative was the loans. Although members paid a lower interest rate than they would have had to pay in a bank (had they been given a loan in the first place), they nonetheless paid significant interest to the cooperative: 1 percent or higher per month, and not infrequently as high as 2 percent or 2.5 percent (corresponding to an annual rate of 24 percent or 30 percent).

Another central source of income for the collective was the commercial agreements worked out with various firms and companies. Elwin provided an illustration:

> Let's say, for example, that I see a drugstore or pharmacy in a place that is convenient for the *socios*. We talk with the owner and ask whether he can give us [the cooperative] one month of credit. A *socio* who needs medicine often needs the medicine immediately; the drugstore delivers it right away and the cooperative pays the bill within a month. The *socio* then pays the amount to the cooperative during some months, three months, four months, six months. But, in this way, the *socio* manages to solve his problem. This is the collective strength that the cooperative has.

The Divina Pérez and Friends cooperative had this type of agreement, at the time of my fieldwork, with two supermarket chains (Olé and La Sirena), a large furniture store, a hardware store, and a couple of pharmacies. The cooperative paid for any purchases from these companies and the members then paid the cooperative, and every time a member bought something, the cooperative earned a small commission. Added up, this secured an important income stream for the cooperative. The cooperative's management used members meetings to promote the agreements and to encourage the members to make use of them.

The consumer cooperatives that Marcel Mauss managed in Paris, for much of his life, were deeply incorporated into, indeed entirely a part of, the market and global capitalism's mechanisms and processes. The same applied, as we have seen, to the savings and credit cooperative that Giovanna and Elwin managed in twenty-first-century Santo Domingo. In his critical assessment of the extent to which "the Bolshevik experiment" proved or disproved socialism, in the first part of the 1920s, Mauss even went so far as to reject as ridiculous any attempt to do away with the market. As he put it:

> Communism of consumption is absurd and should be proscribed from practice. *But what was even more absurd* is the fact that, in order to establish it, *it was necessary to destroy the essential constituent of the economy itself, i.e. the market* . . . But a society without markets is inconceivable. By markets, I do not mean the market places, exchanges and so on that are their external signs, I simply mean the economic fact that prices are publicly self-determining via alternative prices freely "supplied and demanded"—in other words, the legal fact that everyone "on the spot" has the right to buy what he wants in peace and with confidence in his title, and also that no one can be forced to buy what he does not want. This market system, which has grown up slowly in the economic history of mankind, currently governs a very large part of production and consumption. Of course, other systems of social facts contribute to the same function and further new ones are conceivable which could so contribute effectively, but freedom of the market is the absolutely necessary precondition of economic life . . . For the moment and for as long as one can foresee, *socialism—communism—must seek its path in the organisation and not the suppression of the market.* (Mauss 1984 [1924–25]:353, emphasis in original)[7]

The cooperatives in Santo Domingo that I know did what Mauss saw as a necessity: they worked every day with, and through, the market, with its restrictions and possibilities, in order to advance their members' interests. The Divina Pérez and Friends cooperative worked, to a striking extent, on the premises of the market. Two examples further illustrate this. A few members sometimes made larger deposits in the cooperative, for example, 100,000 pesos, if they had made a sale, or were temporarily in control of a sizable sum. The member would deposit the 100,000 in the cooperative for a limited period, such as six months or a year, perhaps while they thought more about what to do with it. During this period, they could not withdraw it, but in return they received a higher rate of interest from the cooperative than they would have earned had the amount been deposited in their ordinary savings account. In addition, the interest was a bit higher than they would have been offered by a bank. Giovanna underscored that these larger deposits were a priority. They gave the cooperative more capital with which to work and produce a surplus. "The *socio* obtains an interest rate that is a bit higher than that of the banks, because it's his money, he is a *socio*—and the 100,000 secures the cooperative possibilities to work. The cooperative pays the *socio*, for example, an annual interest of 12 or 18 percent, and lends out the money [to other members] at 24 or 30 percent."

The Dominican cooperative sector includes an insurance company, the only cooperative insurance company in the country, and all the cooperatives negotiated and bought insurance schemes from COOPSEGUROS. The Divina Pérez and Friends cooperative had a deal with COOPSEGUROS through which the members could buy life insurance. If a member (or a member's close relative) died, the dependents or the family received an agreed amount, half of which was disbursed by the cooperative immediately after the death. When COOPSEGUROS had transferred the whole sum, the cooperative disbursed the remaining half. However, in late 2009, COOPSEGUROS suddenly notified the cooperative that the life insurance agreement was going to be canceled. Giovanna explained drily: "We had a year with many deaths. Many among us died—and in December 2009, COOPSEGUROS told us that they would cancel the policy, because we had many deaths and they were of the opinion that we caused losses." After this, the cooperative entered into another agreement with another (private) insurance company. Three years later, however, in 2013, COOPSEGUROS was under new management, which had new perspectives, and the cooperative negotiated a new life insurance agreement for the members with them.

The Cooperative in Puñal

The cooperative in Puñal differed from most other Dominican cooperatives, in that its basis was not savings and credit but rather agriculture—
the production of acerola cherries. It was also different because it had
been created, and remained anchored, in a place-based community, which
I have called Puñal, in contrast to cooperatives such as the Divina Pérez
and Friends cooperative (discussed above), which emerged out of a geo-
graphically dispersed kin network. Nevertheless, the history of the Puñal
cooperative overlapped with that of Divina Pérez and Friends in an important way: both were dependent on the market. Both entities were, as their
members often acknowledged, *empresas* (companies)—that is, business
operations. Simultaneously, they were also, as Giovanna put it, "different"
from ordinary companies: the Divina Pérez and Friends cooperative, she
explained, was "a social type of company" (*una empresa de carácter social*).

Administratively, the community of Puñal belongs to the La Victoria
district in the municipality of Santo Domingo Norte. It is a 15-minute drive
from downtown Villa Mella, or the capital's northernmost metro station,
Mamá Tingó. Census data show that, in 2010, Puñal had just over 1,500
inhabitants. The community was created on state-owned land in the first
half of the 1970s, as part of the Balaguer regime's agrarian reform projects.
Peasant families moved to Puñal from other parts of the country, and were
offered financial support from the state in the form of a piece of land and
a few cattle. State support ended after some years, and the area proved to
be unsuitable for cattle farming. Quite a few of the families gave up, sold
their land cheaply, and returned to their home communities.

In the 1980s and 1990s, many of the households that remained com-
bined factory work and other forms of wage labor with small-scale or sub-
sistence agriculture, such as growing plantain, yuca, lemons, and so on.
In the late 1990s, some in the community tried to grow *cerezas* (acerola
cherries). The experiment was deemed a success, and the product quickly
developed into the community's first significant cash crop. As one of the
cooperative's leaders put it in 2013: "Here, there are women who previously left for the city to work as domestic workers, and they had to leave
their children alone. Now, they remain instead in the community [growing
and selling *cerezas*]."

The majority in Puñal were poor. According to the 2010 national census data, 85 percent of households lacked an interior water supply, and
75 percent lacked access to streets or paved streets. However, 97 percent

of the houses had access to electricity (although the frequent blackouts were a constant source of frustration). The principal economic activity was agriculture. Other sources of income were small businesses, (regular or temporary) waged work, remittances from relatives abroad, and old-age pensions. Most of the farms were small or tiny, only a few were larger. The average land area per farm (or household) in Puñal dedicated to growing of acerola cherries was 1–1.5 hectares, but many people cultivated smaller patches, and some significantly larger plots, such as 5 or 6 hectares. The acerola tree grows to approximately 3 meters in height. After it has been planted, the cultivator must wait two years before it fruits. Thereafter the yield is continuous, but the trees must be cared for constantly, fumigated in the correct manner, and so on.

There were three reasons why some of the growers had begun discussing establishing a cooperative. First, as Mabel (the cooperative's first president) explained, they wanted to try to cut each grower's costs and reduce competition among themselves:

> The majority of the inhabitants of Puñal began to cultivate acerola cherries. Okay, what happens? In May, June, September, or in the periods of the year when the production is high, we all left for the market [in Villas Agrícolas in La Zona Norte], 30 or 40 producers, each with his or her helpers and a vehicle full of cherries. We went to the market to compete against one another by bidding the price downward.

If they cooperated, they could spend less time and money on the transportation of the product to the market, and strengthen their bargaining power in the price negotiations with the different buyers or intermediaries at the market. Various kinds of buyers purchased acerola cherries at the market in Villas Agrícolas. Some were owners of restaurants or cafeterias. Others represented Dominican factory owners who needed fruit and berries for the production of juices and jams. Still others bought in order to resell in the different neighborhoods of the capital. The price the growers got varied enormously during the year, based on the supply, ranging from 500 to 600, or even 700, pesos per *cubeta* (plastic bucket) of cherries, to 200–250 per bucket. Four hundred pesos was considered good. The cherries must be sold immediately after harvesting, because they are so perishable, so to return home without selling them was not an option.

The second reason why some of the growers wanted to join forces was to explore the possibility of selling directly to purchasers without using the physical market area in Villas Agrícolas. Through selling part of the harvest directly to factory owners and/or others, they would be able to stabilize and better protect the price they got for the cherries. To do this, they would have to be able to deliver larger quantities—in other words, cooperate.

The third reason was, as they put it, an idea, a vision, a (wild) dream that had flourished among at least some people in the community. This was to create a cooperative that could secure a greater economic return from the product (the cherries). The idea was to begin cherry processing in the community, producing pulp, juice, and/or jam. In the words of Fernando, one of the cooperative's founders: "For us this is an agro-industrial project—to process our cherries and then place them on the national and international markets. We wish to get more value out of our cherries. Add value to the product. Get the maximum out of it."

The cooperative was created after two years of discussions, and with assistance from IDECOOP, in late 2010. The constitutive assembly, which took place in the center of Puñal, comprised around a hundred locals, men and women. A year later, the cooperative was formally approved and authorized. The biggest challenge in the two years before the cooperative was founded, Mabel told me, had been to preserve enough unity. People in the community had different interests. One group, for example, lived off the transportation of the cherries to the market, and a few of these had not wanted changes and had worked against the project.

In 2012, the cooperative had around 140 members, and that number grew to 160 by 2013, and to more than 200 in 2017. Most lived in Puñal, but some resided elsewhere: in neighboring communities, in Villa Mella, in other parts of the capital area, in two or three other acerola-producing areas in the country, and in New York. Some of those who resided outside the community owned a piece of land in Puñal where they grew acerola cherries. In addition to cultivating cherries and other agricultural products, members had other forms of work. Some had their own vehicle and worked as drivers, others were engaged in small trade, and a few were public employees. Some were single mothers raising children. In order to be accepted as a new member, one had first to solicit membership and thereafter attend three of the monthly member meetings. The new member had to pay 100 pesos as subscription fee and also deposit 500 pesos (as a contribution to the cooperative's capital), which could not be withdrawn unless the membership was canceled. In addition, all members had to save at least 100 pesos monthly in the cooperative, savings they could withdraw when they liked.

Mabel, the cooperative's first president, was in her late forties and a single mother with a son and a daughter. She had worked as a teacher in Puñal for many years, and also cultivated cherries. Her parents had been among Puñal's founders in the 1970s. Her vice president was Flavio, a peasant in his early sixties, who had been among the first in Puñal to begin to grow cherries. Two of the other original founders of the cooperative were Fernando and Isabel. Fernando had worked for more than twenty years as an accountant in various firms in the center of Santo Domingo, but had now decided to live only off his agriculture in Puñal. Isabel worked as an agronomist for the state in Puñal. In addition, she had her own small farm in the community. In 2016, Dionicio took over Mabel's job as president. He had been an engineer and had recently retired after three decades working for various state institutions. He lived in the southwestern part of the capital but, together with a brother, owned a small property in Puñal where they produced acerola cherries. The cooperative's board, which had eight members (including the president and the vice president), was elected annually by the members. A members' meeting was held in the center of Puñal on the first Sunday of each month.

The cooperative ran a small store in the community that sold insecticides, fertilizer, and necessary equipment and tools for cherry growing. The rustic premises that housed the store had previously belonged to the Instituto Agrario Dominicano (the state), and had been built in the 1970s when the community was founded. When the cooperative was established, in 2010, the Instituto Agrario handed over these premises, two other dilapidated buildings, and a small piece of land situated in the heart of the community.

A central priority when the cooperative was first established had been—and remained—to find Dominican industry owners who wanted to purchase acerola at an acceptable price. Mabel and the other board members spent much time and resources on this, but the outcome remained limited. The cooperative had managed to secure a number of one-off sales of larger quantities, but no regular, ongoing agreements with factory owners. The members therefore continued to sell as individuals at the market in Villas Agrícolas. Only now and then did they sell to the cooperative (which then delivered the cherries to a factory owner). When they sold through the cooperative, the cooperative took a small percentage of the amount to cover expenses associated with the sale.

In early 2013, the European Union's Brussels-based Centre for the Development of Enterprise (CDE), through its Office for the Caribbean (situated in Santo Domingo), granted 48,000 Euro to a project in Puñal. The money was used to bring a Dutch engineer, an expert on the global acerola market and on acerola-processing technology, to the community. His task was to conduct a study on how an acerola-processing plant could best be constructed in Puñal. In the community, he was met by the cooperative's representatives. The expert then wrote two 25-page reports in which he outlined in detail how a plant should technically and practically be built. The total investment, he estimated, would be in the region of US$1.5 million.

Fernando told me about the origins of the project. The goal was to develop cherry processing in Puñal. In 2012, there had been a trade fair in downtown Santo Domingo. The theme was the European Union's trade with the Caribbean. Fernando and a couple of others went to represent the cooperative and give out tasting samples of the community's acerola juice and acerola jam. They met the CDE representatives, and as a result the cooperative put together a funding application. However, there was not much follow-up to the Dutch engineer's prefeasibility study. The cooperative lacked capital; it did not have the necessary US$1.5 million. For its part, the CDE concluded (after having studied the engineer's reports and other data) that the EU would not continue to invest in what it viewed as a project with too limited commercial potential. From the CDE perspective, the aggregate Dominican and Caribbean acerola production was relatively small, and the European consumption market limited.

Later the same year, the cooperative in Puñal secured another grant. The PLD government (funded by the United Nations Development Programme [UNDP]) invested 2.5 million pesos in the cooperative. The purpose was to help strengthen the basis of local development through support to the area's acerola production. A majority of Puñal's inhabitants voted for the PLD. The cooperative's leaders used their contacts in the PLD-controlled state apparatus to secure Medina's financial backing (in return for their loyalty). A part of the grant was invested in the store for the sale of insecticides and fertilizer to the growers. Another part was used to purchase a truck for the cooperative's transport needs. The rest was used to buy two machines for acerola processing: a *lavadora*, or bubble washer, and a simple *despulpadora*, or pulping machine.

When I returned to Puñal a year and a half later, in November 2016, a small plant for the production of acerola pulp and juice was under construction. Some six months later, the plant was up and running. Construction had been funded through a grant of 11 million pesos from the UN

International Fund for Agricultural Development (IFAD) to the Dominican state. The (private) Junta Agroempresarial Dominicana (Dominican
Agribusiness Board), in cooperation with a state institution, the Dirección
General de Cooperación Multilateral (DIGECOOM), administered the
money and the construction. Fernando explained that this was a small plant,
a significantly smaller plant than what the Dutch engineer had outlined in
2013. The goal now was to start up without too much risk, with a limited
production of pulp, and seek to sell to the national market, not export.

The plant was a rebuilt, renovated, and bigger version of what had been
a dilapidated workshop building. The building and the land on which it
stood had belonged to the Instituto Agrario Dominicano. Before the cooperative could start construction and move in, it first had to invest grant
money in building two new private homes elsewhere in the community,
as two local families had, for many years, been living in the closed-down
workshop and it was up to the cooperative to rehouse them. The new plant
had two modern offices for the cooperative's leaders and administration,
with computers and a printer. A small production hall housed the bubble
washer and pulping machine. There were also two cold-storage rooms for
the pulp, and wardrobes for employees and workers. The plant had solar
panels that produced all the electricity it needed.

Acerola pulp has a clear advantage over the fresh product, since the fresh
cherries are, as I said, exceedingly perishable. The pulp, however, is frozen,
and does not leave the cool-storage room until there is a buyer, and this
strengthens the seller's (the cooperative's) bargaining power. In addition,
the pulp is a versatile product that can be used to make a variety of juices,
jams, desserts, and other products.

In spite of the acerola pulp's advantages, however, it proved difficult to
find buyers for the product. When I met Dionicio and his brother Sucre in
November 2017, they seemed both surprised and frustrated by the situation. Since the plant had been completed, it had only been used on three
occasions—three different days—to produce a limited amount of pulp.
Eight female cooperative members from Puñal had been recruited and paid
as day laborers to do the work. The rest of the time the production hall
had stood empty, and the unsold pulp was still in the cold-storage rooms.
Dionicio and Sucre had been working for five months to find national
buyers willing to pay an acceptable price—industry owners, hotel owners,
restaurant owners. They had even sought out agents, but had had little
success selling the pulp. I asked them: "What do industry representatives

say? Is the problem that national industries and others import acerola, or acerola pulp, at a lower price?" "This isn't the problem," Dionicio replied. "The problem is that they all prefer to make, and offer, a product of a low quality, synthetic products, to not use genuine or natural acerola. Instead they produce and sell a *jugo de cereza* [acerola cherry juice] made essentially from cheap imported flavoring, color additive, sugar, and water." Dionicio kept an example in his office—a small carton of one of these synthetically produced cherry juices sold in Dominican supermarkets. He showed it to me, read out the ingredients written on the carton, and said, "The product is legal, and the country has no law that makes it prohibited to label it *jugo de cereza*. This is what we compete against."

Later the same month, Dionicio informed the cooperative's member meeting about the challenges. He told them that he and other board members had recently had three meetings with marketing specialists in order to seek advice. One of the specialists, he said, had explained: "You [in the cooperative] break capitalism's law number one, the law of price based on supply and demand!" The cooperative had decided to pay the growers 350 pesos per *cubeta,* or bucket of cherries. But, the expert had said, this is to begin at the wrong end. "Instead it is necessary to pay only what the market permits, a fluctuating, competitive price." Dionicio finished, "The reason why I tell you about this is only that I want you to know how challenging the situation is."

The cooperative had also tried to sell to the state—but again, so far without result. The Ministry of Education is in charge of and administers *el desayuno escolar* (school breakfasts), a free daily meal served across the country in the state schools. The Puñal cooperative had a goal to become a regular supplier of acerola pulp to the school breakfast scheme, so that the schoolchildren in, for example, northern Santo Domingo could be served a vitamin C–rich *jugo de cereza* at least one day a week. Dionicio's brother, Sucre, was cynical about their lack of success. A handful of large companies, producers of milk products, he said, had acquired a monopoly on the scheme and supplied everything that the ministry purchased. Either they produced the commodity themselves, or they imported it cheaply. "But this is part of the corruption," he continued. "Those in the ministry and those in the companies are friends, relatives. They overbill the state and share the profit. They don't care about the small agricultural producers."[8]

Like other Dominican economic ventures, the Puñal cooperative had to work (produce and sell) in a world of political authoritarianism, patronage practices, and exclusions. The cooperative's political leanings, as we have seen, had been rewarded with grants from the EU system and the PLD regime. At the same time, however, representatives of elite interests (companies, importers, intermediaries) and the PLD-dominated state-system continued to complicate, counteract, or block improved, or more profitable, market access for the growers and the cooperative. Almost half a year after the completion of the plant, the cooperative was still not producing acerola pulp—with the exception of a few sporadic days producing a limited quantity for a one-off sale. In the meantime, the members and the other growers continued to sell their cherries to the highest bidder at the agricultural market in Villas Agrícolas, competing with one another as they always had done. Sometimes the price per bucket was considered high or acceptable, other times, too low.

The views, and the degree of hope, varied from one member to another. Dionicio and Sucre were disappointed and lacked solutions. They did not know what the cooperative should do. However, they continued to struggle, every day, to find possible buyers for the new product. Mabel, Fernando, and others seemed far more optimistic, albeit also realistic. As Mabel put it in an address at the members' meeting in November 2017: "Now we have completed phase one. Now we have our own processing plant here in Puñal. It's what we dreamed of when we started the cooperative. Now begins phase two! Now we have all to be sellers. We must all do everything we can to make our product known, to get the pulp on the market. It's going to be hard work. It's necessary to do it little by little, with patience."

Economic conditions for the majority of the growers have remained precarious, and in early 2018 the cooperative's liquidity was in difficulties. However, it would be wrong to say that the collective economic struggle had been without results. Through the Puñal cooperative, the members now owned resources and *patrimonio* (assets): the piece of land donated by the state through the Agrarian Institute, the small shop that sold agricultural merchandise, and the freshly built processing plant with its offices and cold-storage rooms.

The Ideas behind the Businesses

Cooperative ideologues in England and France in the nineteenth and twentieth centuries frequently conceptualized cooperation as separate from, and an enemy of, capitalism. The cooperative movement, the message was, would transform competitive, capitalist society into a society founded on the principles and practices of mutual association. However, as Nicole Robertson has shown in her fine history of the British cooperative movement in the twentieth century, there was often a distance between the perspectives of national and local cooperative ideologues and activists, and the prevailing ideas and aspirations among ordinary cooperative members at the grassroots level. Robertson maintains that the records of individual cooperative societies complained that

> "many people look upon the co-operative movement as being nothing more than a form of shopkeeping" . . . The apathy of the rank-and-file members, and their indifference to the wider objectives of the co-operative movement, was a cause of dismay amongst local co-operative leaders. This does not appear to have been the product of a particular time period, as this was a source of concern to activists during both the interwar and post-war periods. (Robertson 2016:51)[9]

In today's Dominican cooperative movement, political and economic dreams vary considerably from one member to another. However, nothing in the two cooperatives that I came to know in Villa Consuelo and Puñal suggested socialist leanings. The members' meetings were not spent on abstract or political discourses on cooperation (or the cooperative movement) as something that destroyed or replaced capitalism. Far from it. Instead, the focus in both places was essentially on advertising the services and activities of the cooperative—and upon the turnover (and the production, marketing strategies, and sales) of the enterprise.

Take Elwin, for example, the head of the Surveillance Council of the Divina Pérez and Friends cooperative. He was in his forties and lived with his family in the northern part of the city. For many years he had worked in the Santo Domingo Norte municipal administration, but he now worked as a salesman for a Spanish import firm. The job involved spending about four days per week in the southwestern part of the country, selling merchandise to the region's grocery stores. Elwin had only joined the cooperative in 2008. His most important priority, he said, was to try to grow the cooperative, and ensure that it attracted more members and expanded: "Our objective [in the cooperative] is always to search for sources of income, look for ways to make money." He viewed the cooperative's savings activities as a means to strengthen the development of each individual member by teaching them to save and, through this, to become better organized and more disciplined. He said: "The cooperative helps morally; it helps people to get more organized mentally, as persons."

There is no doubt that the members cultivated the community through the power of mutual help and unity, of solidarity. The members' meetings often included a part where an invited guest spoke on a subject of a moral-social-economic nature—from the cooperative movement's ideas to the value of, and opportunities for, education for the marginalized, to beneficial child-rearing practices. A committee in each cooperative was charged with informing members about seminars and training activities, and quite a few members, both in Giovanna and Elwin's cooperative and in that of Puñal, had attended workshops and courses on cooperative ideals and methods.

In both Villa Consuelo and Puñal, the monthly members' meetings began with a shared prayer. Giovanna or Mabel (and subsequently Dionicio) would invite one of the other members to lead the prayer, and they would stand together and ask God to bless the cooperative and its projects. In addition, members appealed morally and affectively to one another with the help of biblical readings. I attended a members' meeting of the Divina Pérez and Friends cooperative, one Sunday afternoon in June 2013, in Villa Consuelo. Giovanna's sister led the prayer. Afterward, another member, a woman in her twenties, read a lesson from the Bible, and then Giovanna offered a brief interpretation of the reading and asked the audience for their views on it. The reading thus emphasized, Giovanna said, "We Christians have an obligation to attempt to aid one another." Three other members then got up and shared some thoughts on the need for compassion in the light of the Bible's words, before the meeting proceeded.

Members often conceptualized their community as if it were an expression of kinship. They described the cooperative as *la familia, nuestra familia,* or *una hermandad* (a brother- and sisterhood). This does not mean they were not well aware of the dissimilarities among them. Many of them were poor, or very poor, while others were relatively better off. All recognized this. However, they all also saw the value in being able to stand and fight together, as a cooperative, irrespective of differences between the members.

The moral foundations of these cooperativists' collective activities can be summed up simply: for ordinary Dominicans, taking part in mutual aid was an obligation. Through forms of cooperation, it became more feasible, a bit easier, to manage everyday challenges, and to cope with the threatening consequences of emergencies or crises—an accident, sudden illness, or a death in the household. The glue of the cooperative was the (historically produced) will for sufficient unity and shared help.

A history of joint saving and mutual aid among a group of relatives and acquaintances, as we saw, gave rise to the Divina Pérez and Friends savings and credit cooperative. The country's savings and credit cooperatives helped many: while most poor Dominicans found it impossible, or too difficult or too expensive, to borrow through one of the country's banks, many secured access to loans and credit forms through joining a cooperative. As a number of interlocutors (cooperativists) put it, the bank was not a viable alternative; the cooperative worked better.

In Puñal, sufficient solidarity was an imperative. When the cooperative was given the closed-down workshop building by the state to make into a processing plant, it first spent a considerable amount of time and resources on the construction of two new, albeit small, houses in the neighborhood, as compensation for the two (impoverished) families that had been living in the dilapidated building for many years.

In July 2013, I attended a members' meeting. One member, a man in his fifties, got up and began to speak with empathy about Flavio—the cooperative's vice president, mentioned earlier, who had been one of Pu- ñal's first acerola cherry cultivators. He had recently been diagnosed with bowel cancer, had had an operation, and was now convalescing at home. The man proposed that they do something to help him: "He is ill, and he spends money." He said that he himself would give Flavio 500 pesos, and proposed that the others give what they felt they could. He added, "The cooperative must in addition visit him. It's about showing moral support." This triggered a discussion among the attendees. All wished to help Flavio, but a couple proposed that the cooperative should be the donor—that the cooperative should charge all its members 50 pesos (whether they had at- tended the meeting or not) and give this to Flavio. Mabel and a number of others spoke against this, maintaining that the attendees should aid Flavio on a personal, voluntary basis, and that it would not be right if they decided now to allocate funds from the cooperative's money to Flavio, for two reasons. First, the meeting lacked the necessary authority to make such a decision, because only a minority, around forty, of the members were present. Second, the cooperative had not yet established an internal *fondo* (fund) for *ayuda mútua*, mutual aid. The outcome was that immediately after the meeting the attendees, on a voluntary basis, collected a substan- tial sum. In addition, Mabel promised the meeting that the board would now start planning the development of a fund for mutual aid. "We need a 'general' solution," she concluded. "Today, it's Flavio. However, tomorrow it's another *socio*. Around here we're many who experience problems and who need help in crisis situations." Mabel and a handful of others and I then went to Flavio's home, sat down for a chat, and handed over the aid.

The cooperatives' practices (or will for solidarity) also had limitations. The Dominican cooperative movement did not question wage labor, for example. Rather, cooperative enterprises helped to naturalize inequalities between categories of workers (as the Dominican labor market did, in so many different ways, routinely and every day). Both in Villa Consuelo and in Puñal, the cooperatives attempted to treat their employees correctly, and the employees seemed satisfied. Both cooperatives, however, took the existence of the typical wage hierarchy for granted. The Divina Pérez and Friends cooperative paid its older male security guard and young female receptionist modest salaries. It paid its head of office and accountant far better. The cooperative in Puñal paid only low wages to those who worked in the store and the office, and to those whom it recruited as casual labor.

Hierarchy and Equality: The Cooperatives and the Practice of Politics

It was an early Friday afternoon in October 2017 in Puñal, and I was chatting with Dionicio. We had met by chance outside the metro station in Villa Mella an hour earlier and had traveled to the village in the same *concho* (collective taxi). On the first Sunday in November the cooperative would be holding its regular, monthly members' meeting in the center of Puñal. According to Dionicio:

> The member meetings are democratic! Everybody is able to say whatever he wants. The only exceptions are politics and religion. We don't want anybody to talk about politics or religion in the cooperative's meetings. If someone brings up one of these subjects, it only undermines the unity, creates divisions, and we don't want that. Of course, the cooperative acts politically, and we discuss political strategies. But what is banned in the meetings is talk about the parties, the party politics, to act in a partisan manner. It's the same with religion. Around here, there are many small, evangelical denominations, and we have all those who are Catholics. However, if we begin to talk about

God, God's nature or existence, or about a particular denomination, or about the Church, it only creates division.

Virtually all the Dominican cooperatives had the same rule. Elwin, the head of the Surveillance Council of the Divina Pérez and Friends cooperative, summed it up: "The statutes are clear—no politics, no religion. You can refer to something political, or something religious, but you cannot start a discussion [of these issues], because these subjects divide the *socios*. If we begin to take a partisan stance [*Si entramos a la política*], the cooperative gets hurt." Elwin went on to describe how it was sometimes necessary to stop a member in the middle of a statement or comment, because the meeting thought that what they were saying was too "political." Someone in the audience would say or shout the word *política*, and the member would cordially be asked to desist.

Yet, as Dionicio pointed out, this does not mean that the cooperatives did not operate or work politically.[10] Evidently not. The cooperatives' fight was a fight for the rights of the popular masses—a struggle for increased social justice and strengthened democracy. We see this particularly clearly if we look at the Dominican savings and credit cooperatives' persistent struggle to avoid becoming classified and regulated as if they were just banks—ordinary, commercial banks. Powerful, political-economic groups (like parts of the Dominican Central Bank) have argued for years that the growing streams of money that are channeled through the nation's savings and credit cooperatives each year ought to be monitored and taxed in the same way as those of the banks. These forces maintain that the cooperatives should be regulated by the same legal framework that is used to govern the commercial banks: the country's Monetary and Financial Law. Such a measure would radically alter the rules of the game and the conditions for the nation's cooperatives. Through CONACOOP, the Dominican cooperative movement has fought against such a change. In October 2010, CONACOOP's president, Julito Fulcar, summed up the struggle and its significance in a speech to his fellow cooperativists:

Government sectors and multilateral institutions have insisted that the cooperatives need to be regulated with the aid of the Monetary and Financial Law. They argue that the economic growth of the cooperatives makes it necessary for states and governments to take precautions in order to secure the savings of the members. We cooperativists have repeatedly made it clear that we support a reinforced regulation,

monitoring, and control of the cooperatives—but with the aid of special laws and institutions, since the cooperatives are not banks and are
therefore different from the other, traditional financial entities. Those
who assert that the cooperatives ought to be regulated by means of
the Monetary and Financial Law forget about the social background
and the social conditions of our members . . . The experience shows
that in those countries where one has subjected the cooperatives to
bank regulation, the collapse has started immediately—because they
detach the cooperatives from their natural environment, destroy their
social role, ignore their special nature, and reject universal values and
principles like solidarity, commitment, equality, education, cooperation
between cooperatives—but the result is also that they reduce the access
to services for our members! (Fulcar 2011:26–27)

The message was echoed in Villa Consuelo and Puñal. Giovanna, for
example, explained in mid-2013: "The Central Bank and other parts of
the state want to subject the cooperatives to the same laws and systems
of control and taxing that apply to the commercial banking sector.
But the cooperative movement has vigorously opposed this—and we
have been backed by other parts of the state, such as IDECOOP and
others. So far the proposition [of the Central Bank and its allies] has
been fought off."

After Trujillo's death, Dominican society remained, to a conspicuous
extent, permeated by political authoritarianism (Krohn-Hansen 2009; Horn
2014). Since the late 1970s, the dominant parties have continued to build
the state based on (hierarchical, intolerant) patron–client relations. If a
citizen belongs to, or votes for, a party other than the one in power, they
lose access to the state's jobs and services, at least until the next election.

The cooperatives' practices challenge most of this—or at least the hierarchical ideals—through being more democratic, more inclusive. The cooperatives' model for ownership and political activity is different: it is a model
designed to engender greater equality and participation. Each member
has one vote, and the surplus or the profit from the cooperative's activities
is distributed among the members. The business ethic underscores social
responsibility and democratic member control. In both Villa Consuelo and
Puñal, the elected leaders used a significant part of the members' meetings
to report on current activities: projects, meetings, negotiations, forms of
cooperation, and trips. In Puñal, the treasurer also provides an account of

the cooperative's income and expenditure in the last month, reading out and explaining what the enterprise has made and spent.

The meetings entail discussions. Typical was a discussion that took place in the Puñal cooperative's members' meeting one Sunday in November 2017. Some forty members attended. Dionicio, who chaired the meeting, raised a question. The cooperative had been informally contacted (verbally, not in writing) by a couple of locals who wanted to create a *taller de costura* (sewing workshop). The question was whether the cooperative would be willing to donate a piece of its property, situated in the center of Puñal, to this purpose. If the cooperative donated a plot, they would use it to establish the workshop. Dionicio explained: "It's obvious that we cannot give away a plot on the most valuable part of the land, this is evident! But I think that we can find a suitable plot for them on our property."

Leonel, a member in his late thirties, got up and replied with empathy: "People need work! It's only by being able to work that people can put food on the table and raise their children. I therefore back that we donate the plot. However, we have to demand that the workshop is provided with the cooperative's name, carries the name of the cooperative of Puñal!"

His words triggered a debate. Some, like Dionicio and another member, Miguel, maintained that it was unnecessary to force the workshop to carry the cooperative's name. Either way, they argued, the sewing workshop would constitute a contribution, a help, to *la comunidad* (the community).

Leonel, Mabel, and a number of others saw a risk, however. All supported the idea that they should donate a plot. But what if some politician—or a big shot in the area or the community—took credit for the creation of the workshop? Or worse, what if the plot that the cooperative had donated for a shared or collective purpose later became privatized, transformed into a resource, a piece of property, controlled or "owned" by only one individual or by only one household? Leonel backed his position with the example of a family living nearby that had managed, bit by bit, to privatize a water source that had originally been established in order to serve several households.

Mabel backed Leonel. "We often speak of 'the community,'" she maintained. "It's said that something is for, or a contribution to, the community. But we have to ask: *which* community? Who are the people that make up 'the community'? Sometimes these are, in reality, just two or three politicians, or only a handful of others."

Another of the cooperative's founders, Isabel, took the floor and spoke passionately, even dramatically: "We, in the cooperative, have our own assets, and the community of Puñal has its own assets—these are not always exactly the same. We must defend the values of the cooperative. I'll defend to the death the assets of my cooperative!"[11]

The meeting then decided the following: Those who wanted to open the workshop would be invited to submit a written application with the necessary specifications of the prerequisites and a budget. Thereafter the cooperative, through its board and the members' meeting, would make its decision.

Compared to the large political parties, the cooperatives were more dialogic, more inclusive. The members' meeting in Puñal had a regular feature that symbolized and expressed this. Each meeting included a sequence called *el turno libre*, or an opportunity to speak freely. *El turno libre* gave the members a chance to speak to their comrades on whatever political, economic, or moral subject, or problem, they wanted. Each month, a number (five, ten, twelve) chose to use the opportunity.

In Search of Dignity, in Search of Respect

The cooperatives that I got to know in Villa Consuelo and Puñal helped generate dignity and self-respect. They did so by creating and reproducing experiences of belonging. The everyday routines in the office of the Divina Pérez and Friends cooperative bore testimony to this. The members exchanged greetings when they entered and left, and chatted about the family, businesses, the cooperative, and events. Many had known each other for years. A number were relatives. Sonia, the head of the office and the cooperative's accountant, had held the same position for fifteen years. She knew the majority of the members well. Many got her help when they applied for a loan or had to produce and submit something in writing The member would sit down with Sonia in her office and tell her verbally what she needed to know, and Sonia and the secretary would then complete the paperwork on behalf of the member.

The community's existence was celebrated on special occasions. Sunday, 5 August 2012, for example, I attended Divina Pérez and Friends' monthly members' meeting. The meeting was special; it was a celebration of three different occasions. First, the cooperative had just relocated, and this was the first members' meeting in the new, more spacious premises. Second, the cooperative (or the loose network of relatives and acquaintances that later was transformed into a cooperative) was sixteen years old—the cooperative's anniversary was 4 August. Third, the cooperative marked El Día del Padre (Father's Day). The venue was decorated with balloons. On the wall behind the podium we read: "*Felicidades* [Congratulations]—*Aniversario* [Anniversary]—*Papá* [Dad]." There were well over a hundred people there, and the place was packed. While we awaited the opening of the meeting and the celebration, we were shown advertisements on a screen: the cooperative encouraged members to make use of its favorable deals with commercial agents ranging from the two hypermarket chains, Olé and La Sirena, to the furniture store, Pérez Comercial in La Zona Norte, to the firm APR Electronics in eastern Santo Domingo, to the cooperative movement's own insurance company, COOPSEGUROS.

An older member opened the meeting. He spoke enthusiastically of the three reasons to throw a party, before he solicited everyone to support the cooperative. The cooperative, he underscored, is different from the banks. It is a social enterprise. It has two goals: to achieve social and cultural outcomes, and to make money. The cooperative, he went on, is for the family, a family enterprise for the benefit of the family. "We have all to defend *nuestra empresa* [our firm]!" he finished.

After this, a woman led a shared prayer, before Giovanna showed pictures of some of the founders of the cooperative and told the story of how the cooperative had been conceptualized and developed. The rest proceeded cheerfully. Those who were fathers were given a gift by the cooperative, and all the attendees were served food and drink: homemade salads, *bollitos de yuca* (cheese-filled cassava balls), juice, and pieces of a gigantic cake. Many of the attendees took part in the various party games and competitions. A couple of teenagers performed music.

One Sunday in November 2013, I was present when the cooperative in Puñal began planning that year's *actividad de navidad* (Christmas party). It was the monthly members' meeting, and around forty members were present. Mabel led the meeting. Each year, the cooperative in Puñal staged a few ceremonies and fiestas. The Christmas party took place on the Sunday before Christmas and was an informal gathering for families and friends. It started early, around 11 a.m., and lasted until late afternoon or early evening. In 2013, the date was 15 December. Mabel addressed the assembly: "Bring your family. Bring your partner. A couple of friends. This is meant as *un día de compartir* [a day of sharing and being together]. We'll have lots of food, and music. We eat, drink, dance, are together."

The attendees agreed to two mutually dependent premises. First, the party would be entirely based on voluntary contributions from the participants. As Mabel put it, "each participant ought to make a rough estimate: how many [relatives and friends] are we [from my household or from my circle]? And how much can we afford to bring? Every member who participates brings some food, or something else, according to their capacity and according to how many persons they bring to the event." Second, the cooperative's money would not be used, or touched, to cover expenses.

The next half-hour or so was spent on more detailed organizing. Mabel would, she said, prepare and bring to the party a *pierna,* or roast pork leg, as she had done the previous year, and Flavio, the vice president, promised to bring five chickens. Two women would each bring three chickens, and Pedro, another of the board members, would bring a large pot of yuca and a large pot of *guineos con cebolla* (green bananas with onion). "What about the beverages?" a man asked. José then offered to come with a *moro de guandules con coco* (a dish of rice, pigeon peas, and coconut), before two men said that they together would bring a case of beer. One of the attendees made a list of what the various members said they would bring. Four women would prepare different salads, and a young man said that he would come with a half-case of beer. Another promised to bring 25 pounds (11.25 liters) of *jugo* (juice), which triggered cheers and applause. Mabel finally asked a man to bring some Christmas sweets, before she rounded off, "We still lack a number of things, dishes, knives, forks, spoons, more beverages, and more food. The other *socios* who wish to participate will be asked to bring these things, the rest of what we need, so that we'll have plenty of everything."

In 2016 and 2017, the cooperative celebrated the Christmas fiesta in more or less the same manner. All brought something according to their capacity, and they spent the Sunday together. However, the cooperative appointed a committee—three of the members—to organize the event.

Conclusion

Dominican cooperatives offer their members economic advantages. While most poor Dominicans find it more or less impossible to obtain a loan through a commercial bank, many can secure access to loans through joining a savings and credit cooperative. The interest rates on loans are typically lower than in the banks. Many cooperative enterprises are, in addition, multiservice operations. Most combine being a savings and credit cooperative with supplying their members with special offers from firms and businesses—from cheaper medicines and refrigerators, for example, to discounted prices on groceries and furniture, to favorable insurance schemes. Through the cooperative membership, many experience greater dignity, more respect. This is of deep significance in a social reality characterized by sharp inequalities and brutal, marginalization processes.

The cooperatives are best understood as tools in the common Dominican search for *progreso*, a better (more modern) life.[12] They are regarded by the members as *empresas*, or business firms—but firms with a social, more human, purpose. At any rate, these enterprises represent a certain (limited) political—democratic—hope. Most of them seek to train their members—groups of ordinary citizens—in a more inclusive and dialogic way of running affairs and practicing decision-making. At their best, cooperatives' forms and practices challenge the nation's ingrained, authoritarian social and political patterns.

This can be said in a different way. Today's Dominican cooperative is, as we have seen, mostly an instrumentality of insertion into the interstices of capitalist time as a survival strategy.[13] The basis of these cooperative business activities is the (historically and culturally constituted) will for mutual aid. Forms of shared help and cooperation render it easier (or less difficult) to manage everyday challenges, and to tackle crises. My analysis of these Dominican cooperative enterprises rests upon the same understanding of how formations of global capitalism are produced (rather than existing a priori) that I have promoted in the preceding chapters. Capitalism is produced through the intersection of diverse social fields and multiple power relations. Cultural heterogeneity is part and parcel of capitalism. We must distance ourselves from (entrenched) conceptions of capitalism as unilinear, singular, and outside other social formations (Bear et al. 2015).[14]

From a form of radical or leftist, not to say anticapitalist, perspective, these Dominican cooperatives have limitations. These enterprises do not question wage labor, for example. The country's cooperative movement struggles against poverty and other forms of social injustice, and strives for an economy with a human face. However, Dominican cooperativists are far from revolutionary, and they are not socialists.

Does this mean that Dominican cooperatives cannot change? The answer is evidently no, for at least two reasons. First, important parts of the international cooperative movement's history have been marked by forms of anticapitalist ideology and radical political critique, and members of the Dominican cooperative movement are regularly in touch with cooperativists from different countries in Latin America and Europe (CONACOOP 2011, 2018). They participate in international seminars and workshops, and they visit cooperatives abroad. An outcome is that some Dominican cooperativists continually change perceptions and develop new perspectives. Second, as we have seen, the Dominican *cooperativa* is an open, flexible form or institution that can be used by actors with different political-economic-social agendas. At present, this institution is used as a survival technology and in order to create feelings of dignity. In the future, it can come to be used to advance a more profound critique of, and to challenge, capitalism with its principles and inequalities, as has happened in other countries (Ranis 2016). Dominican cooperatives are active, effective, and vital—they are ongoing processes and experiments.

CHAPTER 5

Jobless Growth, "No Labor" Futures, and the Investigation of Popular Economies

> The idea that Africans leaving agricultural village life for the city would be incorporated into a stable, Fordist industrial working class where unemployment and destitution would be atypical conditions, stabilized through insurance mechanisms, is increasingly implausible. But if we make ourselves aware that what is being lost is not any possibility of a decent future but instead just one particular formulation of what such a decent future might look like, then we can perhaps learn to free ourselves from a politics of nostalgia and see new sorts of futures and new sorts of politics. (Ferguson 2015:83)

Formal-sector employment, with a decent wage and workers' rights, remains an unrealistic possibility, a distant dream, for large parts of the world's poor masses. How do we best examine the popular economies in the many vast city landscapes that, in the course of recent decades, have appeared in Latin America, the Caribbean, Africa, and Asia? This chapter formulates some answers to this broad question that have emerged from my attempts to explore the economy in Santo Domingo. My goal, however, is broader: I wish to outline some principles, or analytical tools, for an anthropology of the livelihood activities of the urban masses in today's global South.

Why do so few in today's Dominican Republic bank on a future with wage labor? The long-running Trujillo dictatorship (1930–61) forged, as I have shown in the preceding chapters, an alliance with a significant part of the population in the countryside. The regime–countryside compromise served to protect and sustain a peasant way of life (irrespective of the regime's violent, despotic, and many eccentric features) (Turits 2003;

144

Krohn-Hansen 2009). After the end of the Trujillo rule in 1961, the nation saw continual urbanization, such that today greater Santo Domingo is a city of nearly 3 million inhabitants, almost 30 percent of the country's population. More than 70 percent of the Dominican population now lives in cities. However, to borrow James Ferguson's formulation, few people—hardly anyone of those who left the Dominican countryside for the capital—were "incorporated into a stable, Fordist industrial working class." Instead, most were forced to try to survive from day to day as best they could. The Dominican Republic posted impressive growth rates over a period of twenty-five years. In spite of this, the generation of new, good jobs was remarkably weak. This is how an International Labor Organization (ILO) publication summarized the labor market situation in the country in 2013 (nothing much of significance has changed since then):

> Notwithstanding the strong economic performance of the past 20 years, the Dominican labour market is characterized by: (i) a relatively low level of participation—especially for women—and a large share of workers with primary or no education; (ii) a large portion of the workforce still largely discouraged and underutilized; (iii) high levels of outflows of educated workers and inflows of foreign irregular workers [Haitians]; and (iv) falling real wages and a decline in the wage share. The pattern of sectoral changes in the last decade—the deep crisis of manufacturing with the decline of wage employment in large enterprises and the surge of employment in low productive, precarious occupations in traditional services—has contributed to retain high levels of total informal employment. (Parisotto and Prepelitch 2013:19)

Given this economic and social history, it is small wonder that more and more people in today's Dominican capital appear to disregard a future based on wage employment. People use their experience, and that of relatives and friends, when they make decisions. Many of those I met in Santo Domingo's barrios had previously worked for some years as lowly remunerated employees (in firms or stores, in offices, or as domestic workers for families), but preferred now to try and manage in another way, such as driving their own taxi; dealing in plantains, vegetables, or other foods; or having a workshop, a beauty parlor, or some other micro-enterprise.

Why, to ask a more general question, does the idea of universal wage employment appear so thoroughly unrealistic in so many places in today's world? Most of the vast city landscapes that have emerged in the global

South (from Lima to Luanda to Dhaka) are, in a sense, reminiscent of that of the Dominican capital. How might we provisionally or stenographically characterize these urban societies? Large parts of them seem both urban and rural—they are cosmopolitan, and typically transnationalized, yet, in the main, still poor. They constitute a particular form of modern urban landscape: not particularly industrialized, not preindustrial and not postindustrial, and with little or limited public welfare. There are at least two reasons, or sets of reasons, why I am convinced that these social formations will not, in the foreseeable future, change (or develop) into industrial or wage-labor societies in the way that large parts of social theory have long assumed that they eventually would.

First, researchers (Denning 2010; Smith 2011; Ferguson and Li 2018; Ferguson 2019) have, in recent years, increasingly directed renewed attention toward a process that was already actively and instructively discussed in the 1960s and 1970s with the aid of data from Latin American cities (see Quijano 1966, 1974; Nun 1969; Cardoso 1971; Perlman 1976; de Janvry and Garramón 1977 and the surplus population debate).[1] Global capitalism appears to have no use for a growing number of people, neither as labor-power nor as consumers. This has been solidly confirmed by mainstream economists and politicians recognizing that "full employment" is unfeasible and that structural unemployment levels will increase as an effect of technological changes, developments in supply-chain management and logistics, and robotization. As Tania Li (2010:67) put it some years ago in an Asian context, the exclusion of so many people today from the formal wage-labor economy is "a sign of their very limited relevance to capital at any scale."

Second, the world has to confront climate change and replace fossil fuels with alternative energy resources. It seems doubtful that these badly needed structural changes in themselves will mean many new jobs, or contribute to a strengthening of the bargaining position of the masses in the cities that have emerged in the global South. As Timothy Mitchell's *Carbon Democracy* (2011) brought out powerfully, coal provided working-class people and their unions with new and significant bargaining strength. In Mitchell's analysis, modern Western political democracy emerged as a consequence of organized coal miners leading an effective workers' struggle to develop a strategy of political claims leveraged by their capacity to block or stop the supply of coal for industrial production, beginning in the late nineteenth century in Britain, elsewhere in Europe, and in the United States, and continuing until the 1970s (2011:12–42). Western elites turned to oil rather than coal partly because they wanted to regain power over energy supplies. Oil could be transported via pipelines and tankers that were organized into imperial/transnational networks, rather than along the limited regional "arborescent" supply lines that had been constructed for coal, whose weak links workers and their unions had been able to take physical control of. *Carbon Democracy* tells the history of the defeat of labor through the restructuring of global capitalism to use oil instead of coal as a source of energy: the process lasted at least until the historic defeat of British coal miners by the Thatcher government in 1984.

There can be little doubt that world society, over the next decades, will see massive changes in energy systems. Nevertheless, so far there seems to be a significant contradiction between the imperative to put an end to the use of fossil fuels, on the one hand, and the need for jobs (or for "proper jobs") in the South, on the other. Production of energy from wind, water, and solar power requires limited amounts of labor. Once the necessary technical installations (wind turbines, hydroelectric power plants, ocean-wave devices, solar power plants, and so on) have been constructed and are in place, they require relatively few employees for operation and maintenance (although the installations or the parks can occupy, or block, significant landscape areas, or land properties and, through this, influence—perhaps damage or jeopardize—the conditions for local agriculture, fisheries, and tourism) (Pasqualetti 2011; Howe 2014). The same applies to the expanding production of energy crops on large plantations. This production is mechanized, so is not labor-intensive, and takes up vast areas of land—and it is one of the reasons why dispossessed and poor people from the countryside end up in one of the global South's cities in the first place (Li 2011; Borras Jr. et al. 2012; Vergara-Camus and Kay 2017).

The remainder of the chapter is divided into three parts. In the first part, I argue that we still need to have a strong interest in labor and the labor concept—in spite of the picture of the labor market, or the global lack of "proper jobs," that I have just sketched. The second part insists that we need empirical, grounded analyses of the articulations between labor and time, between particular labor activities and concrete, specific timescapes. The third part emphasizes that it remains important to ask who accesses land and housing, and what exactly they do with these assets.

Is Labor a Useful Concept for Research Today?

If a "proper job" seems so unrealistic for so many people in so many places, does this mean that we should give up the concept of labor as a sine qua non in our investigations? Or does the concept of labor continue to be useful and necessary as an analytical instrument for anthropologists?

The answer is yes to the second question, and no to the first. The contemporary world is a product of connections. We need the concept of labor because it impels us to acknowledge how decisive it still is to continue to focus analytically on the power of contemporary global capitalism. Capitalism has always been transnational, and the traversing of geographical and political borders is immanent in its historical trajectory. I thus stress that it is key to approach specific (national or local) economies in relation to global configurations. Capitalist restructuring or dislocation of labor in one (historically and socially generated) place is intimately connected to capitalist processes and changes in other parts of global society (Kasmir and Carbonella 2014; Harvey and Krohn-Hansen 2018). Susana Narotzky has summed it up this way:

> While capitalism remains hegemonic, I suggest that we do not abandon the concept of labour, as it addresses the connection of people and places in a process that overpowers their will to make a life worth living and abducts them into the aim of the expansion of money value. Even when unpaid and hidden forms of labour may be on the rise, such as neo-bondage, contract farming, or self-employment, these unwaged workers are crucial to capitalist social reproduction. Moreover, the ways in which they become valuable for capital accumulation include their configuration as consumers of commodities, rent, and interest providers. (Narotzky 2018:41)

The focus on labor (as an analytical concept and as an empirically existing practice) has another advantage. The category "labor" connotes something embodied. Labor forms are locally situated, sociomaterial activities. The focus on labor invites one to work ethnographically (some would say phenomenologically) on the concrete. It invites one to discover and explore key features of the sociomaterial processes in question through examining specific interconnections between forms of labor, on the one hand, and forms of gender, forms of kinship, structures of affect, concepts of history, and ideas about politics and the state, on the other.

In sum, to work with, and through, labor is essential. The concern with labor drives us to do two equally necessary things simultaneously: It makes us work historically on structures of domination and exploitation (and through this to document places and people as connected through a historically constituted, globally extended, powerful capitalist process that changes, disrupts, and dislocates places and persons); and it lets us work ethnographically (and through this to highlight how existing forms of economic action, such as labor, are never abstract, but rather are always concrete, specific, and localized).

It is key to operate with a broad concept of labor. What constitutes labor in a given context should be investigated empirically, not assumed. If we take a narrow perspective and treat only financially remunerated wage or contract work as labor, we leave out a broad range of labor activities and, in this manner, contribute to rendering invisible much of the important quotidian labor that is performed within capitalism. It is more useful, more in tune with the actual world (a capitalist order that is shifting and changing constantly), to open up the concept of labor and to acknowledge that there are many different forms. But there is a limit. Not everything is labor. I support Narotzky when she maintains that labor as a concept should be restricted to "work effort (human energy expenditure) *in its relation to capital*, tak[ing] into account, however, that this relation has many forms, including many non-commodified and unwaged forms which can be dominant in certain historical conjunctures" (2018: 41, emphasis added). In today's Dominican capital, or more generally in today's cities in the South, labor's relation to capital has a multitude of faces, including petty trade, precarious family enterprises and small businesses, small-scale entrepreneurship, wage labor, household labor, workshops, communal work, and cooperatives.[2]

I insist on an elastic concept of labor for a reason. Who is it that usually constitutes "the workers" or "the laborers" in historical narratives about capitalism? Marx and Engels imagined capitalism's laboring masses essentially as industrial workers or wage laborers. Their analyses have been, and remain, of unique significance, but rest on historically untenable simplifications. As Anna Tsing has correctly summed up:

> Nineteenth-century Manchester industrialization formed the context for one potent figuration [or representation] in the collaboration of Marx and Engels. Not every oppressed person at that time was a wage laborer—and, of those who were, few were involved in the technologically advanced and well-organized factories of English industry.

Manchester industrial workers, however, proved good to think with . . .
The daily struggles of the Manchester industrial worker allowed critics to glimpse a future of radical change: the proletarian revolution.
He—and it was a *he*—guided Marx's and Engels' thinking in charting
the constraints and possibilities of capitalism . . . In hindsight, we can
see how the gendered, racial, and national character of the Manchester industrial workforce helped Marx and Engels imagine labor as a
universal, progressive category—thus supporting a science of capitalist
transformation . . . These white male industrial workers became figura-
tive protagonists of a social movement that, through the progressive
generalities they seemed to embody, moved far beyond Manchester.
(Tsing 2009:153, emphasis in original)

Marx's and Engels's abstraction—the factory worker/wage laborer—fa-
cilitated the making of a political left focused on the exploitation and the
revolutionary potential of the working class. However, as Michel-Rolph
Trouillot (1995:27) has maintained, "any historical narrative is a particular
bundle of silences"; any voicing of history, or any narrative of the past, present and future, is simultaneously a silencing of history.[3] Marx and Engels
disregarded, or glossed over, important histories, such as the work of the
slaves and the production of commodities for European consumers, including the emergent English working class, in the colonies (Mintz 1985;
Linebaugh and Rediker 2000). Slaves and proletarians, different kinds of
laboring masses, together powered the new world economy, the capitalist
system.

As Susan Buck-Morss, the American political philosopher and social
theorist, has shown in her *Hegel, Haiti, and Universal History* (2009), the
Marxist standard narrative about slavery and wage labor *could, perhaps*,
have been different. Her book documents that it is unthinkable that G.
W. F. Hegel, an avid reader of newspapers and political journals, was not
familiar with French Saint-Domingue's slave revolution that had been going
on for the whole decade immediately before he wrote *The Phenomenology
of Mind* and published it in 1807. The young Hegel, Buck-Morss argues,
knew well about the Haitian Revolution (1791–1804), and he outlined his
influential ideas about the relation between lordship and bondage within
this contemporary setting—within this context of the historical existence of
Western imperial formations; large-scale, routinized use of enslaved African
labor; and a bloody, successful colonial war of liberation fought out by real

ex-slaves. In brief, Haiti and the master–slave dialectic were created at approximately the same time; Hegel was reading about the Haitian Revolution when he wrote his book. However, this connection was subsequently distorted and silenced. Philosophers, intellectual historians, and others soon came to view the master–slave dialectic mainly as a concept, a wholly abstract example. Hegel himself contributed considerably to the production of oblivion and silence. Some years later, in the early 1820s, his views had changed and become less radical, more politically conservative. "Slavery," he wrote in *The Philosophy of History* (1991 [1822]: 99, emphasis in original), "is in and for itself *injustice*, for the essence of humanity is *Freedom*; but for this man must be matured. The gradual abolition of slavery is therefore wiser and more equitable than its sudden removal." Marx and other leading Marxists also contributed to the creation of silence or distortion. As Buck-Morss puts it, "since the 1840s, with the early writings of Karl Marx, the struggle between the master and slave has been abstracted from literal reference and read once again as a metaphor—this time for the class struggle. In the twentieth century, this Hegelian-Marxist interpretation had powerful proponents . . . The problem is that (white) Marxists, of all readers, were the least likely to consider real slavery as significant because within their stagist understanding of history, slavery—no matter how contemporary—was seen as a premodern institution, banned from the story and relegated to the past" (2009:56–57).

In brief, capitalism has not always only been translocal. It has also, from its inception up to the present day, been made and remade with the aid of highly different forms of labor and labor regimes, from slavery to wage labor, from sharecropping to contract farming, from self-employment to small-scale entrepreneurship. In the large cities in today's global South, it is rarely formal-sector employment that prevails. Instead, a significant proportion of the population struggles in precarious family enterprises— small workshops and businesses. Others—typically vast numbers—live off street vending or petty trade. In the next section, I look in more detail at the analysis of these forms of labor. More specifically, I ask: How can the small economic ventures and forms of petty trade and self-employment that characterize the cities of the global South most usefully be analyzed? It has been said that these social and material spheres, or these parts of the economy, scarcely "produce," that the population within them labors but can hardly be said to produce, or to be productive. I disagree. In some ways, these practices and processes—these precarious small businesses and the many forms of self-employment—constitute the bulk of the real economy in these city societies. Through the work that is performed, the urban masses are provided with food and meals, homes and furniture, decisive transport services, and access to necessary repair work, to mention but a few things. We are talking about real production. Car-repair businesses mend cars and other vehicles. An independent driver with his own vehicle transports passengers and goods. A woman who runs a food stall on a pavement makes and sells meals. In the following section, I argue that it is necessary to examine these types of practices and processes (small family enterprises, petty commerce, self-employment) as particular, historically produced relations or articulations between forms of social *time* (disparate time-maps, social rhythms, and chronotopes) *and* labor.

Time and Labor

As I have sought to document in detail, especially in chapter 1, but also in other parts of the book, there is no singular social timespace in contemporary capitalism. Instead, in all places—all around the world—there are complex timespaces in which socioeconomic agents seek, through their labor in and of time, to coordinate activities (May and Thrift 2001; Bear 2014a, 2016; Mankekar and Gupta 2019). It is the same with the field of power and knowledge that we call the state, or the nation-state. There is no uniform social timespace in the (often relatively loose, not to say messy or disorganized) nationally extended system or network of political institutions and practices that, in Philip Abrams's (1988 [1977]) term, constitutes "the state-system" (Auyero 2012; Mathur 2014). As we have seen in the preceding chapters, the Dominican Republic's small-scale economic enterprises and businesses, for example, often experience delays. Instead of speed and well-oiled, effective political-economic integration, there is persistent slowness, blockades, and marginalization. This seems representative: the norm is that most citizens, including the world's poor working masses, in practice are forced to live with inconsistent and contradictory capitalist, political, and bureaucratic rhythms. In turn, the diversity and clashes among and between rhythms have a bearing on everyday experiences of time *and* performances of labor. At the level of the individual, navigating capitalism's and the state's forms of time is replete with challenges, dilemmas, and decisions.

An important task is therefore to analyze empirically the various forms of labor through which inconsistent rhythms are mediated. In such examinations, one has to look in detail at labor practices. It is through particular encounters with the material world and use of the body, technology, infrastructure, and time that humans attempt to reconcile disparate time-maps and social rhythms.

But why bother? When the goal is to be able to better understand livelihood practices in the South, *why* focus on (the implications of varying and contradictory forms of) social time? I view the interest in time—or in the relationship between time and labor—as a tool, a research strategy. Specifically, I see at least two important reasons why we ought to focus on time.

First, we need bottom-up, or ethnographically driven, accounts of the everyday activities and the labor processes that, in so many ways, constitute the masses' livelihood strategies, their small ventures, businesses, and forms of trade and self-employment. The interest in discrepant and clashing forms of social time can help us create and strengthen this type of analysis. By studying contemporary economic, political, and bureaucratic time through a focus on the concrete labor practices in a given place, or in particular family businesses and forms of petty trade, we can track how capitalism's and the state-system's different rhythms influence, disrupt, and dislocate (actual) labor activities. Simultaneously (since it is always through concrete labor practices that persons, or families and workers, constantly seek to reconcile disparate rhythms and, in this way, to cope), we demonstrate how the agents in question attempt to adapt to, and work on the effects of, the conflicts between rhythms. These popular economic activities are thoroughly precarious. The basic condition is shot through with unpredictability and uncertainty. Much of this has precisely to do with agents' encounters with and experiences of social time—with their experiences of the diversity and clashes among economic, political, and bureaucratic rhythms. Ethnographic examinations of the popular navigation of time through everyday labor can generate not only more vivid and concrete analyses of decisive features of the masses' livelihood strategies, but also more realistic ones.

Second, we ought to use the focus on time to work phenomenologically on meanings and moral and affective processes. We should ask, for example, what does it signify for particular agents to have to live with, and seek to reconcile, specific complex timescapes? How are tensions between rhythms experienced at the level of the individual (such as a workshop owner, a food stall operator, a street vendor)? Let me provide an example. Chapter 1 demonstrated how small-scale furniture makers (and others) in the capital are normally forced to try to navigate a diversity of inconsistent or clashing forms of time. Frequent blackouts remain a tough challenge. Electricity supply is unpredictable, and sometimes the power is gone all day. María Paulino, the owner and operator of a small furniture workshop in the eastern part of the city, told me how her mood changed according to the shifting relationship between rhythms: "When I arrive in the morning and there is power," she explained, "I begin to work, filled with energy. But when the workers have arrived but wish to leave because we lack electricity and can't work, I'm at the point of despair." In turn, specific cultural and affective ideas stimulate, or drive, agents to act in particular ways, economically or politically (Yanagisako 2002; Weston 2017).

How the urban masses navigate time thus requires empirical investigation. That said, I consider it useful to distinguish between, and seek to put to use, three questions. In specific analyses, we ought to ask: What is the relationship between social time and labor (or how does the labor in/ of time manifest itself) if we look, respectively, at (1) the access to capital, credit, and loans on the part of the agents (the enterprises, the businesses, the individual); (2) their access to infrastructure, premises, tools and raw materials; and (3) the market situation and their sales opportunities. Let us briefly consider each of these items in turn.

The Access to Capital, Credit, and Loans

As I have said, there is no uniform social timespace in capitalism. The abstract time-reckoning of capitalism in practice helps to produce contradictory social rhythms that must be mediated by agents (capitalists, financiers, workers) through concrete labor (Marx 1993 [1885]; Bear 2014a). For example, the rhythms of the money and credit markets are often in certain conflict with the rhythms and needs of the production of goods and services.[4] These basic connections apply just as much, if not more, to those who lack resources, or are poor. The latter are also dependent on (access to) capital and loans in order to be able to invest and produce. Many people in the cities in the South are not "bankable": they do not qualify for a loan in a bank. Sometimes a small minority can perhaps secure an ordinary commercial bank loan, or a loan through some NGO or aid organization, but only after having first invested considerable time and labor (and probably money) and having waited for weeks or months, if not years. Different forms of time thus encounter one other—on the one hand, the banks' "no" and the slowness and waiting that are then experienced, and, on the other, the imperative to be able to invest and work and make a living right now, at this very moment in time. In turn, the agents (or people with their businesses) must adapt. They might source capital and loans through kin and friends, or resort to loan sharks. Many create and use informal rotating savings and credit associations; others join savings and credit cooperatives. Compared to the services of the banks, those of moneylenders, savings and credit associations, and community-based savings and credit cooperatives are regarded as available, fast, and flexible. The problem is that the interest rates charged by the loan sharks are typically extortionately high—for example, in many places a rate of 30 percent or 50 percent in ten days is common.

With the continual use of kin, moneylenders, and savings and credit associations to obtain capital and loans comes the need to navigate and reconcile further social rhythms or forms of time. For example, chapter 4 told the history of a small savings and credit cooperative situated in Villa Consuelo, one of Santo Domingo's working-class barrios. The savings, credit, and multiservice cooperative, Divina Pérez and Friends, began as a kinship and mutual aid network based on monthly meetings, and was subsequently transformed into a legally approved cooperative. Giovanna, the cooperative's head, told me that it had all begun in 1996 when her grandmother died. The grandmother's home had functioned as a gathering place for the relatives: six adult children with their families, and nephews and nieces. When she died, a number of the remaining kin decided to try to hold the family together. In addition, they wanted to save together, to develop a common financial fund to help cover challenging expenses that resulted when someone in the family died. Giovanna put it this way: "The family then started to meet, my cousins. They had monthly gatherings, and rotated between the homes. In those days, we paid 50 pesos to the fund per person, in case of a death, or for mutual aid, and some—those who didn't have insurance—paid 250 pesos monthly to see if they could obtain a form of insurance sometime later."

Access to Infrastructure, Premises, Tools and Raw Materials

In order to be able to labor and be productive, one needs access to infrastructure (water, electricity, roads) in addition to tools and raw materials (supplies of foods, timber, auto parts). This implies a need to coordinate activities through work on and in time. Why so? Any public or private supplier (of infrastructure services, technology, or other commodities, such as agricultural or industrial raw materials) has their own pattern, including their own pace, tempo, and rhythm. Sometimes specific tempos or rhythms are difficult or impossible to reconcile—such as when the day has just begun and you need to work but lack water (because the water supply has been interrupted or cut off), or experience a long power cut, or the only possible road has become impassable owing to heavy rain in combination with delayed or poor maintenance work (Gupta 2015; Uribe 2017; Anand et al. 2018). The question then becomes, how do you find a material-social solution? or how do you carry out the work despite discrepancies or conflicts between forms of time?

Many individuals or businesses need some kind of (simple) premises for production and/or repair work. This applies to carpenters, sewing workers, glass-cutters, mattress makers, bread makers, and mechanics, to mention a few. Earlier (in the introduction and chapter 1), I recounted the story of Cristian Nolasco and his small family firm. Cristian's furniture manufacturing business, started in the late 1980s, made beds, chairs, mattresses, and other items. The enterprise was located in a small, two-story building that originally had been a home. The family had removed some walls and made some other changes and, in this way, had transformed the house into a workshop. The firm was situated in a narrow street in Villa Consuelo, near downtown Santo Domingo. The workshop's premises had two characteristic features. First, the workshop was located in one of the city's most populous barrios and a residential area, wedged in between dwellings, shops, street trading, and congested roads. Second, the premises were small, and there was no possibility of expansion. Cristian told me how, for years, he had had to time the workshop's production activities and labor (or routinely seek to reconcile inconsistent rhythms) because of the location and size of the premises. The neighboring buildings on each side of the firm, and directly opposite on the other side of the street, were homes and apartments. The family or the workers therefore could not use the workshop late in the evening or during the night; Cristian had received complaints from neighbors about noise from the machines and the smell of the painting work. The firm needed for large trucks to be able to access the narrow street, and Cristian always had to time these deliveries carefully to ensure they did not block the traffic or annoy store owners or neighbors. In the late 1990s and early 2000s the business flourished, so Cristian rented an extra storeroom in a building in another part of the barrio. However, in spite of this, he had to operate with an absolute limit on the number of beds and mattresses he could produce—previously, finished mattresses had been stored in his office, and if the number reached one thousand they had been forced to temporarily stop production.

In the late 1990s and early 2000s, Cristian was looking for new premises, a place that would allow the firm a chance to develop. When the Dominican government started to construct a large industrial park in the western part of the capital in 2004, he decided to invest in the project. According to the plan, the park would be built in two or three years and would house some 200 small and medium-sized enterprises. Instead, construction became a prolonged farce and a nightmare for Cristian and the other small workshop and firm owners who had invested in the project (see the ethnographic vignette that opens the book for the details).

Cristian and other Dominicans often experienced the state apparatus as being idle, and excruciatingly slow. One reason was the notorious corruption. Another had to do with something more basic: As Philip Abrams (1988 [1977]) pointed out long ago, any modern state is best understood, not as if it were an object or "thing" above and outside society, but rather as a (more or less) loose and jumbled structure of political institutions and practices. An implication is that any state-system, including the Dominican one (but also the French, the Norwegian, the Bolivian, the Angolan, the Indonesian), necessarily produces a variety of different, and often unsynchronized and badly coordinated tempos and rhythms. The state institution Proindustria constructed the industrial park in western Santo Domingo. More than thirteen years after construction had begun, the park was far from complete. However, even if in 2017 it finally *had* been ready, there would still have been a big problem: it did not have satisfactory road access, so a new road needed to be built. However, roads were not part of Proindustria's mandate, and it thus had no plan to construct the access road, which was the responsibility of another part of the state apparatus. By 2017, nothing had been done to build it.

Access to the Market and Sales Opportunities

Competition for customers and markets is another domain where there is no uniform timespace. Rather, we typically see the coexistence of dissimilar forms of time—from contemporary capitalism's capacity for striking speed, or time-space compression, to state institutions' divergent rhythms and tempos, to the economic patterns and rhythms that are associated with, or determined by, production cycles in the country's agricultural areas. Let me explain.

The neoliberal restructuring that has been implemented in country after country from the second half of the 1970s onward has had two important effects in significant parts of the global South. First, the working classes often saw a decrease in their wages in real terms, were fired from their jobs, or faced increasingly uncertain working conditions. Second, the number of petty traders and street vendors in the cities grew as real wages fell, workers and employees lost their jobs, and people abandoned the countryside (Harvey 2005; Gregory 2014; Goldstein 2016). More recently, cheaper imported commodities made in China, Mexico, or the world's free zones are increasingly arriving in the markets in most places in the South, both legally and as contraband. A reason for this is the ever growing (technological, logistical, and commercial) capacity for moving products rapidly over large geographical distances, or for transcending time and space. The consequence for self-employed small traders is increased competition and tougher conditions. They seek to survive through working long days with grueling schedules. Sian Lazar provides a good example. In her book on everyday life and politics in El Alto (a satellite city to La Paz, the Bolivian capital), she explains that many street vendors with whom she worked described how their earnings were good in the 1970s and 1980s, but how economic competition had now increased to the point where their markups were tiny:

> Effectively things have changed radically; for example, before there were more sales, we had more income. In contrast, now because there is quite a lot of competition and more traders, the sales themselves have really lowered, too much. Where you used to sell 100 percent of your stock, now you sell 20 percent. And profits too, we've also had to lower our prices in order to compete, for example before, from a [sachet of] shampoo, let's say, we earned at least 2 Bolivianos, now a sachet only earns me 50 cents, sometimes 20 cents. And so we have to sell so that the money circulates and doesn't stagnate.
>
> What you used to sell for 100 Bolivianos now you sell at 20 or 30 Bolivianos. Now it's not like before, because before there was money in circulation, a worker earned, had [money] in order to buy from the streets, and bought from us. But now no, now it's reversed, we only buy and sell between ourselves. For example, you, Doctora, you'll sell books, I sell batteries, you buy batteries from me, and I buy exercise books from you—that's all we do now. (Lazar 2008:181)

If sales to local households, families, and private firms are undermined because of growing competition from imports of foreign commodities, there is nevertheless another possibility: to try to sell your products (bread, cakes, juice, marmalade, chairs, beds) to a part of the state—the armed forces, the police, the education sector, hospitals, ministries. There are, however, the same challenges and obstacles that I mentioned above: the bureaucracy's divergent and clashing forms of time, and corruption (with its impacts, such as enduring uncertainty and unpredictability, foot-dragging, boycotts, and rejections) (Muir and Gupta 2018).

The Significance of Land (and Housing)

As James Ferguson and Tania Murray Li recently pointed out, "contemporary narratives about land-grabbing or primitive accumulation could give the impression that there is a rising tide of global landlessness. As always, the *actual* pattern is more differentiated. In some parts of the world, land frontiers are still open; in others, they have closed down—some recently, some centuries ago" (2018:9, emphasis added). At the same time, the majority of the inhabitants in the cities in the South are typically newcomers from the countryside—and many of these continue to stay in touch with relatives and others in the community that they or their parents left. In the big city (no matter where it is located, irrespective of whether we are talking about New York or Santo Domingo, Tokyo or Manila), the ceaseless struggles over land (access, ownership rights, uses) play a key role. This means that it continues to be essential for researchers studying popular livelihood projects (whether in the global South or North) to ask: Who does access (rural and/or urban) land as part of their livelihood approach? How do they use it? What does it mean to them? Among the urban masses in the South, it is obvious that land rarely is the most important, or the decisive, productive asset. Instead, land forms part of more multiplex economic projects, and is incorporated into sets of relations, activities, and investments that are more diversified. In the rest of this section, I attempt to illustrate this by identifying and analyzing three questions, or sets of questions, that revolve around what land (and housing) facilitates.

What Are the Uses of City-Country Connections?

Many new arrivals in the city keep in close touch with the hometown or home area in the countryside. They reside in the city, and are wage workers or run their own small business, and travel to their home area to see family and friends. Relatives from the countryside seek them out in the city. A range of products, services, money, information (and so on) circulate in both directions in these country–city networks. Some use their connections with the original home area more systematically. Ana, whose history I told in chapter 2, is a case in point. She was a thirty-four-year-old single mother of four who ran a sidewalk food stall in the Cristo Rey barrio. She and the children lived farther north in a part of Villa Mella. Ana was not from Santo Domingo, however. She had grown up and spent most of her life in the countryside in a part of the community of Yamasá, located around 40 kilometers north of Santo Domingo. Six days a week she operated her food stall in Cristo Rey. The seventh day, Sunday, she bought secondhand clothes and textiles at a market in Villa Mella, and then took a bus to Yamasá where she resold the goods to villagers, or relatives and friends. In this way, she achieved at least three things: each week she helped her mother in Yamasá, kept in touch with kin and old neighbors in the community, and made some extra money.

Ana had not inherited land in her home area, but a few people whom I got to know in the Zona Norte owned a small plot, or a field, somewhere in the country, often in a *campo* (rural settlement) far from the capital. The plot might be lying fallow, or be rented out. The general question we need to ask ourselves is what are the shifting uses and significations of access to such plots of land?[5]

What Is the Significance of Urban Farming?

A few plantain trees or a patch of vegetables beside the house, a bit of backyard egg production, or an urban kitchen garden may be of greater economic and social value than at first seems to be the case. Milquella, a Dominican in her late forties, worked six days a week, in the old working-class barrio of San Carlos, as the administrative head of a small savings and credit cooperative. In 2014, she and her husband bought a small house on a relatively large plot on the outskirts of Villa Mella—a 10-minute drive from the northernmost metro station in Santo Domingo, Mamá Tingó. They grew herbs, vegetables, and tubers. A few families in the neighborhood, explained Milquella, had each purchased two plots. They had built their house on one plot, while they provisionally grew plantains, tubers, and vegetables and kept chickens on the other. Some of the families had hired Haitian migrants to do the agricultural work and guard the property. The questions I am interested in here are these: *Who* grows food in the city, and where do they grow it? What exactly do they do with what they produce, and what does the gardening mean to them?

Under particular political and economic (or environmental) conditions (such as in a crisis), urban gardening may become more widespread. A good example can be found in the so-called "Special Period in Times of Peace" that was introduced by the Cuban government in 1990 to refer to the many economic adjustments that were the result of the economic crisis following the breakdown of the Soviet Bloc. While the crisis affected all parts of the Cuban economy, its impact was especially strong in the food and agricultural sectors, as the loss of favorable trade agreements with Soviet Bloc nations translated into a colossal drop in the availability of traditionally imported foodstuffs and agricultural inputs (Rosset and Benjamin 1994). Food insecurity grew quickly to unheard-of levels, and in 1991 the government of the city of Havana allocated resources, including state land, to stimulate individual citizens to engage in farming or food production on every "inch of available land" (Murphy 1999). These agricultural developments in Havana and other Cuban cities in the 1990s, writes Adriana Premat (2009:32–33), "did not just include state land [like parks, baseball fields, and demolition sites] given in usufruct to citizens but also spaces within private homes, where the food security crisis led home-owners to transform their rose gardens and bare rooftops into spaces for chicken coops, pig sties, goat sheds, and vegetable gardens." One striking, and ironic, consequence was that, beginning in the late 1990s, Cuban public officials "began to express concern about the small-scale urban agriculture spaces that had grown uncontrolled since the beginning of the crisis" (Premat 2009:35).

What Part Does Housing (and Land) Play in Strategies for Creating Social Ties, and Utilizing Them to Get By?

Renting out a room, or rooms, can generate important (extra) income in urban areas. Some people might use part of their house for a small store, a beauty parlor, or a workshop. A house (or home) in a poor urban area that contains a store or a workshop may also be a source for cheap labor. The urbanization processes in the Dominican Republic after 1960 illustrate how this occurs. As we have seen in previous chapters of this book, rapid population growth in the Dominican capital resulted in a situation where more and more people lived and worked far away from what had earlier been the main urban supplier of food to families: the public market. The niche was filled by *colmados*, the small barrio or street-corner stores that sold basic foodstuffs, cleaning products, soft drinks, beer, and rum. The *colmados* functioned on family labor. Often a young man left the countryside and started working in a relative's *colmado* in one of Santo Domingo's new neighborhoods. As one *colmadero* explained to me, previously, a poor young man in the Dominican countryside typically had two options if he wanted to try his luck and leave—joining the armed forces or going to work in a *colmado*. In the city, he slept and ate in the *colmado* (or the relative's house). The working day was long and the salary low.

A mother's or father's (or grandmother's or grandfather's) house may function as a gathering place for the extended family. The house functions as a stable, physical-emotional anchorage point for the reproduction of a social network. The members help each other when necessary—but an important basis for the network is the physical meeting point, or the house: the relatives pool their resources; they help one another to raise capital for investments, secure childcare, survive temporary crises, and organize and pay for funerals.

Having a piece of land or a house may enable people to secure credit through a mortgage. The following is an example: One morning in June, 2013, I was on the second floor of Supermercado La Favorita, a large independent supermarket in the densely populated and poor Los Trinitarios barrio, in the east of the Dominican capital. The man sitting with me was Eusebio Rodrigues, one of the owners. Aged around fifty, he owned the store with a brother and sister. A number of their grown children and some nephews worked with them in the store. In 2013, the store was around 2,000 square meters, and had 128 employees. It was located at an important crossroads, where the broad Avenida Charles de Gaulle crosses Carretera Mella, and traffic was constant and congested. Eusebio told me the story of the store's success. It began in 1987 when his eldest brother, who at the time had been working as a public employee for about two decades, together with his oldest sister and the much younger Eusebio, opened a tiny supermarket (*un supermercado pequeñito*), a store of 250 square meters. The store was located in Los Trinitarios, and they rented the premises. Four years later, they wanted to expand, and decided to buy a small house, a family home, located where their store, Supermercado La Favorita, was in 2013. At the time (in the early 1990s), this part of the city was still sparsely populated, had few businesses, and consisted mainly of small family homes. The road northward to Villa Mella (Avenida Charles de Gaulle) had not yet been constructed. The family tore down the house, prepared the ground, and erected a new (albeit small) building for their supermarket. How did they obtain the necessary capital? According to Eusebio, at the time they had a bank account in order to run their business, but the store's accounts were not formal enough. The man who handled their affairs in the bank did them a favor. He visited the store, and helped them to organize their accounts and the necessary documentation and put together an application for the loan that they needed. Subsequently, the family had had, and paid off, a series of bank loans. In the years that followed the family bought up more of the houses in the area—Eusebio told me that they gradually purchased and demolished ten small homes. In 2005, they built a much larger supermarket, and their last major expansion and remodeling was in 2010.

The question of who accesses land and housing (and what they do with it) is key to analyzing the (re)production of socioeconomic inequality. To put it another way, the most impoverished people are normally those who are not only without income-generating work, but also without a secure physical place or home in which to produce and reproduce social relations and belonging.

Conclusion

My goal in this chapter has been to broaden the perspective and outline some general answers to a broad question: How might one usefully investigate and analyze popular economic action—or the masses' livelihood strategies—in the many large cities in the global South? These urban formations are often thoroughly transnationalized, but large numbers of residents remain poor. Significant parts of the population run their own economic enterprises and seek to survive from day to day as best they can. For the large majority, formal-sector employment with a decent wage and workers' rights appears unattainable. In spite of this, or in spite of the fact that the idea of universal wage employment seems so unrealistic or irrelevant in so many places in today's world, I have nonetheless argued that we should not give up the concept of labor as a sine qua non in our analyses. What constitutes labor in a given setting has to be discovered empirically, not presupposed. In today's cities in the South, the relation of labor to capital, or its integration into the global capitalist order, takes a great number of shapes, from forced labor, to household or family labor, to wage labor, to street vending and petty trade, to a multitude of forms of small business and varying scales of entrepreneurship.

I have insisted, throughout the chapter, that we need specific investigations of the articulations between labor and time. The norm is that workers and citizens, including the South's urban masses, must live with inconsistent and conflicting economic, political, and bureaucratic rhythms, and that the diversity and contradictions among rhythms affect the everyday experiences of time and the performance of labor. An essential research task is to examine, from the bottom up—or concretely—the various and shifting forms of work through which incongruent forms of time are mediated. Much of the instability and unpredictability that ordinary citizens in the South face lies in their encounters with and experiences of social time (see also Guyer et al. 2002; Auyero 2012; Taylor 2014; Millar 2018). What is it like to be compelled to live with the type of vulnerability that comes with seemingly permanent uncertainty or unpredictability? with repeated and enduring waiting? with tremendous volatility?

More specifically, I demonstrated the importance of asking three questions: What is the connection (or the articulation) between social time and labor when we investigate (1) agents' (small businesses', economic ventures', individuals') access to capital, credit, and loans; (2) their access to infrastructure, premises, tools and raw materials; and (3) their access to the market.

In addition, I have underscored the need to continue asking questions about land. Who has access to urban or rural land? What are the uses of city–country connections? What is the role of urban farming? And what role does land (and housing) play in people's livelihood projects and business strategies?[6]

In all parts of the world, there have been enormous changes in political-economic practices and thinking since the 1970s and 1980s. Most states adopted, sometimes voluntarily and in other cases in response to coercive pressures, some version of neoliberal theory and practice. Restructuring through deregulation and privatization was the order of the day. An outcome became changed structures of power, and changed and new types of contradictions in society. Common livelihood strategies should not be studied as if they develop in isolation from forms of rule. On the contrary. The exploration of popular economic action has to include the examination of popular politics. Let me highlight two forms of popular politics that are often important (there are, of course, other types—the forms of political action that are of most significance need to be determined and investigated empirically). Many who run their own small enterprises are often also members of a small business association or a similar (neoliberal) entity (for example, a kind of trade union for independent drivers, an interest organization for mobile vendors of fruit and vegetables, an association for the vendors who run their business at the same publicly operated market area). Bread makers often have their own interest organization, as do furniture makers, mattress makers, glass-cutters, and small-scale store owners. These forms of political engagement are anchored in the agents' economic strategies or forms of labor. Another widespread type is the barrio or neighborhood association—an interest community based on where the members reside. These webs of usually fragmented or loosely allied associations—the multitudes of small business associations and place-based neighborhood associations—may be tremendously important because it is through these organizations and communities that people exercise what Partha Chatterjee (2004) has described as "the politics of the governed": they fight for, and seek to defend and secure, their material, social, legal, political, and moral rights.

Many people today lead a wageless life. I have argued that if we want to understand the popular economies in the cities in the global South, we need an undogmatic, open approach. Hence, the importance of the ethnographic project. Things (out there in the world and in the social sciences) are not what they used to be; but then they never were. People seem to be living and working at the margins of, or outside, the state—but they participate nonetheless in the construction, reconstruction, and transformation of the state. People live without work, or decently paid jobs, but work long days nonetheless, six or seven days a week. They presuppose (operate with) a future "without labor," but are nonetheless busy trying to create a future for themselves and their loved ones.

Afterword: The End of an Era?

The Dominican Republic was the first country in the Western Hemisphere to conduct presidential and congressional elections during the COVID-19 global pandemic. It did so on 5 July 2020, after its national electoral authority, the Central Electoral Board, had consulted with the Pan American Health Organization to produce standardized sanitary protocols for implementation during the election, specifically: (1) sterilization of all polling stations; (2) wearing of masks and surgical gloves by polling station officials; (3) hand sanitizing and wearing of masks by all voters entering and exiting polling stations; (4) social distancing of 6 feet while in line to enter and while inside polling stations; and (5) wiping down of all polling station surfaces, voter ID cards, and markers used to fill paper ballots.

The nation experienced a seismic political shift on election night. Once all ballots were tabulated, the ruling PLD (the party that had governed the Dominican Republic since 1996, with the exception of the four years from 2000 to 2004) was handed an overwhelming defeat, nullifying any need for a runoff election three weeks later.

Luis Abinader—the presidential candidate for the opposition Modern Revolutionary Party (Partido Revolucionario Moderno [PRM])[1]—won the presidential election by a substantial 15 point margin, capturing 52 percent of the total vote, with PLD presidential candidate Gonzalo Castillo placing second with 37 percent. Abinader won twenty-four of the thirty-two provinces (including the National District) and was also the favorite of Dominicans who voted abroad. As for voter turnout, the pandemic definitely affected the numbers both at home and abroad, with many foreign governments prohibiting expatriate Dominicans from voting to avert the risk of further COVID-19 spread in their respective countries. Thus, overall voter turnout registered at just 55 percent—well below the 70 percent average of the past three presidential elections (in 2008, 2012, and 2016). However, given that the election took place in the middle of a pandemic, voter turnout was remarkably high, indicating voter resolve to see political change.

As in the presidential election, the PRM swept to victory in the Senate races, capturing nineteen of thirty-two Senate seats. The PLD won only five Senate races—from a total of twenty-eight between 2016 and 2020. The PRM captured ninety seats in the Chamber of Deputies (the lower house), six votes short of the ninety-six required to obtain a majority in the 190-seat Chamber of Deputies. The PLD won seventy-five seats.

Abinader is a US-educated economist. He comes from a family that has extensive business holdings in the Dominican Republic, especially in the tourism sector. Up until the election, he was the executive president of Grupo Abicor, a tourism real estate development company, and vice president of the cement company Cementos Santo Domingo. This was the second time Abinader had run for the top job in the country. In 2016, he lost to Danilo Medina in the second round.

One of the main challenges for the new regime will be to revive the nation's economy. For twenty-five years, the Dominican Republic was one of the fastest growing economies in the Americas, reporting a 6 percent average yearly GDP growth rate for the 2015–19 period. However, the situation changed in 2020, when the country's economy showed no growth in the first quarter (having expanded almost 6 percent in the previous quarter), and was then hit by the tremendous consequences of the global pandemic. In particular, social distancing measures restrained domestic activity, while border closures and reduced travel crushed the island's tourism industry.

Abinader's victory was more a reflection of Dominicans' growing discontent with the ruling PLD than of pro-PRM feelings. To illustrate this, let me highlight four factors, or sets of factors, that contributed to the PLD's defeat after sixteen years in power:

Glaring economic inequality. The country has seen conspicuous growth. The results of this striking economic performance, however, have scarcely trickled down to society as a whole. A small minority became much richer, while the bulk of the population (80–85 percent) continued to earn little.

Hence this book. The party that presided over this entrenched and enduring social inequality was the PLD.

Persistent impunity: Over the last few years, the immense levels of corruption in the country have angered many Dominicans and triggered protests. Specifically, we can trace (a big part of) the PLD's downfall to 2016,
when Brazilian construction giant Odebrecht admitted to paying enormous
sums in bribes to Dominican officials in order to obtain contracts. Investigations ranging from the United States to Brazil uncovered a pervasive
scheme in which Odebrecht used money to influence elections, and bribed
politicians and public officials in order to win billions of dollars' worth of
public works contracts in many countries in Latin America and Africa.[2]
However, few countries other than Brazil played so large a role as the Dominican Republic. In a settlement in US federal court in December 2016,
the Brazilian company admitted to doling out US$788 million in bribes in
the period 2001–16. Of that, US$92 million was paid in the Dominican
Republic, the third highest share after Brazil's and Venezuela's. According
to the Dominican attorney general's own investigations, Odebrecht money
made its way to at least a dozen prominent Dominican politicians, including a member of Medina's cabinet, as well as to executives of state-owned
companies. Yet, more than three years later, in July 2020, no one had been
convicted. As one of my friends in Santo Domingo put it, "The country
was sick and tired of it. A long time stealing, they managing everything
and taking everything themselves" (*El país estaba cansado. Mucho tiempo
cogiendo, administrando todo ellos y todo para ellos*).

*The handling of the municipal elections in February 2020 and of the
COVID-19 pandemic*: Two factors that clearly influenced the election were
the regime's handling, first, of the municipal elections earlier the same year
and, thereafter, of the pandemic. Having switched from paper-based voting
to electronic voting in 2018, the country experienced a series of technical
malfunctions with the voting machines during the municipal elections on
February 16, 2020, which rapidly enveloped the PLD in a political crisis.
The elections were hastily rescheduled to March 15, which engendered
antigovernment protests in the capital and strong accusations of potential
electoral fraud. At the same time, the advent of COVID-19 in the Caribbean in mid-March aggravated the situation (and intensified feelings of
political dissatisfaction), and quarantine and lockdown measures were met
with accusations of authoritarianism directed at President Medina. When
the presidential and legislative elections were also postponed, from May 17

to July 5, due to the pandemic, the government's guarantee that they would use paper-based voting and permit international observers to take part did not calm the opposition. In brief, the elections were held in an atmosphere of pervasive political uncertainty, suspicion, and distrust of the government.

The PLD's divisions: Much of the PLD's downfall was due to the party's own internal rivalries and conflicts, and many of its actions over the past years had dramatically undermined its chances of retaining power. In 2018, Medina followed in his predecessor's steps and declared his intention to run for a third consecutive term. His decision implied the need for constitutional reform and was met with immediate resistance from the opposition, the party faction of former president (and then-chief of the PLD) Leonel Fernández (who had made clear his intention to seek the nomination—yet again), and civil society. Although Medina pressured the legislature to allow his reelection, as Fernández had done in the past, he failed to garner sufficient support—and meanwhile protests grew in strength. He then announced he would not seek a third term. The decision triggered a race for the PLD to nominate a presidential candidate. The primary, held in October 2019, was another showdown between pro-Medina and pro-Fernández forces. Medina backed Gonzalo Castillo, the fifty-eight-year-old minister of public works and communications. Castillo, who lacked charisma and was generally seen as Medina's puppet, competed against Fernández in a disputed primary race, and won by fewer than 30,000 votes. Fernández, in turn, alleged the vote was fraudulent and left the party, running in the 2020 presidential race under the banner of the new People's Force party (Fuerza del Pueblo [FP]). Fernández's decision and the ensuing party split profoundly affected the election result. One consequence was that twenty-seven deputies and two senators quit the PLD and joined the FP. In the election, Fernández came third as the candidate for the FP, with almost 9 percent of the vote. Although persistent caudillo and former president Fernández clearly lost, he nevertheless managed to succeed in reestablishing himself as an important political force in the country, with prospects for future political gains if other elected and/or powerful PLD members align with him in the future.

When he took office on August 16, 2020, the country's new president, Abinader, stressed that the Dominican Republic faced stiff challenges from a flagging economy and the coronavirus pandemic. "Recovery will not come quickly or easily," he said in his first speech to Congress, noting the damage inflicted by the pandemic on tourism, exports, and remittances, three key sources of national income. He also deplored how public debt had doubled over the past decade, and how fiscal deficit had reached historic levels. "Never has any government faced such a combination of challenges and threats," he claimed (Abieu Lopez 2020). By September 1, 2020, the country registered some 95,000 confirmed COVID-19 cases and 1,738 fatalities. The same day, to try to curb the spread of the virus, Abinader extended the countrywide curfew (from 7 p.m. to 5 a.m., Mondays to Fridays, and 5 p.m. to 5 a.m. on Saturdays and Sundays), for another twenty-five days and the state of emergency for a further forty-five days. Eight months later, as of April 29, 2021, the country reported 265,818 confirmed COVID-19 cases and 3,467 deaths.[3]

In 2019, more than half (55 percent) of the working population in the Dominican Republic worked in unregistered jobs, street vending, and other precarious activities—without governmental protection or labor rights (Barinas and Viollaz 2020:10). With the government's order to stop non-essential activities and its other emergency measures to contain the virus, those people saw their income suddenly diminish or disappear entirely. For many poor people it was more than the job or the business that vanished. Although the Dominican Republic has plenty of water, nearly one in every two households in the country has no running water, relying instead (as mentioned in chapter 3) on private deliveries that have been badly disrupted by the coronavirus, just when they are most needed. According to authorities, there were 560 new cases of malaria infections in the country in the first five months of 2020, compared with 186 reported in 2019. Also in May 2020, a record 3,165 cases of dengue were registered. Both diseases are spread by mosquitos that breed in standing water (Suero Acosta 2020). The situation has led to an adjustment of the economic projections for the country for 2021–22. According to World Bank forecasts from late 2020, the Dominican Republic's GDP was expected to contract by 4.3 percent in 2020 and "projected to remain below its potential in 2021 and 2022." The pandemic's effects are, of course, global. According to the Economic Commission for Latin America and the Caribbean, the COVID-19 crisis with its consequences pushed up poverty levels in the Latin American and Caribbean region in 2020 from 185 million to 209 million people (from 30.3 percent to 33.7 percent of the total population), while extreme poverty increased from 70 million to 78 million people (ECLAC 2021:1).

Did the elections in the Dominican Republic in 2020 mark the end of a period—of a regime? It is hard to say. The country has a new president from another party, and the state is now in the hands of other political forces (the PRM and its allies). For the vast majority of Dominicans in the countryside and in the cities, however, much will remain the same. The country will continue to lack decent-paying, rights-based jobs. Access to public services and public welfare will continue to be limited. The corruption that has, for years, haunted the country and the state apparatus is unlikely to disappear overnight. Access to water and/or electricity will, in many places, remain challenging (or nonexistent). While the coronavirus pandemic has inevitably aggravated the situation, the employment problems are not new, nor are they transient. Precarity has been, and remains, the norm among the urban masses in most places in the South. This is why we need the sort of malleable, bottom-up approach to political-economic analysis I advocate in this book.

Acknowledgments

The ethnographic research on which this book about economic processes in the Dominican capital is based started in the period from early May to late August 2012. In this period, I lived in Santo Domingo and gathered data. Subsequently I returned to the city for shorter stays in 2013, 2014, 2016, and 2017. I could not have carried out the field research that I did, without the help I received from a large number of Dominicans who live and work in many different areas of greater Santo Domingo. I would like to thank all whom I met and got to know in the Dominican capital. Not only did they give readily of their time, hospitality, and knowledge, but also overall they shaped my investigation by offering contexts, insights, and perspectives decisive for creating this book. I thank especially the following persons for their openheartedness and assistance: Yuri Chez, Isabel De Los Santos, Arismendi Díaz, Héctor Gonzalez Villalona, René Japa, Lety Melgen Bello, Cristian Patrocinio, Dionicio Quiñones, Manuel Roa, and Lorenzo Rosario. My major debt in Santo Domingo is to Fernando Pellerano and his extended family. I am deeply grateful.

The Department of Anthropology at the University of Oslo supported my research economically through financing my trips to Santo Domingo in 2012–17. At the department, I have on several occasions presented work in progress, that is, a part of my research on Dominican society. I thank my colleagues at the department for lively exchanges and for backing, critique, and help.

I began writing the manuscript that became this book in late 2015, when I spent seven months as a visiting researcher at the Department of Anthropology at the University of Chicago. I sincerely thank this institution for the opportunities and the aid that it offered me—and for the intellectual benefit and the friendliness I experienced in this place. Special thanks go to Stephan Palmié for his generosity and assistance.

Important parts of this book emerged from an extended conversation on "labor" that began in a reading group at the University of Oslo in 2013. One of the excitements of this conversation was that it did not arise from a sense of prior specialization. Our agenda was more exploratory and ethnographically driven, as we read and discussed how a more systematic return to the concept of labor might inform our ethnographic analyses in new ways. Different people came in and out of the group—as visitors to Oslo, as participants in panels and workshops that we organized, and as contributors to an edited collection that we produced. I thank especially the following persons for their significant contribution to these conversations on labor: Susanne Brandtstädter, Ben Campbell, Alanna Cant, Jan Grill, Penny Harvey, Ingjerd Hoëm, Keir Martin, Marit Melhuus, Massimiliano Mollona, Susana Narotzky, Knut Nustad, Ruth Prince, Elisabeth Schober, Astrid Stensrud, and Sylvia Yanagisako. In addition, I would like to thank the Research Council of Norway for the funding of the project "Anthropos and the Material: Challenges to Anthropology," which supported our group discussions on labor. Thanks go as well to Ove Olsen for his preparation of maps of the Dominican Republic and the Dominican capital, and to Sarah A. Bologna for help with editing and language.

I owe a great deal to Steve Catalano at Stanford University Press for helping me through the last phases of this intellectual project. Many thanks also to my anonymous reviewers for your acute and generous readings.

An earlier version of chapter 1 appeared in *Journal of the Royal Anthropological Institute* 24, S1 (2018): 180–97.

Notes

Introduction

1. Some words are in order here on the use of names and pseudonyms in this book. I have used real names of powerful business families, political and economic leaders, and familiar political activists in Santo Domingo. All other names of persons have been changed. I have used the real names of organizations and associations—but in a handful of cases I have changed the name of a business, a cooperative, or a place to protect informants' anonymity.

2. The continuous growth in annual gross domestic product started in the early 1990s. The Dominican economy expanded by an average growth rate of 6 percent per year from 1993 to 2000.

3. While the bulk of this book was shaped and written before the COVID-19 crisis unfolded, its ethnographic descriptions and analytical insights remain highly relevant for the postcrisis period. As in other countries, the early projections of the impact of the crisis on employment, livelihood strategies, and poverty outcomes were worrisome. In late 2020, the World Bank expected the GDP of the Dominican Republic to contract by 4–5 percent in 2020. (For more on how the global shock triggered by the COVID-19 pandemic significantly affected the Dominican Republic's society and economy, see the afterword.) However, this book does not seek to dwell on the COVID-19 crisis. Rather, its goal is to outline and analyze various structural and decisive features of the Dominican Republic's and the Dominican capital's social and economic processes, in the belief that these features are likely to remain important even after the crisis has passed.

4. The country has seen a continual decline in real wages. Real average hourly

wages in the Dominican Republic in 2010, for example, were 20 percent below the level reached in 2000 (Parisotto and Prepelitchi 2013:12–13).

5. Banco Intercontinental (or BANINTER) was the second-largest privately held commercial bank in the Dominican Republic before it collapsed in 2003 owing to gigantic fraud tied to political corruption. The resulting central bank bailout spurred a 30 percent annual inflation and, as mentioned, increased poverty.

6. The opposition candidate, Hipólito Mejía, and the Dominican Revolutionary Party (Partido Revolucionario Dominicano [PRD]) won the election in 2000 and held power for the next four years.

7. The term "jobless growth" was coined by the US economist Nicholas Perna in the early 1990s.

8. Throughout this book, I am preoccupied with other processes and other questions than those with which Weeks essentially concerns herself—but I am nonetheless inspired by some of her perspectives and arguments.

9. The project to conceptualize and build a postwork society has a long, diverse, and rich history. Among Weeks's most important precursors are Marxists, autonomist Marxists, feminists, and others. A conspicuous example is Karl Marx's son-in-law, Paul Lafargue, who early on (at least some 140 years ago), committed to the theory or doctrine of "refusal of work" and was interested in the possibilities of a postwork future. See the bitingly critical and satiric essay collection *The Right to Be Lazy: Essays by Paul Lafargue* (Lafargue 2011).

10. When I speak of "the global North" and "the global South," I refer to positions or locations within the global political-economic system, or a globally extended structure of domination and inequality, not to geographic places or territories.

11. Based on data supplied by the US Census Bureau. See, in addition, Ricourt (2002:35).

12. The brilliance of Weeks's book lies in its refreshing, strong insistence that work must be seen as a fully *political* rather than a simply economic phenomenon. The inquiry into labor regimes and labor forms cannot be isolated from the exploration of political life and of the making of the state (something that I seek to show in historical and ethnographic detail). Weeks argues that the question of work ultimately is a question of freedom (2011:20–23). I agree. As Susan Buck-Morss has instructively demonstrated in her *Hegel, Haiti, and Universal History* (2009), the Enlightenment's thinkers, while liberating in the abstract, refused to address the enduring existence, in their midst, of violence and inequality in the form of slavery. The slave revolution that created independent Haiti showed the possibility of a broader and more inclusive—in brief, more revolutionary—democratic project, but that was glossed over or silenced. "Liberty" was regarded by eighteenth-century European political philosophers as the highest political value.

"Slavery" operated as freedom's conceptual antithesis and, quite simply, as an image, a key metaphor: "For eighteenth-century thinkers who contemplated the subject, slavery stood as the central metaphor for all the forces that debased the human spirit" (Davis 1975:263). Rousseau, for example, writes in *On the Social Contract* ([1762] 2019:10), "[T]he right of slavery is null, not simply because it is illegitimate, but because it is absurd and meaningless. These words *slavery* and *right* are contradictory. They are mutually exclusive." But the same author had nothing to say about the French empire's and Europe's actual, enormous, legalized use of Africans as slaves. In today's world, forced labor and slave labor have, as we know, by no means disappeared (Calvão 2016). The case of slavery is extreme and demonstrates the depths of human suffering and tragedy—but it is also a case that shows, with exceptional clarity, how labor regimes (with their recruitment of workers and organizations of work forms) can hardly be understood in isolation from the wider structures of domination that shape and surround them—or the basic conditions of freedom. The labor question is, in the last instance, a matter of human sovereignty, freedom, and dignity.

13. The use of the concept of "the informal sector" (or "the informal economy") is, to be sure, fraught with intellectual difficulties. Indeed, Keith Hart, the originator of the very category "informal sector," has suggested that in many nations informalization has now become so widespread that it no longer makes any sense to seek to identify a distinct sector or form of activity. As he claims, "when most of the economy is 'informal,' the usefulness of the category becomes questionable" (2006:28). In this book, I employ the term loosely and just occasionally. For the purposes of the book, the informal economy refers to activities that evade (the state's) labor market regulations (such as those governing the minimum salary, social security, and hiring and firing, or regulations about working conditions, such as health and safety). For more on the term "informal sector" and the use of the conceptual distinction between "form" and "lack of form," or between "formalization" and "informalization," see Hart (1973, 1992, 2006) and Lazar (2012).

14. For more on my understanding and use of the concept "dislocation," see Harvey and Krohn-Hansen (2018).

15. See, in addition, Baca et al. (2009), Palmié (2013), and Stoler (2016).

16. Mainly a sugarcane economy, the country moved to import-substitution industrial policies, fostering the appearance of a certain, limited, new industrial sector. In the mid-1980s, however, it shifted to an aggressive export-oriented policy stance, beginning with a major devaluation, conspicuous incentives to the tourism industry, and the creation of *zonas francas*, or special economic zones, for the establishment of export-oriented garment assembly and other types of industry. Yet the total number of accessible jobs for representatives of the Dominican

urban and rural masses in both places—both in the tourist enclaves and in the *zonas francas*—has, in practice, been strongly limited (Gregory 2014). Moreover, most of the accessible jobs in both sectors pay only low or miserable wages. The total number of jobs in the Dominican *zonas francas* has decreased, over the past couple of decades, from 140,000 in 2000 to about 40,000 in 2012 (Carneiro and Sirtaine 2017:6).

17. Dominican migrants originate from households across the entire socioeconomic spectrum. Remittances have grown over time with the stock of migrants, and accounted for 7.7 percent of the Dominican GDP in 2016—and in 2016, around 18 percent of households in the country received remittances from abroad (World Bank Group 2018:55). At the same time, the country has received large numbers of poor migrant workers from neighboring Haiti, many of whom are illegal and work for very low wages. According to an official Dominican survey, around half a million Haitians were living in the country in 2017 (World Bank Group 2018:55; see also Wooding 2018). For a set of ethnographic explorations of everyday life and survival strategies among Haitians and Dominicans of Haitian descent in the Dominican Republic, see Martínez (1995, 2010); Gregory (2014:166–208); Wynne (2015); and Hippert (2021).

18. Economically, the number-one spot presumably goes to the Vicini family. Other enormously powerful business families in today's Dominican Republic include the Corripio family, the Bonetti family, the León Jimenes family, the Grullón family, the Rainieri family, the Estrella family, the Martí Garden family, and the Gonzalez Cuadra family. Some of these Dominican tycoon families are "old money," in that their wealth came from land, properties, agriculture, and trade. Others have amassed large fortunes principally through trade, imports, and/or profiting from the development (from the 1970s onward) of the large-scale tourism industry.

19. International and national observers saw the 1996 election as fair.

20. See, for example, Tania Molina's "Se gasta RD$39,000 millones en 'botellas,' revela estudio" (2017).

21. In the period 2014–16, the average number of public employees per million inhabitants for seventeen countries in Latin America (including the Dominican Republic) was 48,351; the average for the countries in Central America in the same period was 45,463 per million inhabitants. The figure for the Dominican Republic was 58,313. The only countries with a higher number were Venezuela (82,657), Panama (73,139), Uruguay (70,709), Argentina (63,231), and Costa Rica (59,626). Chile had 50,363; Peru, 44,021; Bolivia, 39,746; Honduras, 26,730; and Guatemala, 25,037 (Oxfam 2017: 8). The PLD's political and economic project has been, and remains, complex and many-sided. On the one hand, the PLD state implemented a sharply neoliberal project. The party deregulated,

privatized, and radically opened up the economy through free-trade agreements. On the other hand, the party continued to enlarge the (already in the 1990s large or overstaffed) public sector through establishing ever more public bodies and jobs. For more on the colossal variations in how neoliberalism has been put into practice in different countries since the 1970s, see Harvey (2005) and Ferguson (2007, 2009, 2015).

22. For some general sociological-anthropological discussions of the issue of how to best think, conceptualize, and study "the modern state," see Abrams (1988 [1977]), Gupta (1995, 2012), Coronil (1997), Ferguson and Gupta (2002), Aretxaga (2003), Das and Poole (2004), Krohn-Hansen and Nustad (2005), Reeves (2014), Uribe (2017), and Kivland (2020). In my treatment of the Dominican state-system in this book, I am inspired by the basic views that are found in these (and related) works. See, in addition, Krohn-Hansen (2015).

23. For more on the economic scope, and the effects, of corruption in the last couple of decades, see Oxfam (2017:18–28).

24. In the period 2007–11 (during Fernández's rule), the country spent on average only 2.3 percent of GDP on education; in the same period, the average for all the Latin American countries was around 4.5 percent (World Bank Group 2016:21).

25. The term "precariat," meaning a precarious proletariat, burst onto the mainstream scene some years ago with the publication of Guy Standing's book *The Precariat: The New Dangerous Class* (2011). The difficulty with Standing's perspective on the precariat (defined by Standing mostly by what it is *not*—an imagined, stable working class with full social and political rights) is that it elides the historical and contemporary experiences of the global South. The book has few references to any part of the world outside the North Atlantic. The North Atlantic is simply assumed to be the norm that will apply in most places. There is little recognition that the economic, social, and political condition described by the term "precarity" has always been the typical, the norm, in the South. In reality, from a global perspective, it is Fordism and the welfare state that is the anomaly.

26. Population growth in the Dominican Republic was high for most of the twentieth century. The country's overall fertility rate was estimated at 6.8 in 1970. It declined substantially in the 1970s, and in the late 1990s was estimated at around 2.8. Whatever the case, many Dominicans have had a substantial number of brothers and sisters and often many uncles, aunts, and male and female cousins.

27. That businesses may be undermined through "uncontrolled solidarity" was brilliantly shown in Clifford Geertz's classic ethnographic study of entrepreneurial activity, *Peddlers and Princes* (1963:123).

Chapter 1

1. In this chapter, I am inspired by Bear's stimulating thinking (2014a, 2014b, 2016). For another instructive work, see Mankekar and Gupta (2019).

2. For discussions of the notion of "time-maps," see Bear (2014a) and Gell (1992:235–41), and also Kjaerulff (2020).

3. For a relevant comparative perspective, see Michael Herzfeld's (2004) study of the production of tradition through an analysis of small-town Cretan artisans' workshops and their forms of labor.

4. Mahogany, the reddish brown timber of the genus *Swietenia*, is indigenous to the Americas. The wood first came to the notice of Europeans when Spanish colonization began. The two main species of New World mahogany are the short-leafed West Indian *Swietenia mahagoni*, generally considered the best quality for cabinetmaking, and the big-leaf Central American [Honduran] *Swietenia macrophylla*, which initially (before the early extinction of the West Indian variety of mahogany in the last part of the eighteenth century) was used by European and American cabinetmakers only as a secondary wood. For a brilliant book about the mahogany trade and mahogany consumption on both sides of the Atlantic, see historian Jennifer L. Anderson's *Mahogany: The Costs of Luxury in Early America* (2012). See also Anderson (2004). For more on the environmental history of the island of Hispaniola, see Moya Pons (1994).

5. For a history of the creation and emergence of the world's export processing zones, see Neveling (2015).

6. For classic works on power, memories, and mimicry, see Taussig (1993) and Stoller (1995).

Chapter 2

1. A series of barrios located in the north of the city are collectively known as the Zona Norte (Northern Zone) in Santo Domingo. These barrios were the main sites of urban growth and social conflict between the 1950s and the 1990s (although newer shantytowns outside the municipal boundaries now absorb the largest proportion of new rural migrants).

2. To carry out my field research in the Dominican capital effectively, I decided to recruit and pay a young Dominican to assist me. In June 2012, I hired Lety Melgen Bello, who at the time was completing her undergraduate studies in the Economics Department at the Universidad Autónoma de Santo Domingo (UASD). Lety collaborated with me from June 2012 to March 2013. The ethnographic material on the ten women and their businesses that I explore in this chapter was thus produced in collaboration with Lety, whom I thank for her contribution. Lety's job was to conduct taped interviews, semi-structured, or fairly open and informal, with women and men working in Santo Domingo's popular

economy. She did the interviews in the street and in markets—that is, where the persons worked. Some interviews were conducted with female and male sellers of fruit, vegetables, plantains, meat, and fish; others with female owners of food stalls; and yet others with male drivers. Lety had a gift for ethnographically oriented exploration. Her long, taped conversations covered life stories, business activities, everyday routines, social networks, and the management of money, credit, and debt. After Lety's interviews, I conducted follow-up research. In the years 2012–14, I sought out and visited the different places where she had interviewed people, observed, and written notes. I continued, through informal conversations, the dialogues that Lety had begun with her interviews. In this chapter, I draw on both Lety's observations and taped interviews, and my own observations and conversations with the women in question.

3. Over the last ten or fifteen years, the concept of precarity has occupied a more central position within the social sciences, including anthropology—although anthropologists and ethnographers have long mapped and analyzed historically and socially specific forms of precarity and how these are conceptualized, experienced, and lived by groups and individuals in different contexts. For a set of discussions on the concept of precarity and on the analysis of (forms of) precarity, see the following: Stewart (2012), Muehleback (2013), Millar (2014, 2018), Das and Randeria (2015), Bear (2016), and Harvey (2018). In my treatment of forms of precarity in contemporary Dominican society in this chapter and this book, I am inspired by the general perspectives that are found in these works.

4. For an ethnographically driven analysis from one of these areas in the Zona Norte, the infamous squatter settlement La Ciénaga, located on the banks of the Ozama River, see Erin B. Taylor's *Materializing Poverty: How the Poor Transform Their Lives* (2013). The book maps and examines in detail residents' efforts to construct housing and the barrio, and more generally to achieve a measure of control of their environment (see especially chapters 2, 3, and 5).

5. Trujillo was assassinated in 1961, and Balaguer died in 2002. However, before he died, Balaguer helped Leonel Fernández and the PLD rise to power. In 1996, PLD candidate Fernández won the presidency. Fernández, who had been brought up in the United States, secured more than 51 percent of the votes through an alliance with the old despot, Balaguer, and his party. Before the election, Fernández worked to move the PLD toward a less radical or more "centrist" position, advocating economic liberalization and the privatization of state enterprises. Fernández ruled from 1996 to 2000 and subsequently from 2004 to 2012. For more on the PLD rule and its authoritarian, corrupt, and excluding forms and practices in the years 1996–2020, see the introduction and chapter 1.

6. See Junot Díaz's three books, *Drown* (1996), *The Brief Wondrous Life of Oscar Wao* (2007), and *This Is How You Lose Her* (2012). For a fine reading of

Díaz on Dominican/Dominican American masculinity in *The Brief Wondrous Life of Oscar Wao*, see Ramírez (2018:123–48). Two detailed ethnographic studies of sex tourism and sex work in the Dominican Republic—Denise Brennan's *What's Love Got to Do with It?* (2004), and Mark Padilla's *Caribbean Pleasure Industry* (2007)—contain some of the best and most nuanced analyses that we have of (shifting) gender norms and sexual identities among ordinary Dominicans.

7. These insights—or Smith's general views—have relevance for the understanding of most of the Caribbean, including colonial and postcolonial Santo Domingo. As Anne Eller argues, "Dominican colonial elites shared the aspirations of their neighbors, even if a lack of capital frustrated them. Anguished appeals of some eighteenth-century *letrados* to the Crown demonstrate how some colonists dearly hoped the spoils of cattle sales to [French] Saint-Domingue might bring more bondage in the east as well. The relentless will to increase the purchase of people for slave labor ought to be instructive of the proslavery mindset of Dominican colonists with a degree of prosperity, no matter the steady failure of their pleas. Traditional historiography that emphasizes Santo Domingo as isolated or fundamentally different from its plantation neighbors elides the continued presence of slavery and racism in the territory, how many Dominicans responded to these pressures, and the reborn plantation state that almost was" (2014:84).

8. The central meaning of this label, the *tíguere* (the word is spelled the way Dominicans pronounce *tigre*, the Spanish word for "tiger"), is "survivor in his environment." In today's Dominican society, the term is used to classify men in a wide range of positions (e.g., an engineer or a worker, a congress deputy or a lower level public employee, a professor or a student). Those whose conduct is classified with this label are mainly men. But the label is also used about women (in which case one employs the female form, *tiguerona*). The *tíguere* is the type who acts according to the situation, has a gift for improvisation, surmounts obstacles, challenges conventions, and skillfully, if not always ethically or legally, manipulates the surroundings to his advantage. Common to most of those men referred to by this label is that they seem to embody a moral and political force or power that is ambiguous. The ideas about the *tíguere* have shaped, and continue to shape, a man who is both courageous and smart, both cunning and convincing, and a gifted talker who gets out of most situations in a manner acceptable to others, while he himself at no moment steps back, stops chasing, or loses sight of his aim (be that women, money, a job, a promotion . . .). For more on the subject of the Dominican uses of the label *tíguere*, see Collado (1992), Krohn-Hansen (1996), de Moya (2003), Padilla (2007:132–40), Derby (2009:114–15), and Gregory (2014:41–42).

9. Sidney Mintz (1996:104) defines cuisine as "the ongoing foodways of a region, within which active discourse about food sustains both common

understandings and reliable production of the foods in question." For a brilliant historical discussion of the interpenetration between food and nationalism in the Dominican Republic, see Derby (1998). For a book that seeks to map the emergence of the Dominican cuisine, see Hugo Tolentino Dipp's *Itinerario histórico de la gastronomía dominicana* (2014). For an essay that traces the emergence of the *comida criolla*, or national cuisine, in neighboring Cuba, see Dawdy (2002).

10. According to Richard Turits (2003:28), the sudden collapse of the colony's sugar industry was "caused not primarily by local conditions but rather by the constraints imposed by Spain's evolving commercial policies toward the New World: limitations on trade with ports other than Seville, high prices demanded by Spanish merchants for imports, licensing restrictions hindering the expansion of the slave trade (thus raising slave prices), and, most decisively, a dramatic decline in the number of vessels docking on Santo Domingo's shores and hence the colony's inability to market its sugar."

11. For instructive descriptions (as well as contested discussions) of the Dominican peasantry's slash-and-burn cultivation methods, agricultural products, daily diet, and use of the plantain in the 1890s and early 1900s, see two classic essays by the Dominican writer and social reformer, José Ramón López: "La alimentación y las razas" (1975 [1896]) and "La caña de azúcar en San Pedro de Macorís, desde el bosque virgen hasta el mercado" (1991 [1907]:76–78).

12. This was representative. Because of women's domestic responsibilities, they often needed their enterprise to be in, or right by, the home. Cely (1996:62) found that between the years 1992 and 1995, 88–97 percent of Dominican female entrepreneurs reported that they were engaged simultaneously in domestic activities alongside their businesses (compared to less than 15 percent of male entrepreneurs during the same period).

13. It is essential to recognize this. The business was these women's tool, a means—not a decisive goal in itself. Poor female micro-entrepreneurs' enterprises in the so-called informal sector must be assessed in terms of a composite (and shifting) set of criteria. I back Sherry Grasmuck and Rosario Espinal when they assert (in a study from 2000 of the impact of gender on the relative economic success of micro-entrepreneurs in the Dominican Republic): "women's businesses must be evaluated not only in terms of market criteria but in terms of their social contributions as well. From a gendered perspective, two areas of strategic concern in any analysis of this sector should be the contributions of their businesses to household income and welfare and the empowerment of women as a result of their business activities" (235).

14. In the 1980s, several nongovernmental organizations (NGOs), such as ADEMI (Association for the Development of Micro-enterprises), PROAPE (Program for the Assistance of Small Firms), and Banco de la Mujer (Women's Bank),

began providing credit to small-business owners in the country's informal sector and expanded their lending programs (Grasmuck and Espinal 2000:232).

15. Banks (such as BanReservas, Banco Popular Dominicano, Banco BHD Leon, Citibank, Scotiabank República Dominicana) are the main formal source of private-sector financing in the Dominican Republic. Most of the banks' lending is short term (one to five years), although financing for construction or tourist projects with government funding has terms of twelve years and more. *Empresas financieras,* or finance firms, provide short- and medium-term loans to commercial and industrial sectors. These firms provide loans when commercial banks are unable or reluctant to do so, and with the highest rate of the market. Some finance firms are large, others small. Some of them have been created with the aid of money made in other sectors of the Dominican economy, others by means of money earned abroad, and yet others by means of capital derived from mystical and/or illegal activities. Others who were providing loans to poor Dominicans at the time of my fieldwork were individual *prestamistas* or moneylenders (loan sharks) and Dominican savings and credit cooperatives. I discuss the savings and credit cooperatives' significance and practices in chapter 4. For a fine overview and study of Dominican formal and informal credit providers in the years 2005–7, see Derek Brandon Lewis's thesis, "The Head of the Mouse: Dominican Microenterprises' Formal and Informal Credit Decisions" (2007).

16. Two monographs—Clara Han's *Life in Debt* (2012) from neoliberal Chile, and Deborah James's *Money from Nothing* (2015) from postapartheid South Africa—offer some of the richest and most nuanced studies that we have of credit and debt processes among urban poor. For more on the anthropology of credit and debt (in general, and among poor populations), see Peebles (2010), Graeber (2011), Guérin et al. (2013), Guérin (2014), Villarreal (2014), and Bear (2015b).

17. In the Dominican Republic, there is no current regulation limiting the amount of interest that can be charged by lenders, and there is thus no usury rate or maximum allowable rate of interest in the Dominican jurisdiction. The country's banking law and regulations provide that financial operations shall be done under free market conditions, and that the interest rate of transactions will be freely determined among market agents.

18. The data in this chapter support Tsing's (2009, 2015) argument about how we should think (conceptualize) the structure of contemporary capitalism. In sharp contrast with theories of growing capitalist homogeneity, Tsing argues that cultural diversity is structurally central to capitalism, and not an epiphenomenon. In the Zona Norte, women gravitate into the niches that are the focus of this chapter through a process of structural violence *and* their own creative forms of agency. These niches (with their labor forms) are reproduced, as Tsing insists, in

performances of cultural identity. They are given shape by the women's gender, notions of foodways, and ideas about creoleness and Dominicanness, and so on. The finance firms that provide small-business owners in Santo Domingo's poor areas with loans make good money. The debt relations in question are, as we have seen, intensively extractive over time—sharply exploiting. Women in today's Zona Norte who run precarious *ventorrillos* and food stalls are entirely incorporated into the global capitalist economy. In Tsing's (2009:159) words, in their "conflations of self- and superexploitation" they help to make contemporary capitalism possible. See in addition Bear et al. (2015).

Chapter 3

1. My first encounter with Dominican *colmados* was in 1991–92 when I carried out my first fieldwork among Dominicans in the southwestern region of the country, in the community of La Descubierta. From 2002 to 2008, I conducted ethnographic research on Dominican New Yorkers' small businesses, including street-corner grocery stores and small and medium-sized independent supermarkets. From mid-2012 to 2017, I gathered ethnographic material on different types of small economic ventures in various parts of the Dominican capital; the research included *colmados* and small independent supermarkets. This chapter is based on all this research, in addition to my reading of other scholars' works, as well as Dominican and US newspaper articles.

2. My reconstruction of La Descubierta's history is based mainly on two kinds of sources: oral histories produced through my thirteen months of fieldwork in the early 1990s, and Jesús María Ramírez's autobiographic book *Mis 43 años en La Descubierta* (My 43 Years in La Descubierta; 2000). For more on the sources and La Descubierta's history, see Krohn-Hansen (2009, especially 49–94).

3. Joaquín Balaguer, who held important positions under Trujillo and was one of the regime's leading ideologues, ruled the country from 1966 until 1978. Eight years later, he regained the Dominican presidency and thereafter stayed in power until 1996.

4. For a vivid, instructive ethnographic description of one such trip to the market, Santo Domingo's Mercado Nuevo in the north of the city, see Murray (1996:65–96).

5. In Puerto Rico and Cuba, small neighborhood grocery stores are called bodegas, and New York's Latinos also call the city's small groceries bodegas. In 1991, Dominican immigrants owned and ran around 80 percent of the approximately 9,000 bodegas and independent groceries controlled by Latinos in New York City (Martinez Alequin 1991; Silverman 1991).

6. See note 1, above in this chapter, for more on my field research in Dominican New York.

7. See also Purnima Mankekar's "'India Shopping': Indian Grocery Stores and Transnational Configurations of Belonging" (2002). Mankekar shows how Indian-owned grocery stores in the San Francisco Bay Area enable the making and remaking of India and Indian culture in today's United States. For more on (the comparative study of) the relationship between food memories and the construction and reconstruction of identity, see Abarca and Colby (2016).

8. For more on this, see Krohn-Hansen (2013:185–87), and Pessar (1995:24).

9. For more on the restructuring and the opening of the Dominican economy from the early 1990s onward, see Moya Pons (2010:444–48, 458–59) and Gregory (2014:1–30). See also the introduction and chapter 1 in this book.

10. For more on the history and the economic activities of Dominicans of Chinese descent, see del Castillo (1984:171–75).

11. In this and the following paragraphs, I outline some important changes in the Dominican grocery business since the late 1990s. A main source has been oral histories. From mid-2012 to 2014, I recorded long conversations and informal interviews with ten different owners and operators of independent supermarkets in Santo Domingo. In addition, I have talked with many others and written notes. In addition, I have used the following sources: Lara Batista et al. (2003) and Ramos (2011).

12. My interlocutors (that is, representatives of the industry) estimated, in 2013, that there were around 600–700 independent supermarkets in the country. In the capital, they estimated, there were around 200–300.

13. Two other important works on the supermarket and its history are Hamilton (2018) and Lorr (2020).

14. For more on the concept of transculturation, see Ortiz (1995 [1940]), Coronil (1995), and Palmié (2013).

15. The main source for my data on the foundation and development of the Grupo Ramos is a presentation given by Mercedes Ramos (current head of the company) at a conference in Santo Domingo in July 2011 (see Ramos 2011).

16. In 1963, Juan Bosch's government was overthrown by a military coup (after only seven months in power). In April 1965, civil war broke out in the capital between pro-Bosch and anti-Bosch forces. Peace, or a Pax Americana, was then imposed, when President Johnson ordered 42,000 US Marines to Santo Domingo in order to stop Bosch and prevent "a second Cuba in America." This was the prelude to the era of Joaquín Balaguer.

17. The Ramos Group is now among the country's largest private employers. In 2020, the number of employees was approximately 10,000. A large proportion of the workers in the stores are women who are paid something around the national minimum wage, which is low, not to say miserable—well below what any ordinary household needs to manage. In 2015, it was 11,300 pesos, or about US$248, a month.

18. For an impressive ethnographic exploration of the important place of *colmados* in the provisioning strategies of poor people in the northern coastal town of Cabarete, an international tourism destination, see Christine Hippert's *Not Even a Grain of Rice* (2021). The book demonstrates in detail how a common practice in most of the country—*comprando fiao*, or buying food on credit from *colmados*—offers a window into relationships between Dominicans, Dominicans of Haitian descent, and Haitian (im)migrants in this part of the Dominican Republic.

19. The Dominican Labor Code, which became law in June 1992, is a comprehensive piece of legislation that establishes policies and procedures for many aspects of the employer-employee relationships.

Chapter 4

1. Fournier quotes from Marcel Mauss, "L'action socialiste," *Mouvement socialiste* (15 October 1899): 458, 461–62.

2. Fournier's quotation is from Marcel Mauss, "Le Congrès international des coopératives socialistes," *Mouvement Socialiste* 2 (15 October 1900): 499–501.

3. It is true that the dictatorship saw some labor unrest in the early and mid-1940s that concurred with a flourishing foreign trade. Sugar workers managed to get wage increases, but the incipient social movement was rapidly suppressed by the regime (Cassá 1990:341–498).

4. For more on the *colmado*, see chapter 3.

5. "Puñal" is a pseudonym.

6. I did intermittent fieldwork in these cooperatives from 2012 to 2017, and chose them because they were relatively small, accessible, and different. Both were members of CONACOOP, and that organization's leaders assisted me in establishing initial contact with the leaders of the two cooperatives. I talked with, and interviewed, leaders and ordinary members; sought out the cooperatives' offices; spent a significant amount of time in the community of Puñal; and attended a series of members' meetings in both cooperatives.

7. As David Graeber, among others, has pointed out, it seems obvious that Mauss must have written his most famous work, his "Essay on the Gift," in 1925 (or at about the same time as he wrote his "A Sociological Assessment of Bolshevism (1924–5)"), in response to the crisis of socialism: "If it was impossible to simply legislate the money economy away, even in Russia, the least monetarized society in Europe, then perhaps revolutionaries needed to start looking at the ethnographic record to see what sort of creature the market really was, and what viable alternatives to capitalism might look like. Hence his 'Essay on the Gift'" (Graeber 2004:17).

8. For more on the comprehensive corruption in the country and on how it

works, see the introduction and chapter 1. For an instructive comparative perspective, see Muir and Gupta (2018).

9. Robertson's quotation is from the *Birmingham Co-operative Society Quarterly Report*, 3 October 1953.

10. I use the word "politics" in a wide, anthropological sense (Krohn-Hansen 2015).

11. As several authors have underscored, it is essential, when we look at cooperatives, to always seek to read "community" ideologies or "community" discourses sufficiently critically (Narotzky 1988; 1997:120; Narotzky and Smith 2006; Rakopoulos 2015). As Theodoros Rakopoulos (2015:57) argues, the members of cooperatives (and of the communities to which the cooperatives in question belong) "may well belong to different 'communities' and hence appeals to 'community mutuality' can very well contradict economic democracy in cooperativism." My discussion about Puñal shows that many in Puñal, and in the cooperative of Puñal, knew well that their own and others' use of the term "community" had to be decoded—that it was an expression of interests and political positioning.

12. *Progreso* corresponds to an idea of historical change: over time, things get better. For more on the concept and ideal of *progreso* among Dominicans, see chapter 3. See also Hoffnung-Garskof (2008:11–43).

13. For a study of a related (but different) case, that of entrepreneurial Dominican livery cab cooperatives in New York, see Krohn-Hansen (2019).

14. See also Yanagisako (2002) and Tsing (2015).

Chapter 5

1. For more on the surplus population debate, see Kay (1991:42–46).

2. This is in line with the perspective of Marcel van der Linden in his *Workers of the World: Essays toward a Global Labour History* (2008). Van der Linden proposes a greater focus on the way in which labor power is commodified by capitalism in different forms and suggests, for example, that the concept of "subaltern labor" should be extended to also include self-employment, sharecropping, indentured labor, and chattel slavery (2008:331).

3. "Silences," explains Trouillot, "enter the process of historical production at four crucial moments: the moment of fact creation (the making of *sources*); the moment of fact assembly (the making of *archives*); the moment of fact retrieval (the making of *narratives*); and the moment of retrospective significance (the making of *history* in the final instance)" (1995:26, emphasis in original).

4. For more on this, see chapter 1.

5. See also James Ferguson's many-faceted analyses in his great book, *Expectations of Modernity: Myths and Meanings of Urban Life on the Zambian Copperbelt* (1999).

6. In this book, and specifically in this chapter, I do not attempt to be exhaustive, or to cover all significant or possible research tasks. In addition to posing a series of questions about land, housing, labor, and time, the researcher should also ask what are the other livelihood resources, or income-generating activities, that are significant in a given social field. Two income sources that are of varying importance for households in many places are migrant remittances (Pedersen 2013; Sandoval-Cervantes 2017; Zharkevich 2019; Wright 2020) and state welfare or protection programs dispensing cash transfers (Ferguson 2007, 2015).

Afterword

1. The Partido Revolucionario Moderno (PRM) emerged after a new split within the Partido Revolucionario Dominicano (PRD), a party that was founded in 1939 by a group of expatriate Dominicans living in Havana, Cuba, led by Juan Bosch. The PRM was founded in September 2014, when most senior leaders of the PRD (widely known as *los viejos robles*, "the ancient oaks") joined Luis Abinader to create a new party.

2. Here, I draw on an instructive article about the fall of the Odebrecht corruption empire and the Medina regime, Ezra Fieser's (2017) "A Graft Machine's Collapse Sows Chaos in the Caribbean."

3. Based on the Johns Hopkins Coronavirus Resource Center, the Ministry of Public Health of the Dominican Republic, and the World Health Organization.

References

Abarca, Meredith E., and Joshua R. Colby. 2016. "Food Memories Seasoning the Narratives of Our Lives." *Food and Foodways* 24, nos. 1–2:1–8.

Abdullaev, Umidjon, and Marcello Estevão. 2013. "Growth and Employment in the Dominican Republic: Options for a Job-Rich Growth." IMF Working Paper WP/13/40. Washington, DC: International Monetary Fund.

Abieu Lopez, Ezequiel. 2020. "Dominican Republic's New President Takes Office Warning of Tough Recovery." *Reuters*, 16 August. https://www.usnews.com/news/world/articles/2020-08-16/dominican-republics-new-president-takes-office-warning-of-tough-recovery.

Abrams, Philip. 1988 [1977]. "Notes on the Difficulty of Studying the State." *Journal of Historical Sociology* 1, no. 1:58–89.

Anand, Nikhil, Akhil Gupta, and Hannah Appel, eds. 2018. *The Promise of Infrastructure*. Durham, NC: Duke University Press.

Anderson, Jennifer L. 2004. "Nature's Currency: The Atlantic Mahogany Trade and the Commodification of Nature in the Eighteenth Century." *Early American Studies: An Interdisciplinary Journal* 2, no. 1:47–80.

Anderson, Jennifer L. 2012. *Mahogany: The Costs of Luxury in Early America*. Cambridge, MA: Harvard University Press.

Appel, Hannah, Nikhil Anand, and Akhil Gupta. 2018. "Introduction: Temporality, Politics, and the Promise of Infrastructure." In N. Anand, A. Gupta, and H. Appel, eds., *The Promise of Infrastructure*, 1–38. Durham, NC: Duke University Press.

Aretxaga, Begoña. 2003. "Maddening States." *Annual Review of Anthropology* 32:393–410.

Aristy Escuder, Jaime. 2012. *El lado oscuro de la SunLand*. Santo Domingo: Editora Búho, S.R.L.

Auyero, Javier. 2012. *Patients of the State: The Politics of Waiting in Argentina*. Durham, NC: Duke University Press.

Baca, George, Aisha Khan, and Stephan Palmié, eds. 2009. *Empirical Futures: Anthropologists and Historians Engage the Work of Sidney W. Mintz*. Chapel Hill: University of North Carolina Press.

Barinas, Sócrates, and Mariana Viollaz. 2020. "Social and Economic Impacts of the COVID-19 and Policy Option in the Dominican Republic." UNDP Latin America and the Caribbean COVID-19 Policy Document Series No. 15. New York: UN Development Programme.

Bear, Laura. 2014a. "Doubt, Conflict, Mediation: The Anthropology of Modern Time." *Journal of the Royal Anthropological Institute* 20, S1:3–30.

Bear, Laura. 2014b. "For Labour: Ajeet's Accident and the Ethics of Technological Fixes in Time." *Journal of the Royal Anthropological Institute* 20, S1:71–88.

Bear, Laura. 2015a. "Beyond Economization: State Debt and Labor." In "Fieldsights—Theorizing the Contemporary," special section, *Cultural Anthropology* online, March 30. https://culanth.org/fieldsights/beyond-economization-state-debt-and-labor.

Bear, Laura. 2015b. *Navigating Austerity: Currents of Debt along a South Asian River*. Stanford: Stanford University Press.

Bear, Laura. 2016. "Time as Technique." *Annual Review of Anthropology* 45:487–502.

Bear, Laura, Karen Ho, Anna Tsing, and Sylvia Yanagisako. 2015. "Gens: A Feminist Manifesto for the Study of Capitalism." In "Fieldsights—Theorizing the Contemporary," special section, *Cultural Anthropology* online, March 30. https://culanth.org/fieldsights/gens-a-feminist-manifesto-for-the-study-of-capitalism.

Benítez-Rojo, Antonio. 1992. *The Repeating Island: The Caribbean and the Postmodern Perspective*. Durham, NC: Duke University Press.

Betances, Emelio. 1995. *State and Society in the Dominican Republic*. Boulder, CO: Westview Press.

Borras, Saturnino M., Jr., Jennifer C. Franco, Sergio Gómez, Cristóbal Kay, and Max Spoor. 2012. "Land Grabbing in Latin America and the Caribbean." *Journal of Peasant Studies* 39, nos. 3–4:845–72.

Bosch, Juan. 1988 [1970]. *Composición social dominicana. Historia e interpretación*. Santo Domingo: Alfa y Omega.

Bourdieu, Pierre. 2002. *Masculine Domination*. Trans. R. Nice. Stanford: Stanford University Press.

Brennan, Denise 2004. *What's Love Got to Do with It? Transnational Desires and Sex Tourism in the Dominican Republic*. Durham, NC: Duke University Press.

Bryer, Alice R. 2012. "The Politics of the Social Economy: A Case Study of the Argentinean *Empresas Recuperadas.*" *Dialectical Anthropology* 36:21–49.

Buck-Morss, Susan. 2009. *Hegel, Haiti, and Universal History.* Pittsburgh: University of Pittsburgh Press.

Calvão, Filipe. 2016. "Unfree Labor." *Annual Review of Anthropology* 45:451–67.

Candelario, Ginetta E. B. 2007. *Black behind the Ears.* Durham, NC: Duke University Press.

Carbonella, August, and Sharryn Kasmir. 2014. "Introduction: Toward a Global Anthropology of Labor." In Kasmir and Carbonella, eds., *Blood and Fire: Toward a Global Anthropology of Labor*, 1–29. New York: Berghahn Books.

Cardoso, Fernando H. 1971. "Comentario sobre los conceptos de sobrepoblación relativa y marginalidad." *Revista latinoamericana de ciencias sociales* (Chile) 1–2:57–76.

Carneiro, Francisco G., and Sophie Sirtaine. 2017. "Overview." In Carneiro and Sirtaine, eds., *When Growth Is Not Enough: Explaining the Rigidity of Poverty in the Dominican Republic*, 1–14. Washington, DC: World Bank Group. https://openknowledge.worldbank.org/handle/10986/26711.

Carr-Saunders, A. M, P. Sargant Florence, and Robert Peers. 1938. *Consumers' Co-operation in Great Britain: An Examination of the British Co-operative Movement.* London: George Allen & Unwin.

Cassá, Roberto. 1990. *Movimiento obrero y lucha socialista en la República Dominicana.* Santo Domingo: Editora Taller.

Cassá, Roberto, and Fred Murphy. 1995. "Recent Popular Movements in the Dominican Republic." *Latin American Perspectives* 22, no. 3:80–93.

Castree, Noel. 2009. "The Spatio-Temporality of Capitalism." *Time and Society* 18:26–61.

Cely, Patricia. 1996. *Dinámica de las microempresas y pequeñas empresas de mujeres en La República Dominicana: 1992–1995.* Santo Domingo: Fondo para el financiamiento de la microempresa, Inc. (FondoMicro).

Chatterjee, Partha. 2004. *The Politics of the Governed: Reflections on Popular Politics in Most of the World.* New York: Columbia University Press.

Checker, Melissa, and Julie Hogeland. 2004. "Views on Policy: The Future of Cooperatives, Interdisciplinary Perspectives." *Anthropology News* 45, no. 5:33–34.

Coates, David. 2000. *Models of Capitalism: Growth and Stagnation in the Modern Era.* Cambridge: Polity Press.

Collado, Lipe. 1992. *El Tíguere Dominicano.* Santo Domingo: Editora El Mundo.

CONACOOP (Consejo Nacional de Cooperativas de la República Dominicana). 2010. *Estudio diagnóstico del sector cooperativo de la República Dominicana.* Santo Domingo: CONACOOP.

CONACOOP (Consejo Nacional de Cooperativas de la República Dominicana), ed. 2011. *Cuarto Congreso CONACOOP: Cooperativismo, identidad y responsabilidad social.* Santo Domingo: CONACOOP.

CONACOOP (Consejo Nacional de Cooperativas de la República Dominicana). 2018. *Estudio: Impacto socioeconómico del cooperativismo en República Dominicana.* 1st ed. Santo Domingo: CONACOOP. https://elcooperadordigital. com/wp-content/uploads/2018/08/estudio-de-impacto-socioecnocmico- -del-cooperativismo-rd-6.pdf.

Coronil, Fernando. 1995. "Introduction to the Duke University Press Edition. Transculturation and the Politics of Theory: Countering the Center, Cuban Counterpoint." In Fernando Ortiz, *Cuban Counterpoint: Tobacco and Sugar,* introd. Bronislaw Malinowski, new introd. F. Coronil, ix–lvi. Durham, NC: Duke University Press.

Coronil, Fernando. 1997. *The Magical State: Nature, Money, and Modernity in Venezuela.* Chicago: University of Chicago Press.

Damirón, Rafael. 1938. "El Friquitin." In Damirón, *Estampas,* 67–72. Ciudad Trujillo, Distrito de Santo Domingo: Imp. Listín Diario.

Das, Veena, and Deborah Poole, eds. 2004. *Anthropology in the Margins of the State.* Santa Fe, NM: School of American Research Press.

Das, Veena, and Shalini Randeria. 2015. "Politics of the Urban Poor: Aesthetics, Ethics, Volatility, Precarity: An Introduction to Supplement 11." *Current Anthropology* 56, S11:S3–S14.

Davis, David B. 1975. *The Problem of Slavery in the Age of Revolution, 1770–1823.* Ithaca, NY: Cornell University Press.

Davis, Mike. 2006. *Planet of Slums.* London: Verso.

Dawdy, Shannon L. 2002. "'La Comida Mambisa': Food, Farming, and Cuban Identity, 1839–1999." *New West Indian Guide / Nieuwe West-Indische Gids* 76, nos. 1–2:47–80.

de Janvry, Alain, and Carlos Garramón. 1977. "The Dynamics of Rural Poverty in Latin America." *Journal of Peasant Studies* 4, no. 3:206–16.

del Castillo, José 1984. *Ensayos de Sociología Dominicana.* 2nd ed. Santo Domingo: Editora Taller, C por A.

de Moya, E. Antonio. 2003. "Power Games and Totalitarian Masculinity in the Dominican Republic." In Rhoda E. Reddock, ed., *Interrogating Caribbean Masculinities: Theoretical and Empirical Analyses,* 68–102. Kingston: University of the West Indies Press.

Denning, Michael. 2010. "Wageless Life." *New Left Review* 66:79–97.

Derby, Lauren. 1998. "Gringo Chickens with Worms: Food and Nationalism in the Dominican Republic." In Gilbert M. Joseph, Catherine C. LeGrand, and Ricardo D. Salvatore, eds., *Close Encounters of Empire: Writing the Cultural*

History of U.S.–Latin American Relations, 451–93. Durham, NC: Duke University Press.

Derby, Lauren. 2003. "The Dictator's Seduction: The Moral Economy of Domination during the Trujillo Regime in the Dominican Republic." Paper presented at the American Association for Anthropology Annual Meetings, Chicago.

Derby, Lauren. 2009. *The Dictator's Seduction*. Durham, NC: Duke University Press.

Díaz, Junot. 1996. *Drown*. New York: Riverhead Books.

Díaz, Junot. 2007. *The Brief Wondrous Life of Oscar Wao*. New York: Riverhead Books.

Díaz, Junot. 2012. *This Is How You Lose Her*. New York: Riverhead Books.

ECLAC (Economic Commission for Latin America and the Caribbean). 2021. "Financing for Development in the Era of COVID-19 and Beyond." COVID-19 Special Report 10, Santiago.

Eller, Anne. 2014. "'Awful Pirates' and 'Hordes of Jackals': Santo Domingo/The Dominican Republic in Nineteenth-Century Historiography." *Small Axe* 18, no. 2:80–94.

Espinal, José A. 2017. "Fiscal dice funcionarios vagos, corruptos obstaculizan Justicia." *Hoy*, 27 October, 12B.

Espinal, Rosario. 1987. "Labor, Politics, and Industrialization in the Dominican Republic." Working Paper 96. Notre Dame, IN: Kellogg Institute for International Studies at the University of Notre Dame.

Espinal, Rosario. 2017. "¿Populismo penal? Oh No!" *Hoy*, 25 October, 10A.

Ferguson, James. 1999. *Expectations of Modernity: Myths and Meanings of Urban Life on the Zambian Copperbelt*. Berkeley: University of California Press.

Ferguson, James. 2006. "Decomposing Modernity: History and Hierarchy after Development." In Ferguson, *Global Shadows*, 176–93. Durham, NC: Duke University Press.

Ferguson, James. 2007. "Formalities of Poverty: Thinking about Social Assistance in Neoliberal South Africa." *African Studies Review* 50, no. 2:71–86.

Ferguson, James. 2009. "The Uses of Neoliberalism." *Antipode* 41, S1:166–84.

Ferguson, James. 2013. "Declarations of Dependence: Labour, Personhood, and Welfare in Southern Africa." *Journal of the Royal Anthropological Institute* 19, no. 2:223–42.

Ferguson, James. 2015. *Give a Man a Fish: Reflections on the New Politics of Distribution*. Durham, NC: Duke University Press.

Ferguson, James. 2019. "Proletarian Politics Today: On the Perils and Possibilities of Historical Analogy." *Comparative Studies in Society and History* 61, no. 1:4–22.

Ferguson, James, and Akhil Gupta. 2002. "Spatializing States: Toward an Ethnography of Neo-Liberal Governmentality." *American Ethnologist* 29, no.
4:981–1002.

Ferguson, James, and Tania M. Li. 2018. "Beyond the 'Proper Job': Political-Economic Analysis after the Century of Labouring Man." PLAAS Working Paper
51. Cape Town: Institute for Poverty, Land and Agrarian Studies, University
of the Western Cape.

Fieser, Ezra. 2017. "A Graft Machine's Collapse Sows Chaos in the Caribbean." *Bloomberg*, 12 June. https://www.bloomberg.com/news/fea-
tures/2017-06-12/odebrecht-corruption-machine-s-collapse-sows-chaos-in-
the-dominican-republic.

Fournier, Marcel. 2006. *Marcel Mauss: A Biography*. Trans. J.M. Todd. Princeton:
Princeton University Press.

Freeman, Carla. 2014. *Entrepreneurial Selves. Neoliberal Respectability and the
Making of a Caribbean Middle Class*. Durham, NC: Duke University Press.

Fulcar, Julito. 2011. "Discurso Central." In CONACOOP, ed., *Cuarto Congreso
CONACOOP: Cooperativismo, identidad y responsabilidad social*, 23–29. Santo
Domingo: CONACOOP.

García, Pablo. 2017. "Parques públicos de zonas francas, a media capacidad."
elDinero (Santo Domingo) 3, no. 115 (17–23 April): 10–11.

Geertz, Clifford 1962. "The Rotating Credit Association: A 'Middle-Rung' in Development." *Economic Development and Cultural Change* 10, no. 3:241–63.

Geertz, Clifford. 1963. *Peddlers and Princes*. Chicago: University of Chicago
Press.

Gell, Alfred. 1992. *The Anthropology of Time: Cultural Constructions of Temporal
Maps and Images*. Oxford: Berg.

Goldstein, Daniel M. 2016. *Owners of the Sidewalk: Security and Survival in the
Informal City*. Durham, NC: Duke University Press.

Gordon, Sarah M. 2016. "The Foreign Corrupt Practices Act: Prosecute Corruption and End Transnational Illegal Logging." *Boston College Environmental Affairs Law Review* 43. https://lawdigitalcommons.bc.edu/ealr/vol43/
iss1/5/.

Graeber, David. 2001. *Toward An Anthropological Theory of Value*. New York:
Palgrave.

Graeber, David. 2002. "The Anthropology of Globalization (with Notes on Neo-
medievalism, and the End of the Chinese Model of the Nation-State)." *American Anthropologist* 104, no. 4:1222–27.

Graeber, David. 2004. *Fragments of an Anarchist Anthropology*. Chicago: Prickly
Paradigm Press.

Graeber, David. 2011. *Debt: The First 5,000 Years*. Brooklyn, NY: Melville Publishing House.

Grandin, Greg. 2013. "Empire's Ruins: Detroit to the Amazon." In Ann L. Stoler, ed., *Imperial Debris: On Ruins and Ruination*, 115–28. Durham, NC: Duke University Press.

Granovetter, Mark. 1995. "The Economic Sociology of Firms and Entrepreneurs." In Alejandro Portes, ed., *The Economic Sociology of Immigration*, 128–65. New York: Russell Sage Foundation.

Grasmuck, Sherri, and Patricia R. Pessar. 1991. *Between Two Islands*. Berkeley: University of California Press.

Grasmuck, Sherri, and Rosario Espinal. 2000. "Market Success or Female Autonomy? Income, Ideology, and Empowerment among Microentrepreneurs in the Dominican Republic." *Gender & Society* 14, no. 2:231–55.

Greenberg, James B. 1997. "A Political Ecology of Structural-Adjustment Policies: The Case of the Dominican Republic." *Culture and Agriculture* 19, no. 3:85–93.

Gregory, Steven. 1998. *Black Corona*. Princeton: Princeton University Press.

Gregory, Steven. 2014. *The Devil behind the Mirror: Globalization and Politics in the Dominican Republic*. Berkeley: University of California Press.

Guarnizo, Luis E. 1992. "One Country in Two: Dominican-Owned Firms in New York and the Dominican Republic." PhD diss., Johns Hopkins University.

Guérin, Isabelle. 2014. "Juggling with Debt, Social Ties, and Values: The Everyday Use of Microcredit in Rural South India." *Current Anthropology* 55, S9:S40–S50.

Guérin, Isabelle, Solène Morvant-Roux, and Magdalena Villarreal, eds. 2013. *Microfinance, Debt and Over-Indebtedness: Juggling with Money*. London: Routledge.

Guisarre, Carlos A. 2007. "Las butacas extranjeras 'sientan' a las nacionales." *Listín Diario*, 28 July. https://listindiario.com/economia/2007/07/28/22283/las-butacas-extranjeras-sientan-a-las-nacionales.

Gupta, Akhil. 1995. "Blurred Boundaries: The Discourse of Corruption, the Culture of Politics, and the Imagined State." *American Ethnologist* 22, no. 2:375–402.

Gupta, Akhil. 2012. *Red Tape: Bureaucracy, Structural Violence, and Poverty in India*. Durham, NC: Duke University Press.

Gupta, Akhil. 2015. "An Anthropology of Electricity from the Global South." *Cultural Anthropology* 30, no. 4:555–68.

Guyer, Jane I. 2004. *Marginal Gains: Monetary Transactions in Atlantic Africa*. Chicago: University of Chicago Press.

Guyer, Jane I. 2012. "Obligation, Binding, Debt and Responsibility: Provocations about Temporality from Two New Sources." *Social Anthropology* 20:491–501.

Guyer, Jane I., LaRay Denzer, and Adigun Agbaje, eds. 2002. *Money Struggles and City Life: Devaluation in Ibadan and Other Urban Centers in Southern Nigeria 1986–1996*. Portsmouth, NH: Heinemann.

Hamilton, Shane. 2018. *Supermarket USA: Food and Power in the Cold War Farms Race*. New Haven: Yale University Press.

Han, Clara. 2011. "Symptoms of Another Life: Time, Possibility, and Domestic Relations in Chile's Credit Economy." *Cultural Anthropology* 26, no. 1:7–32.

Han, Clara. 2012. *Life in Debt: Times of Care and Violence in Neoliberal Chile*. Berkeley: University of California Press.

Han, Clara. 2018. "Precarity, Precariousness, and Vulnerability." *Annual Review of Anthropology* 47:331–43.

Hart, Keith. 1973. "Informal Income Opportunities and Urban Employment in Ghana." *Journal of Modern African Studies* 11, no. 3:61–89.

Hart, Keith. 1992. "Market and State after the Cold War: The Informal Economy Reconsidered." In Roy Dilley, ed., *Contesting Markets*, 214–27. Edinburgh: Edinburgh University Press.

Hart, Keith. 2006. "Bureaucratic Form and the Informal Economy." In Basudeb Guha-Khasnobis, Ravi Kanbur, and Elinor Ostrom, eds., *Linking the Formal and Informal Economy: Concepts and Policies*, 21–35. Oxford: Oxford University Press.

Hartlyn, Jonathan. 1998. *The Struggle for Democratic Politics in the Dominican Republic*. Chapel Hill: University of North Carolina Press.

Harvey, David. 1989. *The Condition of Postmodernity: An Enquiry into the Origins of Cultural Change*. Oxford: Blackwell.

Harvey, David. 2003. *The New Imperialism*. Oxford: Oxford University Press.

Harvey, David. 2005. *A Brief History of Neoliberalism*. Oxford: Oxford University Press.

Harvey, Penny. 2018. "Interrupted Futures: Co-operative Labour and the Changing Forms of Collective Precarity in Rural Andean Peru." *Journal of the Royal Anthropological Institute* 24, S1:120–33.

Harvey, Penny, and Christian Krohn-Hansen. 2018. "Introduction: Dislocating Labour: Anthropological Reconfigurations." *Journal of the Royal Anthropological Institute* 24, S1:10–28.

Hegel, Georg W. F. 1991 [1822]. *The Philosophy of History*. Trans. John Sibree. Buffalo: Prometheus Books.

Hendricks, Glenn. 1974. *The Dominican Diaspora*. New York: Teachers College Press.

Hernández, Ramona, Francisco Rivera-Batiz, and Roberto Agodini. 1995.

Dominican New Yorkers: A Socioeconomic Profile, 1990. New York: CUNY Dominican Studies Institute.

Herzfeld, Michael. 2004. *The Body Impolitic: Artisans and Artifice in the Global Hierarchy of Value.* Chicago: University of Chicago Press.

Hippert, Christine. 2021. *Not Even a Grain of Rice: Buying Food on Credit in the Dominican Republic.* Lanham, MD: Lexington Books.

Hirschman, Albert O. 2013 [1977]. *The Passions and the Interests: Political Arguments for Capitalism before Its Triumph.* Princeton: Princeton University Press.

Hoetink, Harry. 1986. "The Dominican Republic, c. 1870–1930." In Leslie Bethell, ed., *The Cambridge History of Latin America,* 5:287–306. Cambridge: Cambridge University Press.

Hoffnung-Garskof, Jesse. 2008. *A Tale of Two Cities.* Princeton: Princeton University Press.

Horn, Maja. 2014. *Masculinity after Trujillo: The Politics of Gender in Dominican Literature.* Gainesville: University Press of Florida.

Howe, Cymene. 2014. "Anthropocenic Ecoauthority: The Winds of Oaxaca." *Anthropological Quarterly* 87, no. 2:381–404.

Hoy 2012a. "El parque industrial DISDO se ha convertido en un potrero." 15 February. https://hoy.com.do/el-parque-industrial-disdo-se-ha-convertido-en-un-potrero/.

Hoy 2012b. "Comerciantes Villa Consuelo se quejan por tanda de apagones." 8 May, 5E.

Hoy 2012c. "Deuda con generadores sube a US$1,000 millones." 26 July, 1E.

Hoy 2017. "Amplia mayoría considera alarmante niveles corrupción." 30 October, 8A.

Humphery, Kim. 1998. *Shelf Life: Supermarkets and the Changing Cultures of Consumption.* Cambridge: Cambridge University Press.

Ianni, Vanna. 1987. *El Territorio de las Masas: Espacios y movimientos sociales en República Dominicana abril 1984–abril 1986.* Santo Domingo: Editora Universitaria de la Universidad Autónoma de Santo Domingo.

ILO (International Labor Organization). 2018. *Women and Men in the Informal Economy: A Statistical Picture.* 3rd ed. Geneva: ILO.

Itzigsohn, José. 2000. *Developing Poverty: The State, Labor Market Deregulation, and the Informal Economy in Costa Rica and the Dominican Republic.* University Park: Pennsylvania State University Press.

James, Deborah. 2015. *Money from Nothing: Indebtedness and Aspiration in South Africa.* Stanford: Stanford University Press.

Jensen, Carsten B. 2017. "Pipe Dreams: Sewage Infrastructure and Activity Trails in Phnom Penh." *Ethnos* 82, no. 4:627–47.

Jiménez, Ramón E. 1929. "Platos Nacionales." In Jiménez, *Al Amor del Bohío*

(Tradiciones y costumbres Dominicanas), 2:69–72. Santiago, R.D.: Editora La Información C. por A.

Kasmir, Sharryn. 1999. "The Mondragón Model as Post-Fordist Discourse: Considerations on the Production of Post-Fordism." *Critique of Anthropology* 19, no. 4:379–400.

Kasmir, Sharryn. 2005. "Activism and Class Identity: The Saturn Auto Factory Case." In June Nash, ed., *Social Movements: An Anthropological Reader*, 78–96. Oxford: Blackwell.

Kasmir, Sharryn. 2012. "Alternatives to Capitalism and Working-class Struggle: A Comment on Alice Bryer's 'The Politics of the Social Economy.'" *Dialectical Anthropology* 36:59–61.

Kasmir, Sharryn, and August Carbonella, eds. 2014. *Blood and Fire: Toward a Global Anthropology of Labor*. New York: Berghahn Books.

Kay, Cristóbal. 1991. "Reflections on the Latin American Contribution to Development Theory." *Development and Change* 22, no. 1:31–68.

Kearney, Richard C. 1986. "Spoils in the Caribbean: The Struggle for Merit-Based Civil Service in the Dominican Republic." *Public Administration Review*, March–April: 144–51.

Kivland, Chelsey L. 2020. "The Spiral of Sovereignty: Enacting and Entangling the State from Haiti's Streets." *American Anthropologist* 122, no. 3: 501–13.

Kjaerulff, Jens. 2020. "Situating Time: New Technologies of Work, a Perspective from Alfred Gell's Oeuvre." *HAU: Journal of Ethnographic Theory* 10, no. 1:236–50.

Krohn-Hansen, Christian. 1995. "Magic, Money and Alterity among Dominicans." *Social Anthropology* 3, no. 2:129–46.

Krohn-Hansen, Christian. 1996. "Masculinity and the Political among Dominicans: 'The Dominican Tiger.'" In Marit Melhuus and Kristi A. Stølen, eds., *Machos, Mistresses, Madonnas*, 108–33. London: Verso.

Krohn-Hansen, Christian. 1997. "The Construction of Dominican State Power and Symbolisms of Violence." *Ethnos* 62, nos. 3–4:49–78.

Krohn-Hansen, Christian. 2001. "A Tomb for Columbus in Santo Domingo: Political Cosmology, Population and Racial Frontiers." *Social Anthropology* 9, no. 2:165–92.

Krohn-Hansen, Christian. 2005. "Negotiated Dictatorship: The Building of the Trujillo State in the Southwestern Dominican Republic." In Krohn-Hansen and Knut G. Nustad, eds., *State Formation*, 96–122. London: Pluto Press.

Krohn-Hansen, Christian. 2009. *Political Authoritarianism in the Dominican Republic*. New York: Palgrave Macmillan.

Krohn-Hansen, Christian. 2013. *Making New York Dominican: Small Business, Politics, and Everyday Life*. Philadelphia: University of Pennsylvania Press.

Krohn-Hansen, Christian. 2015. "Political Anthropology." In James D. Wright, ed., *International Encyclopedia of the Social and Behavioral Sciences*. 2nd ed. Oxford: Elsevier.

Krohn-Hansen, Christian. 2016. "The Dominican *Colmado* from Santo Domingo to New York." In William Beezley, ed., *Oxford Research Encyclopedia of Latin American History*. New York: Oxford University Press. latinamericanhistory. oxfordre.com/.

Krohn-Hansen, Christian. 2019. "Contemporary Capitalism and Dominican New Yorkers' Livery-Cab Bases: A Taxi Story." In Penny Harvey, Christian Krohn-Hansen, and Knut G. Nustad, eds., *Anthropos and the Material*, 59–80. Durham, NC: Duke University Press.

Krohn-Hansen, Christian, and Knut G. Nustad, eds. 2005. *State Formation: Anthropological Perspectives*. London: Pluto Press.

Lafargue, Paul. 2011. *The Right to Be Lazy: Essays by Paul Lafargue*. Ed. Bernard Marszalek. Oakland, CA: AK Press.

Lara Batista, Robin F., Marie-Andreé Amy, and Diomaris L. Díaz Núñez. 2003. "Las Alianzas Estratégicas como herramienta competitiva ante los retos de la globalización. Caso: Unión Nacional de Supermercados Económicos (UNASE)." BA thesis, Universidad Católica Santo Domingo.

Lazar, Sian. 2008. *El Alto, Rebel City: Self and Citizenship in Andean Bolivia*. Durham, NC: Duke University Press.

Lazar, Sian. 2012. "A Desire to Formalize Work? Comparing Trade Union Strategies in Bolivia and Argentina." *Anthropology of Work Review* 33, no. 1:15–24.

Lazar, Sian. 2017. *The Social Life of Politics: Ethics, Kinship, and Union Activism in Argentina*. Stanford: Stanford University Press.

Lewis, Derek B. 2007. "The Head of the Mouse: Dominican Microenterprises' Formal and Informal Credit Decisions." MA thesis, University of Florida.

Lewis, John. 1976. "Washington Heights and Changing Times." *New York Daily News*, 25 January.

Li, Tania M. 2010. "To Make Live or Let Die? Rural Dispossession and the Protection of Surplus Populations." *Antipode* 41, S1:66–93.

Li, Tania M. 2011. "Centering Labour in the Land Grab Debate." *Journal of Peasant Studies* 38, no. 2:281–98.

Li, Tania M. 2014. *Land's End: Capitalist Relations on an Indigenous Frontier*. Durham, NC: Duke University Press.

Linebaugh, Peter, and Marcus Rediker. 2000. *The Many-Headed Hydra: Sailors, Slaves, Commoners, and the Hidden History of the Revolutionary Atlantic*. Boston: Beacon Press.

López, José R. 1975 [1896]. "La Alimentación y las Razas." In López, *El Gran*

Pesimismo Dominicano, 29–68. Santiago, R.D.: Universidad Católica Madre y Maestra.

López, José R. 1991 [1907]. "La Caña de Azúcar en San Pedro de Macorís, desde el Bosque Virgen hasta el Mercado." In López, *Ensayos y artículos*, 63–89. Biblioteca de clásicos dominicanos 10. Santo Domingo: Ediciones de la Fundación Corripio.

Lorr, Benjamin. 2020. *The Secret Life of Groceries: The Dark Miracle of the American Supermarket*. New York: Avery.

Lozano, Wilfredo. 1997. "Dominican Republic: Informal Economy, the State, and the Urban Poor." In Alejandro Portes, Carlos Dore-Cabral, and Patricia Landolt, eds., *The Urban Caribbean: Transition to the New Global Economy*, 153–89. Baltimore: Johns Hopkins University Press.

MacGaffey, Janet, and Rémy Bazenguissa-Ganga. 2000. *Congo-Paris*. Bloomington: Indiana University Press (in association with International African Institute).

Mains, Daniel. 2012. "Blackouts and Progress: Privatization, Infrastructure, and a Developmentalist State in Jimma, Ethiopia." *Cultural Anthropology* 27:3–27.

Maldonado, Rainier. 2009. "Se reducen las ventas de muebles." *Listín Diario*, 13 May. https://listindiario.com/economia/2009/05/13/100977/se-reducen-las-ventas-de-mueblesnbsp.

Maldonado, Rainier. 2013. "Denuncian empresas grandes crean Pymes." *Diario-Libre*, 8 August, 21.

Mankekar, Purnima. 2002. "'India Shopping': Indian Grocery Stores and Transnational Configurations of Belonging." *Ethnos* 67, no. 1:75–98.

Mankekar, Purnima, and Akhil Gupta. 2019. "The Missed Period: Disjunctive Temporalities and the Work of Capital in an Indian BPO." *American Ethnologist* 46, no. 4:417–28.

Martínez, Samuel. 1995. *Peripheral Migrants: Haitians and Dominican Republic Sugar Plantations*. Knoxville: University of Tennessee Press.

Martínez, Samuel. 2010. "Excess: The Struggle for Expenditure on a Caribbean Sugar Plantation." *Current Anthropology* 51, no. 5:609–28.

Martinez Alequin, Rafael. 1991. "Who's Running the Bodega?" *New York Newsday*, 29 August.

Marx, Karl. 1993 [1885]. *Capital*. Vol. 2. Trans. David Fernbach. London: Penguin.

Mateo, Andrés L. 2017. "Seis ensayos de interpretación de lo que está ocurriendo." *Hoy*, 26 October, 11A.

Mathur, Nayanika. 2014. "The Reign of Terror of the Big Cat: Bureaucracy and the Mediation of Social Time in the Indian Himalaya." *Journal of the Royal Anthropological Institute* 20, no. 1:148–65.

Mauss, Marcel. 1923–24. "Essai sur le don. Forme et raison de l'échange dans les sociétés archaïques." *L'Année sociologique*, 2nd ser., 1:30–186.

Mauss, Marcel. 1984 [1924–25]. "A Sociological Assessment of Bolshevism (1924–5)." *Economy and Society* 13, no. 3:331–74.

May, Jon, and Nigel Thrift. 2001. "Introduction." In May and Thrift, eds., *Timespace: Geographies of Temporality*, 1–46. New York: Routledge.

Mazzarella, William. 2009. "Affect: What Is It Good For?" In Saurabh Dube, ed., *Enchantments of Modernity*, 291–309. London: Routledge.

Mbembe, Achille. 1992. "The Banality of Power and the Aesthetics of Vulgarity in the Postcolony." *Public Culture* 4, no. 2:1–30.

Millar, Kathleen M. 2014. "The Precarious Present: Wageless Labor and Disrupted Life in Rio de Janeiro, Brazil." *Cultural Anthropology* 29, no. 1:32–53.

Millar, Kathleen M. 2018. *Reclaiming the Discarded: Life and Labor on Rio's Garbage Dump*. Durham, NC: Duke University Press.

Mintz, Sidney W. 1985. *Sweetness and Power*. Harmondsworth, UK: Penguin.

Mintz, Sidney W. 1989 [1974]. *Caribbean Transformations*. New York: Columbia University Press.

Mintz, Sidney W. 1996. *Tasting Food, Tasting Freedom*. Boston: Beacon Press.

Mitchell, Timothy. 2011. *Carbon Democracy: Political Power in the Age of Oil*. London: Verso.

Molina, Tania. 2017. "Se gasta RD$39,000 millones en 'botellas,' revela estudio." *DiarioLibre*, 23 October, 22.

Moya Pons, Frank. 1984. "Haiti and Santo Domingo, 1790–c.1870." In Leslie Bethell, ed., *The Cambridge History of Latin America*, 3:237–75. Cambridge: Cambridge University Press.

Moya Pons, Frank. 1990. "The Dominican Republic since 1930." In Leslie Bethell, ed., *The Cambridge History of Latin America*, 7:509–44. Cambridge: Cambridge University Press.

Moya Pons, Frank. 1994. "Historia y medio ambiente en la isla de Santo Domingo." *Eco-Hispaniola*. https://ecohis.jmarcano.com/estudios-diversos/moyapons/.

Moya Pons, Frank. 2010. *The Dominican Republic: A National History*. 3rd ed. Princeton, NJ: Marcus Wiener Publishers.

Muehlebach, Andrea. 2013. "On Precariousness and the Ethical Imagination: The Year 2012 in Sociocultural Anthropology." *American Anthropologist* 115, no. 2:297–311.

Muir, Sarah, and Akhil Gupta. 2018. "Rethinking the Anthropology of Corruption: An Introduction to Supplement 18." *Current Anthropology* 59, S18:S4-S15.

Munck, Ronaldo. 2013. "The Precariat: A View from the South." *Third World Quarterly* 34, no. 5:747–62.

Murphy, Catherine. 1999. *Cultivating Havana: Urban Agriculture and Food Security in the Years of Crisis*. Oakland, CA: Food First, Institute of Food and Development Policy.

Murray, Gerald F. 1996. *El colmado*. Santo Domingo: Fondo para el Financiamiento de la Microempresa (FondoMicro).

Murray, Gerald F. 2005. *El colegio y la escuela: Antropología de la educación en la República Dominicana*. Santo Domingo: Fondo para el Financiamiento de la Microempresa (FondoMicro).

Narotzky, Susana. 1988. "The Ideological Squeeze: 'Casa,' 'Family' and 'Cooperation' in the Processes of Transition," *Social Science Information* 27, no. 4:559–81.

Narotzky, Susana. 1997. *New Directions in Economic Anthropology*. London: Pluto Press.

Narotzky, Susana. 2018. "Rethinking the Concept of Labour." *Journal of the Royal Anthropological Institute* 24, S1:29–43.

Narotzky, Susana, and Gavin Smith. 2006. *Immediate Struggles: People, Power, and Place in Rural Spain*. Berkeley: University of California Press.

Neveling, Patrick. 2015. "Export Processing Zones and Global Class Formation." In James G. Carrier and Don Kalb, eds., *Anthropologies of Class: Power, Practice and Inequality*, 164–82. Cambridge: Cambridge University Press.

Nun, José. 1969. "Superpoblación relativa, ejército industrial de reserva y masa marginal." *Revista Latinoamericana de Sociología* 5, no. 2:178–235.

Ortiz, Fernando. 1995 [1940]. *Cuban Counterpoint: Tobacco and Sugar*. Introd. Bronislaw Malinowski; new introd. Fernando Coronil. Durham, NC: Duke University Press.

Ortiz, Marina, Miguel Cabal, and Rita Mena. 2014. *Micro, pequeñas y medianas empresas en la República Dominicana 2013*. Santo Domingo: Fondo para el Financiamiento de la Microempresa (FondoMicro).

Ortiz, Marina, and Rita Mena. 2007. *Microempresas y seguridad social en la República Dominicana*. Santo Domingo: Fondo para el Financiamiento de la Microempresa (FondoMicro).

Ortner, Sherry. 2011. "On Neoliberalism." *Anthropology of this Century* 1 (May). http://aotcpress.com/articles/neoliberalism/.

Oxfam. 2017. *Se buscan: recursos para garantizar derechos*. Santo Domingo: Oxfam. https://d1tn3vj7xz9fdh.cloudfront.net/s3fs-public/file_attachments/story/informe_malgasto_limita_derechos_web.pdf.

Pacini Hernandez, Deborah. 1995. *Bachata: A Social History of a Dominican Popular Music*. Philadelphia: Temple University Press.

Padilla, Mark. 2007. *Caribbean Pleasure Industry: Tourism, Sexuality, and AIDS in the Dominican Republic.* Chicago: University of Chicago Press.

Palmié, Stephan. 2013. *The Cooking of History: How Not to Study Afro-Cuban Religion.* Chicago: University of Chicago Press.

Parisotto, Aurelio, and Gustavo Prepelitchi. 2013. "Growth, Employment and Social Cohesion in the Dominican Republic." ILO Background Paper. Geneva: International Labor Organization. https://www.ilo.org/wcmsp5/groups/public/—-dgreports/—-integration/documents/meetingdocument/wcms_204604.pdf.

Pasqualetti, Martin J. 2011. "Social Barriers to Renewable Energy Landscapes." *Geographical Review* 101, no. 2:201–23.

Pastore, Chaela. 2007. "Mahogany as Status Symbol: Race and Luxury in Saint Domingue at the End of the Eighteenth Century." In Dena Goodman and Kathryn Norberg, eds., *Furnishing the Eighteenth Century. What Furniture Can Tell Us about the European and American Past,* 37–48. New York: Routledge.

Pedersen, David. 2013. *American Value: Migrants, Money, and Meaning in El Salvador and the United States.* Chicago: University of Chicago Press.

Peebles, Gustav. 2010. "The Anthropology of Credit and Debt." *Annual Review of Anthropology* 39:225–40.

Perlman, Janice E. 1976. *The Myth of Marginality.* Berkeley: University of California Press.

Pessar, Patricia R. 1995. *A Visa for a Dream.* Boston: Allyn & Bacon.

Portes, Alejandro. 1995. "Economic Sociology and the Sociology of Immigration: A Conceptual Overview." In A. Portes, ed., *The Economic Sociology of Immigration.* New York: Russell Sage Foundation.

Portes, Alejandro, and Luis E. Guarnizo. 1991. *Capitalistas del Trópico.* 2nd ed. Santo Domingo: Facultad Latinoamericana de Ciencias Sociales, Programa República Dominicana.

Premat, Adriana. 2009. "State Power, Private Plots and the Greening of Havana's Urban Agriculture Movement." *City and Society* 21, no. 1:28–57.

Quijano, Aníbal. 1966. "Notas sobre el concepto de marginalidad social." Mimeo. Santiago: CEPAL.

Quijano, Aníbal. 1974. "The Marginal Pole of the Economy and the Marginalized Labour Force." *Economy and Society* 3, no. 4:393–428.

Rakopoulos, Theodoros. 2015. "Which Community for Cooperatives? Peasant Mobilizations, the Mafia, and the Problem of Community Participation in Sicilian Co-ops." *Focaal—Journal of Global and Historical Anthropology* 71:57–70.

Rakopoulos, Theodoros. 2017. *From Clans to Co-ops: Confiscated Mafia Land in Sicily.* New York: Berghahn Books.

Ramírez, Dixa. 2018. *Colonial Phantoms: Belonging and Refusal in the Dominican Americas, from the 19th Century to the Present.* New York: New York University Press.

Ramírez, Jesús M. 2000. *Mis 43 años en La Descubierta.* Santo Domingo: Editora Centenario.

Ramos, Mercedes. 2011. "Conferencia dictada por Mercedes Ramos, Presidenta Ejecutiva de Grupo Ramos, en el marco del ciclo de conferencias 'Nueva Generación y Liderazgo Empresarial.'" Paper presented at Universidad Iberoamericana (UNIBE), Santo Domingo, 5 July.

Ranis, Peter. 2016. *Cooperatives Confront Capitalism: Challenging the Neoliberal Economy.* London: Zed Books.

Reeves, Madeleine. 2014. *Border Work: Spatial Lives of the State in Rural Central Asia.* Ithaca, NY: Cornell University Press.

Reyes, Patria. 2013. "Desmiente Educación escogiera pymes para pupitres." *Hoy,* 6 July, 1A, 4A.

Ricourt, Milagros. 2002. *Dominicans in New York City.* New York: Routledge.

Ricourt, Milagros, and Ruby Danta. 2003. *Hispanas de Queens.* Ithaca, NY: Cornell University Press.

Robertson, Nicole. 2016. *The Co-operative Movement and Communities in Britain, 1914- 1960: Minding Their Own Business.* London: Routledge.

Rodríguez Bencosme, Angélica M. 2013. *El Mueble de Madera Dominicano.* Santo Domingo: Instituto Tecnológico de Santo Domingo/Editora Búho, S.R.L.

Roorda, Eric P. 1998. *The Dictator Next Door.* Durham, NC: Duke University Press.

Rosario, Yamalie. 2013. "Mipymes cuestionan política del Poder Ejecutivo para impulsar ese sector." *DiarioLibre,* 13 November, 20.

Rosset, Peter, and Medea Benjamin, eds. 1994. *The Greening of the Revolution: Cuba's Experiment with Organic Agriculture.* N.p.: Ocean Press.

Rousseau, Jean-Jacques. [1762] 2019. *On the Social Contract.* 2nd ed. Trans. Donald A. Cress. Ed. and introd. David Wootton. Cambridge, MA: Hackett Publishing.

Sánchez, Miguel E., and Roby Senderowitsch. 2012. "The Political Economy of the Middle Class in the Dominican Republic: Individualization of Public Goods, Lack of Institutional Trust and Weak Collective Action." Policy Research Working Paper 6049. Washington, DC: World Bank.

Sandoval-Cervantes, Iván. 2017. "Uncertain Futures: The Unfinished Houses of Undocumented Migrants in Oaxaca, Mexico." *American Anthropologist* 119, no. 2:209–22.

Sanjek, Roger. 1998. *The Future of Us All.* Ithaca, NY: Cornell University Press.

San Miguel, Pedro L. 1997. *Los Campesinos del Cibao*. San Juan: Editorial de la Universidad de Puerto Rico.

Sassen-Koob, Saskia. 1987. "Formal and Informal Associations: Dominicans and Colombians in New York." In Constance R. Sutton and Elsa M. Chaney, eds., *Caribbean Life in New York City*, 261–77. New York: Center for Migration Studies.

Schwab, Klaus, ed. 2017. *The Global Competitiveness Report 2017–2018*. Geneva: World Economic Forum.

Schwenkel, Christina. 2015. "Spectacular Infrastructure and Its Breakdown in Socialist Vietnam." *American Ethnologist* 42:520–34.

Severino, Jairon. 2011. "La ley 488–08 se acostó a dormir junto al Disdo," *Listín Diario*, 11 November. https://listindiario.com/economia/2011/11/11/210526/la-ley-488-08-se-acosto-a-dormir-junto-al-disdo.

Silverman, Edward. 1991. "The New Nueva York: Taking Care of Business." *New York Newsday*, 21 October.

Smith, Gavin. 2011. "Selective Hegemony and Beyond—Populations with 'No Productive Function': A Framework for Enquiry." *Identities: Global Studies in Culture and Power* 18, no. 1:2–38.

Smith, Raymond T. 1996. *The Matrifocal Family: Power, Pluralism and Politics*. New York: Routledge.

Standing, Guy. 2011. *The Precariat: The New Dangerous Class*. London: Bloomsbury Academic.

Stephen, Lynn. 2005. "Women's Weaving Cooperatives in Oaxaca: An Indigenous Response to Neoliberalism." *Critique of Anthropology* 25, no. 3:53–78.

Stewart, Kathleen. 2012. "Precarity's Forms." *Cultural Anthropology* 27, no. 3:518–25.

Stoler, Ann L. 2013. "Introduction: 'The Rot Remains': From Ruins to Ruination." In A. L. Stoler, ed., *Imperial Debris. On Ruins and Ruination*, 1–35. Durham, NC: Duke University Press.

Stoler, Ann L. 2016. *Duress: Imperial Durabilities in Our Times*. Durham, NC: Duke University Press.

Stoller, Paul. 1995. *Embodying Colonial Memories: Spirit Possession, Power, and the Hauka in West Africa*. London: Routledge.

Suero Acosta, Indhira. 2020. "Dominican Poor Struggle for Water as Coronavirus Lockdown Hits Supplies." *Reuters*, 12 June. https://news.trust.org/item/20200612162804-or8uw.

Taussig, Michael. 1993. *Mimesis and Alterity*. New York: Routledge.

Taylor, Erin B. 2013. *Materializing Poverty: How the Poor Transform Their Lives*. Lanham, MD: Rowman & Littlefield.

Taylor, Erin B. 2014. "When Crisis Is Experienced as Continuity: Materialities of Time in Haiti." *Ethnologie française* 44, no. 3:491–502.

Tolentino Dipp, Hugo. 2014. *Itinerario histórico de la gastronomía dominicana.* Santo Domingo: Amigo del Hogar.

Torres-Saillant, Silvio. 1999. *El Retorno de las Yolas.* Santo Domingo: Ediciones Librería La Trinitaria y Editora Manatí.

Torres-Saillant, Silvio, and Ramona Hernández. 1998. *The Dominican Americans.* Westport, CT: Greenwood Press.

Trouillot, Michel-Rolph. 1988. *Peasants and Capital: Dominica in the World Economy.* Baltimore: Johns Hopkins University Press.

Trouillot, Michel-Rolph. 1995. *Silencing the Past: Power and the Production of History.* Boston: Beacon Press.

Trouillot, Michel-Rolph. 2003. *Global Transformations: Anthropology and the Modern World.* New York: Palgrave Macmillan.

Tsing, Anna L. 2009. "Supply Chains and the Human Condition." *Rethinking Marxism: A Journal of Economics, Culture & Society* 21, no. 2:148–76.

Tsing, Anna L. 2013. "Sorting Out Commodities: How Capitalist Value Is Made through Gifts." *HAU: Journal of Ethnographic Theory* 3, no. 1:21–43.

Tsing, Anna L. 2015. *The Mushroom at the End of the World: On the Possibility of Life in Capitalist Ruins.* Princeton: Princeton University Press.

Turits, Richard L. 2003. *Foundations of Despotism: Peasants, the Trujillo Regime, and Modernity in Dominican History.* Stanford: Stanford University Press.

Uribe, Simón. 2017. *Frontier Road: Power, History, and the Everyday State in the Colombian Amazon.* Hoboken, NJ: Wiley Blackwell.

van der Linden, Marcel. 2008. *Workers of the World: Essays Toward a Global Labour History.* Amsterdam: Brill.

Vargas-Cetina, Gabriela. 2005. "From the Community Paradigm to the Ephemeral Association in Chiapas, Mexico." *Critique of Anthropology* 25, no. 3:229–51.

Vargas-Cetina, Gabriela. 2011. "Corporations, Cooperatives, and the State: Examples from Italy." *Current Anthropology* 52, S3:S127–S136.

Vergara-Camus, Leandro, and Cristóbal Kay. 2017. "Agribusiness, Peasants, Left-Wing Governments, and the State in Latin America: An Overview and Theoretical Reflections." *Journal of Agrarian Change* 17, no. 2:239–57.

Villarreal, Magdalena. 2014. "Regimes of Value in Mexican Household Financial Practices." *Current Anthropology* 55, S9:S30–S39.

Weeks, Kathi. 2011. *The Problem with Work: Feminism, Marxism, Antiwork Politics, and Postwork Imaginaries.* Durham, NC: Duke University Press.

West, Paige. 2016. *Dispossession and the Environment: Rhetoric and Inequality in Papua New Guinea.* New York: Columbia University Press.

Weston, Kath. 2017. *Animate Planet: Making Visceral Sense of Living in a High-Tech Ecologically Damaged World*. Durham, NC: Duke University Press.

Williams, Raymond. 1977. *Marxism and Literature*. Oxford: Oxford University Press.

Winkler, Hernan, and Miriam Montenegro. 2021. *Dominican Republic Jobs Diagnostic*. Washington, DC: World Bank Group.

Wooding, Bridget. 2018. "Haitian Immigrants and Their Descendants Born in the Dominican Republic." In William Beezley, ed., *Oxford Research Encyclopedia of Latin American History*. New York: Oxford University Press. latinamericanhistory.oxfordre.com/.

World Bank Group. 2016. *Building a Better Future Together: Dominican Republic Policy Notes*. Washington, DC: World Bank Group. https://openknowledge.worldbank.org/handle/10986/26045.

World Bank Group. 2018. *Dominican Republic Systematic Country Diagnostic*. Washington, DC: World Bank Group. https://openknowledge.worldbank.org/handle/10986/30055.

Wright, Andrea. 2020. "Making Kin from Gold: Dowry, Gender, and Indian Labor Migration to the Gulf." *Cultural Anthropology* 35, no. 3:435–61.

Wynne, Kimberly. 2015. "Blood, Sweat and Bananas: Making a Moral Life on the Margins of the Dominican Republic." PhD diss., University of Oslo.

Yanagisako, Sylvia J. 2002. *Producing Culture and Capital*. Princeton: Princeton University Press.

Yanagisako, Sylvia J. 2013. "Transnational Family Capitalism: Producing 'Made in Italy' in China." In Susan McKinnon and Fenella Cannell, eds., *Vital Relations: Modernity and the Persistent Life of Kinship*, 63–84. Santa Fe, NM: School for Advanced Research Press.

Zharkevich, Ina. 2019. "Money and Blood: Remittances as a Substance of Relatedness in Transnational Families in Nepal." *American Anthropologist* 121, no. 4:884–96.

Index

216

INDEX

27–28, 30; in Santo Domingo,
25–26; sizes, 26; strategies, 29, 30,
31–35; workshops, 2–3

Gallup polls, 19–20
Gender, of workers, 10–11. *See also*
Men; Women
Gender differences: in accepted sexual
behavior, 56–57, 58, 59; in access
to capital, 91; division of house-
hold labor, 63
Global capitalism: Dominican econ-
omy and, 16; labor and, 9–10, 13,
146–47, 148, 149; state roles, 27.
See also Capitalism
Graeber, David, 187n7
Grandin, Greg, 56
Gregory, Steven, 85
Groceries, *see* Food; Supermarkets
Grupo Ramos (Ramos Group), 98,
99–100, 102, 186n17
Guarnizo, Luis E., 93
Guyer, Jane I., 8
Guzmán, Antonio, 17
Guzmán Santos, Yocasta, 42

Haiti: furniture exports to, 28; inde-
pendence, 176n12; revolution,
150–51; workers from, 15, 111,
160–61, 178n17
Han, Clara, 50, 73
Hart, Keith, 177n13
Harvey, David, 26
Hegel, G. W. F., 150–51
Hoffnung-Garskof, Jesse, 13, 52–56,
89, 188n12
Horn, Maja, 60–61
Housing, 72, 161, 162
Hoy, 19–20
Humphery, Kim, 98–99

IDECOOP, *see* Instituto de Desarrollo
y Crédito Cooperativo

ILO, *see* International Labor
Organization
IMF, *see* International Monetary Fund
Imperialism, *see* Colonialism
Incomes: of food stalls, 70–71,
75, 76; per capita, 5. *See also*
Economic growth; Wages
Industrial parks (parqes industriales),
1–2, 3–4, 157
Inequality, social and economic, 5–6,
17, 54, 85, 135, 168–69
Informal economies: in cities, 11,
144, 151–52, 158–59; COVID-
19 pandemic effects, 171; jobs, 5,
11–12, 21, 145; street vendors,
47, 158–59; use of term, 177n13.
See also Small businesses; Wageless
labor
Infrastructure: access to, 22, 68,
124–25, 155–57, 172; water, 22,
68, 103, 124, 156, 171. *See also*
Electric power
Insecurity, *see* Precarity
Instituto Agrario Dominicano, 127,
129
Instituto de Desarrollo y Crédito
Cooperativo (Institute for
Development and Cooperative
Credit [IDECOOP]), 112, 115,
118, 126, 137
Insurance cooperative
(COOPSEGUROS), 123, 140
International Labor Organization
(ILO), 11, 145
International Monetary Fund (IMF),
5, 28, 30, 45, 55, 97
Inversiones Taveras, 75
Investments: foreign, 28; use of term,
8

Japa, René, 100–101
Jiménez, Ramón Emilio, "Platos
Nacionales," 62